ST. CHARLES COUNTY COMMUNITY COLLEGE

3 9835 00083376

D1527282

ONE NATION,
ONE BLOOD

ONE NATION, ONE BLOOD

Interracial Marriage
in American Fiction,
Scandal, and Law,
1820–1870

Karen Woods Weierman

University of Massachusetts Press
Amherst & Boston

ST CHARLES COMMUNITY COLLEGE
WITHDRAWN
LIBRARY

Copyright © 2005 by University of Massachusetts Press
All rights reserved
Printed in the United States of America
LC 2004026483
ISBN 1-55849-483-9

Designed by Jack Harrison
Set in Adobe Garamond by Binghamton Valley Composition
Printed and bound by The Maple-Vail Book Manufacturing Group

Library of Congress Cataloging-in-Publication Data

Weierman, Karen Woods, 1971–
One nation, one blood: interracial marriage in American fiction,
scandal, and law, 1820–1870 / Karen Woods Weierman.
p.   cm.
Includes bibliographical references and index.
ISBN 1-55849-483-9 (cloth : alk. paper)
1.   American fiction—19th century—History and criticism.
2.   Marriage in literature.   3.   Interracial marriage—Law and legislation—
United States—History—19th century.
4.   Interracial marriage—United States—History—19th century.
5.   Scandals—United States—History—19th century.   6.   Interracial marriage in literature.
7.   Married people in literature.   8.   Race relations in literature.
9.   Racism in literature.   10.   Race in literature.   I.   Title.
PS374.M35W45   2005
813'.3093543—dc22
2004026483

British Library Cataloguing in Publication data are available.

For Bob and Dylan

Boast not proud English of thy birth and blood,
Thy brother Indian is by birth as good.
Of one blood God made him, and thee, and all,
As wise, as fair, as strong, as personal.

Roger Williams

If He has "made of one blood all nations of men for to dwell on all the face of the earth," then they are one species, and stand on a perfect equality; their intermarriage is neither unnatural nor repugnant to nature, but obviously proper and salutary; it being designed to unite people of different tribes and nations.

William Lloyd Garrison

CONTENTS

ACKNOWLEDGMENTS

This book was made possible by funding from many sources. I conducted the final stages of research as an American Antiquarian Society–National Endowment for the Humanities Fellow. I wish to thank the entire staff at AAS, especially Joanne Chaison, John Hench, Marie Lamoureux, and Caroline Sloat, for an inspiring and productive experience. Research fellows Cathy Corman, Vince DiGirolamo, Richard Fox, Melissa Homestead, and Alan Taylor also offered their collegiality and expertise. The research was completed and the manuscript revised with the help of two summer Faculty Mini-Grants from Worcester State College. I am grateful to my colleagues there for their enthusiastic support. An earlier incarnation of the project benefited from a Doctoral Dissertation Fellowship and a Supplemental Research Fellowship from the Graduate School at the University of Minnesota.

Many generous scholars and librarians have assisted me in my research. I especially thank Barbara Allen at the Stockbridge Library Historical Room; Michael Gannett at the Cornwall, Connecticut, Historical Society; Laura Glisson at the Fulton, New York, Public Library; Catherine Hanchett at the State University of New York–Cortland; Daniel Littlefield at the University of Arkansas–Little Rock; Lion G. Miles of Stockbridge, Massachusetts; Marcia Pankake at Wilson Library, University of Minnesota; Suzanne Thorpe at the Law Library, University of Minnesota; and James Walsh, S.J., at Georgetown University. I am also indebted to the staff at the Boston Public Library, the Cortland County Historical Society, the Massachusetts Historical Society, the Wilson Library at the University of Minnesota, and the Worcester State College Library.

Among the many readers who have responded to portions of the manuscript, my dissertation director at the University of Minnesota, Edward M. Griffin, shaped this project with his wisdom, expert editing, and good humor. Lisa Norling, Donald Ross, Art Geffen, John Wright, and the members of the Early American History Workshop and the American Literature Subfield were also essential early readers. They have continued to cheer me on at every step of the way. More recently, Ruth Haber, Lion G. Miles, Alan Taylor, Sarah Wadsworth, the American Civilization writing group at Harvard, and the anonymous reviewers for the University of Massachusetts Press helped me clarify my argument. Paul

Wright, Carol Betsch, and Amanda Heller have guided me through the publishing process.

Finally, I thank my family and friends for their encouragement during this long process, especially my parents, Susan and John Woods; my sister and brother-in-law, Christine Woods Krueger and Dan Krueger; the Weiermans; the Hedenbergs; "Crafts"; the "Howard-Thomas" cousins; the Brooklyn Biestys; the JVC crowd; Erin Fodero, Tim Neary, Dave Noon, Maria Spinelli, Emily Todd, Cathy Trinkle, and Colleen York. Special thanks to the late Nana Boyle, the only family member who read the entire manuscript, and to Maura Tully and Angela Dinger for their hospitality during my research and conference travels.

Most of all, my deepest gratitude to Bob and our sweet Dylan.

ONE NATION,
ONE BLOOD

INTRODUCTION

Narratives of Disruption

> For God hath made of one blood all nations of men for to
> dwell on all the face of the earth.
>
> ACTS 17:26

In 1853 William G. Allen narrowly escaped death "at the hands of an armed mob" in upstate New York. The cause? The African American professor's rumored engagement to his former student, the white Mary King. Despite the fact that their interracial marriage would have been legal in New York State, Allen later recalled, "we were still overpowered by the physical force of the community." Allen and King therefore decided to exercise their rights by eloping and fleeing the country. Their plight seemed the stuff of romance; as one friend wrote, "Your flight is a flight for freedom, and I can almost call you *Eliza*," referring, of course, to the fugitive slave in the recently published *Uncle Tom's Cabin*. Their harrowing tale prompted a letter of encouragement from Harriet Beecher Stowe herself. The stories surrounding the Allen-King scandal were as important as the marriage itself; all parties reverted to legal, religious, and fictional narratives in order to explain their positions.[1]

The American taboo against interracial marriages has always been historically specific and responsive to changing circumstances. The Puritan settlers were concerned about the heathen character of the Indians, for example, whereas nineteenth-century white Americans rejected interracial marriage on the grounds of black inferiority. This study of the taboo against interracial marriage between 1820 and 1870 examines only one phase of an ongoing process, but this period was a pivotal one, establishing the tenor of race relations in the United States and extending the taboo against interracial marriage into the present.

During this time, attitudes toward interracial marriage grew out of a changing understanding of race. The Enlightenment conception of human differences as a consequence of physical and social environment gave way to a belief in the fixed, biological nature of racial identity. By 1830 the majority of white Americans saw Indians as unassimilable and incapable of civilization and believed that blacks were "natural slaves" by virtue of their inferior racial status. In other words, the dominant culture constructed nonwhites as separate races, inferior and inescapably other. This categorization developed under particular historical circumstances—the desire for Indian land and African labor—and means by which Euro-Americans achieved these goals. As Cheryl I. Harris explains, "Although the systems of oppression of blacks and Native Americans differed in form—the former involving the seizure and appropriation of labor, the latter entailing the seizure and appropriation of land—undergirding both was a racialized conception of property implemented by force and ratified by law."[2] The decimation of Indian populations through warfare and removal and the practice of African chattel slavery were justified by the alleged inferiority of the nonwhite people.[3]

Under these circumstances, marriage between Indians or blacks and whites became unthinkable: the legal recognition of such relationships would challenge the basis of racial caste that organized society. This system of absolute racial identities, developed in the struggle for power and property in colonial British America and later in the United States, was undermined by any transgressions of the color line. Interracial marriage was a dangerous threat, both in its production of biracial children and in its implication of equality for people of color. Interracial marriage thus formed a powerful narrative of disruption, threatening the very foundation of this racialized society. During the years 1820–1870, as the nation grappled with the moral issues of Indian removal and African slavery, narratives of interracial marriage abounded in fiction, scandal, and law.[4]

Stories featuring interracial marriages are often "about" something else: Indian land, African labor, the nature of racial identity, or the place of people of color in the United States. In addition to their political dimension, these narratives revealed the racism in American culture, prompting defensive reactions from white supremacists and progressive reformers alike. Repeatedly, the inflammatory question "Would you want your daughter to marry a black man?" (or an Indian) was answered with the equally provocative "better off dead" response, that is, that parents would rather see their child dead than married to a person of color. In American culture, the political goals of the miscegenation taboo became intensely personal, governing the most intimate details of family life.

Despite the overwhelming rejection of people of color as marriage partners, citizens, and social equals, a small minority challenged the social taboo against intermarriage. Rejecting the new "race science" supposedly proving white superiority, they held on to the religious narrative of human unity and the republican rhetoric of freedom and equality, countering that God made all people "of one blood." These arguments offered rhetorical challenges to the growing belief in race science and absolute racial categories that dominated American culture. While the taboo against interracial marriage served as a narrative of control, used to promote exclusion and racial superiority, the disruptive narrative of interracial marriage also challenged Americans, as believers in democracy and Christian brotherhood, to live up to their ideals.

The taboo against intermarriage rests on a complex web of storytelling about the color line and the dangers of crossing it. More than just cautionary tales, these stories shaped lived experience. The philosopher David Carr suggests that "the actions and sufferings of life can be viewed as a process of telling ourselves stories, listening to those stories, and acting them out or living them through. . . . Sometimes we must change the story to accommodate the events, sometimes we change the events to accommodate the story."[5] The intermarriage taboo might best be understood as an evolving series of negative stories: narratives of racial hierarchy, scientific disorder, pollution of the blood, and so on. These stories, while controversial in their subject matter, follow the standard model of narrative structure: (1) equilibrium, (2) equilibrium disrupted, (3) conflict/struggle, and (4) equilibrium restored.[6] In narratives of intermarriage, the forbidden marriage causes disruption, followed by the attempts of competing parties to restore order—either by promoting tolerance or by rejecting the marriage through intense social pressure or even physical force. It is the latter narrative that is usually victorious.

These narratives of disruption frequently appeared in fiction, scandal, and law in nineteenth-century America. While fiction and law are familiar genres, scandal is a more amorphous category. The expression of a community's private codes forms an important counterpoint to both fiction and law; it encompasses a wide range of texts and actions, including newspaper articles, private letters, and vigilantism. According to Judge Barry R. Schaller, "private codes define, govern, and restrict the individuals living in particular communities. In a sense, they constitute a type of private law that regulates and classifies individuals within communities."[7] Private codes are created through narratives about the boundaries of acceptable behavior and the consequences of crossing them. In the case of interracial marriage, scandals result from the powerful narrative of disruption threatening to undermine the private codes of behavior.

While narratives of interracial marriage have much in common across genres, generic purpose and convention shape narrative possibility in important ways. Although law and scandal can express a society's values and highest aspirations, they also can define norms of behavior and guard boundaries. The power of fiction lies in its capability to imagine something different.[8] Fiction creates a vision of what might have been and what could still be. The novelists I study here explore the foundations of American culture and the disruptive narratives of intermarriage, with creative responses both reactionary and revolutionary. The generic expectations of readers make this an interactive process as readers react to the provocative revision of the traditional "marriage plot." This interracial plot twist challenges readers and creates an opportunity for empathy. Of course, as the philosopher and legal scholar Martha Nussbaum acknowledges, there are limits to what fiction can accomplish, but the literary imagination can be a powerful first step toward social change: "Novel-reading will not give us the whole story about social justice, but it can be a bridge both to a vision of justice and to the social enactment of that vision."[9] It is also important to remember that fiction is not necessarily a force for social change: fictional narratives of intermarriage are told within the context of strict legal and social taboo, and the desire to restore equilibrium through the suppression of intermarriages can also function powerfully in fiction.

Part I of this book focuses on Indian-white marriages in the 1820s, a time when removal of Indians from the southeastern United States became a rallying cry for New England intellectuals. The first chapter features the interracial marriage scandal at the Foreign Mission School in Cornwall, Connecticut, and the challenging question it raises: Why would reformers, so eager for the assimilation of Indians into the larger society, reject intermarriage, which seemed to offer a commonsense solution to the problem of assimilation? In chapter 2 I trace the origins and development of Indian-white intermarriage bans, arguing that attitudes toward Indian-white marriages depended on evolving beliefs about religion and culture and about heredity or "blood." This new understanding of race made racial identity the fundamental criterion for citizenship and land rights, for both Indian nations and the U.S. government. In chapter 3, fiction by Catharine Maria Sedgwick, James Fenimore Cooper, and Lydia Maria Child reveals the link between intermarriage and land in American culture. Their work explores the relationship between race and culture and looks to the colonial past for answers to the dilemmas facing a multiracial society. What emerges from this interdisciplinary study of Indian-white marriages is the conclusion that the taboo is never just about racial or sexual anxiety: the supposedly uncrossable gulf between the races was a justification for dispossessing Indians of their land.

In Part II we turn to black-white marriages from the antebellum period through the early years of Reconstruction. Chapter 4 offers a detailed case study of the Allen-King intermarriage scandal at New York Central College, a radical abolitionist institution that accepted students and faculty of all races and both sexes but drew the line at interracial marriage. Chapter 5 shows how the development of slave law and the development of miscegenation law were closely intertwined and explores why the taboo against intermarriage has endured long past the demise of slavery. In chapter 6 I argue that for the novelists Lydia Maria Child, Frank J. Webb, and Frances E. W. Harper, fiction provides a forum for the dramatization of the consequences of miscegenation laws and the likely outcome of their repeal.

One final note on the word choices I make in this book. Because interracial marriage, and not illicit sex, is my central focus, I most often refer to the "taboo against interracial marriage," or, more concisely, "intermarriage." As readers will note, the laws are overwhelmingly about marriage, the fictional plots are driven by marriage, and the scandals are ignited by marriage. This is not a matter of marriage being a more polite topic than sex. The controversy during this period was about giving legal recognition to interracial liaisons, a dispute having serious implications for a society organized along racial lines. I should also add that my use of "interracial" does not endorse an understanding of race as a fixed, biological category; along with Werner Sollors, I find that the term has a "lesser semantic burden" than much of the problematic vocabulary applied to this subject.[10]

The word "miscegenation" also appears, but with less frequency. Because "miscegenation" was not coined until 1864, it is somewhat anachronistic to use it in an antebellum context. The lawmakers, authors, characters, and dramatic actors I discuss use the word "amalgamation" when discussing "race mixing," and, for the sake of accuracy, so do I when presenting their fears or attitudes. Legal historians have found "miscegenation law" to be a useful term for the body of laws banning interracial sex and marriage dating back to colonial times; likewise, I follow this scholarly convention when discussing the law. Some scholars argue that the use of "miscegenation" endorses its dubious racist origins, but I agree with Peggy Pascoe that erasing the term "avoids naming the ugliness that was so much a part of the laws." Following her lead, I "retain the term *miscegenation* when speaking of the laws and court cases that relied on the concept, but not when speaking of people or particular relationships."[11]

The complexity in defining my terms reflects the sensitivity of this issue at the heart of American life and literature. In the pages that follow I tackle these challenging narratives of disruption and the powerful metaphor of "blood" that has shaped our national life.

I

INDIAN-WHITE MARRIAGES

1

"How Our Ladies Marry Indian Men":
The Closing of the Foreign Mission School
in Cornwall, Connecticut

And what a dreadful, doleful sound
Is often heard from town to town,
Reflecting words from every friend,
How our ladies marry Indian men.

EMILY FOX
"The Indian Song, Sarah and John"

Elias Boudinot and John Ridge are notorious in American history as the Cherokees who signed the 1835 removal treaty with the U.S. government at New Echota, the treaty that led to the "Trail of Tears." Although they initially fought for Cherokee land rights, they later decided that further resistance to the government was futile and that removal was the only way to prevent decimation of the Cherokee Nation. As members of the "treaty party," they were branded by opponents of removal as traitors for acquiescing to the demands of the state of Georgia and the federal government, and they were later assassinated. According to an 1829 law passed by the Cherokee General Council, the cession of tribal land was a capital offense.[1] Those who signed the treaty were well aware of the potentially fatal consequences. Ridge acknowledged that he "may yet die by the hand of some poor infatuated Indian. . . . I am resigned to my fate, whatever it may be."[2] Ridge and Boudinot are remembered as the villains of the Cherokee tragedy, but from our vantage point, merely assigning ambition or treachery as the motive behind their decisions seems too reductive. What experiences led them to sign the treaty? Surely one of the most significant of these experiences was their pyrotechnic involvement in the closing of the Foreign Mission School in Cornwall, Connecticut, following their marriages to local white women. Perhaps their experience of white racism in Cornwall—and the limits of the missionary spirit—led them to conclude that the Cherokees' best chance for survival was separation from white society.[3]

The Foreign Mission School

The American Board of Commissioners for Foreign Missions (ABCFM) was founded in 1810 in the midst of the religious zeal of the Second Great Awakening. Ostensibly nondenominational, the organization was nevertheless dominated by Congregationalists. As Donald Philip Corr notes, the ABCFM viewed "the entire world as the mission field" and "considered propagating the Gospel to be the highest priority, with Bible translation an important complement to preaching."[4] Its ministry targeted American Indians, as the organization had less anti-Indian prejudice than other missionary groups. Far from being a disinterested religious group, the ABCFM also served as a quasi-government agency. One strain of federal Indian policy at this time was the promotion of Indian assimilation; the various missionary groups thus played a major role in the federal government's plan to "civilize" the Indians.

In May 1816 William Crawford, secretary of war under President Madison, agreed to a partnership between the government and the ABCFM in which the government would provide some funding for buildings and equipment for the latter's Indian missions. Three years later Congress established a Civilization Fund, which Secretary Crawford divided among the various missionary agencies, giving the majority of the funding to the ABCFM. With the patronage of the president and Congress, the ABCFM dwarfed the small-scale efforts by the Presbyterians and the Moravians and dominated the missionary scene among the southeastern tribes.[5] The historian Robert F. Berkhofer takes a cynical view of this deal, whereby "the missionaries received some federal money and moral support, the Indians supposedly obtained 'civilization,' and the government leaders salved the American conscience while they hoped soon to acquire native lands no longer needed by their transformed inhabitants."[6]

The ABCFM also planned to open an institution in New England to train native missionaries. When it began plans for a Foreign Mission School in 1816, the town of Cornwall in northwestern Connecticut bid for the school and donated a building and property. The *History of the American Board* indicates that the school opened in May 1817 with widespread public support: "This institution and the fund for educating heathen children were received by the Christian public with particular favor."[7] The ABCFM wanted its graduates to become "missionaries, schoolmasters, interpreters, and physicians among heathen nations and to communicate such information in agriculture and the arts as should tend to promote Christianity and civilization."[8]

Boudinot (previously Gallegina or Buck Watie) and his cousin Ridge were among the first pupils at Cornwall. Their fathers, Oo-watie (David Watie) and The Ridge (Major Ridge), were brothers. Education was very important to them; they were among the Cherokees who had begun to adopt white ways of farming, and they believed that literacy was crucial to their nation's survival against white encroachment. John's parents sent him to a Moravian mission school at Spring Place in northwestern Georgia in 1810, when he was seven, and, owing to John's good progress, the Waties sent their son Buck to join him there. Beginning in 1817, both boys attended the new ABCFM Brainerd School along Chickamauga Creek in Tennessee.

In that same year, Elias Cornelius, agent for the ABCFM, arrived at Brainerd to propose additional ABCFM schools in the Cherokee Nation; he also offered to enroll the brightest students in the new school at Cornwall. In May 1818 Cornelius took Buck Watie and Leonard Hicks, son of the Cherokee assistant principal chief, with him to Cornwall. Along the way they stopped at Monticello to meet Thomas Jefferson, who was very interested in the Foreign Mission School, and visited Washington, D.C., to see President Monroe.[9]

In Burlington, New Jersey, they also met Elias Boudinot, the first president of the American Bible Society and former president of the Continental Congress. Two years earlier Boudinot had published *The Star of the West*, a book advancing the proposition that North American Indians were descendants of the lost tribes of Israel. He had developed a particular concern for the situation of Indians, and he took a special interest in Buck Watie.[10] When Buck enrolled at school, he changed his name to Elias Boudinot in keeping with the "ancient Cherokee custom of changing names and the more recent practice of adopting the names of prominent whites and benefactors."[11] John Ridge joined him at school the next fall, and the cousins soon became the best students there.[12] Their parents were extremely proud of their achievements; Susannah Watie dictated in a letter to her son Elias, "When you shall have finished your education, I shall rejoice, just as if I had got the education."[13]

At first the town was fascinated by the "exotic" students, whose numbers included "one Abnaki Indian, two Choctaws, two Chinese, two Malays, one Bengalese, one Hindu, several Hawaiians, two Marquesans, three white Americans, . . . and [several] Cherokees."[14] The Cornwall community embraced the potential converts with a mixture of curiosity and missionary zeal. It apparently never occurred to the residents that these dashing strangers could attract the interest of the local young women.

Sarah and John

John Ridge had suffered from a scrofulous condition of the hip (a swelling of the lymphatic glands, not uncommon among the Cherokees) since he was a boy, and the northern climate only aggravated his problem. By the spring of 1821 he had been removed from the student quarters to a private room, where he could be nursed by Mrs. John Northrup, the wife of the school steward. Major Ridge, very concerned about his son's health, arrived to visit his son in October 1821; he dazzled the town with his fine clothes and carriage. Because John was not well enough to make the long trip home, Major Ridge returned south alone, leaving John in the care of the Northrups and the physician Samuel Gold.[15]

The busy Mrs. Northrup often sent her fourteen-year-old daughter, Sarah, to take care of the patient, and the student and his nurse soon fell in love. The doctor and the Northrups saw John's health rally, but they also may have suspected the budding romance. Both John and Sarah admitted their feelings when questioned by Mrs. Northrup. In an attempt to discourage the relationship, the Northrups sent Sarah off to her grandparents in New Haven, in the hope that the whirl of social life there would distract her from this unsuitable relationship. They were disturbed by the thought of their daughter's marrying an Indian.

In addition to the race question, the Northrups were very likely to have been concerned about Sarah's young age. At fourteen she was well below the average age for white women to marry, which in the early republic was between twenty-two and twenty-three. The nineteen-year-old John was also young for marriage by white standards: men were generally in their middle to late twenties when they married.[16]

John's parents were also less than enthusiastic when he wrote for permission to marry Sarah. They had plans for him to be a great Cherokee leader, and they wanted him to marry the daughter of a chief. Like the Northrups, the Ridges would have preferred John to marry within his race. But his parents reluctantly agreed when they realized how much he loved Sarah.

The Northrups, however, soon raised another objection to the marriage: they were worried about John's health and his need for crutches. In 1822 Mrs. Northrup advised him to go home and rest in the southern climate. He would be allowed to marry Sarah only if he could return in two years without his crutches.[17] The records are ambiguous on the question of whether they had moved beyond race-based objections at this point or whether they just used his health as an easier excuse.

By December 1823 John was well enough to return to Cornwall and to ask again for permission to marry Sarah. The Northrups agreed that he was healthy enough to wed their daughter, but the rest of the town did not react so calmly to his return. The news of the courtship soon became public, and editors and preachers used their forums to denounce the engagement.[18] The Northrups were accused of arranging the marriage for material gain, for the Ridges were a wealthy family. The planned marriage, furthermore, was seen as a threat to the school's mission. Mr. Northrup's employment at the school ended at this time; it is not clear whether he quit or was fired, but his daughter's impending marriage made a continued relationship with the school impossible.[19]

Sarah and John were married on January 27, 1824, and, in the face of an angry mob, they decided to leave Cornwall immediately. At almost every stage of their journey, they were met by outraged crowds who had read about the marriage in the newspapers. Ridge confronted the crowds with pride and dignity, and he rejected the premise that he was inferior to his white wife.[20]

Some Cornwall residents blamed the missionaries for this shocking intermarriage. The local newspaper, the *American Eagle*, chose not to mention the Northrup family by name, but it was quick to denounce the clergymen (including Lyman Beecher and Timothy Stone) who allegedly brought about the "unnatural connection." The paper also deplored the fact that the young ladies of Cornwall received the Indian students as "the most favored gallants, and beaux" and that school officials knew about this situation.[21] The school agents, shocked by this attack, quickly forbade any additional marriages across the color line.

The March 1824 quarterly report of the Foreign Mission School assured the public "that the teachers and authority, had no concern *directly* or *indirectly* in promoting this marriage." It also claimed that no additional Indian-white marriages were in the works and denied the "slander" that Cornwall's young women had been seen walking arm in arm with "foreign" scholars.[22] The principal, Herman Daggett, also tried to counter the bad publicity with a letter in the missionary press in which he again insisted that the school was not to blame for the marriage: "Neither the Agents not the Principal of the F.M. School have had any concern, directly or indirectly, in advising, aiding, or assisting, respecting this marriage: nor have they done or said any thing which had a tendency to lead to it. . . . The intercourse of the scholars generally with the inhabitants, has been marked with strict decorum and propriety."[23] The *Boston Recorder* defended the school administrators:

The marriage of John Ridge, a Cherokee Indian, to Miss Northrop, of Corn-wall, has been represented by some of the political papers in Connecticut and Massachusetts, as contrary to the wishes of the parents, and disgraceful to the Cornwall School, and some of the most respectable Clergy in Connecticut. A letter which has recently been published from Mr. Dagget, Principal of the school, to Charles Sherman, Esq. states, that the marriage was solemnized at the house of the father, with the consent of both the parents, and that the circumstances which led to it were such, as are not likely to occur again: Ridge having been sick, while a member of the school, and confined at the house of the father of the young lady.[24]

In January 1825 the school's agents were still struggling with the "nu-merous false reports" that followed the unexpected marriage; they urged mission supporters not to let "slanderous tongues" undermine their finan-cial support of the school.[25] A local historian, the Reverend Edward C. Starr, notes that in 1825 two Choctaw students, Miles Mackey ("half-breed") and James Terrell were dismissed "for a proposed matrimonial union."[26] It is likely that these young men also planned to marry white women and that school officials wanted to prevent this wave of inter-marriages.

Harriet and Elias

Colonel Benjamin Gold, a leading supporter of the Cornwall school, was also offended by the *Eagle*'s attack and wrote an angry letter denying any improper relationships between Cornwall families and the missionary stu-dents.[27] To Gold's great surprise, soon after the letter appeared in the *Connecticut Journal*, his nineteen-year-old daughter, Harriet, asked for per-mission to marry Elias Boudinot. For reasons of health, Boudinot had returned to Cherokee country in late 1822 after a short enrollment at the Andover Theological Seminary.[28] He and Harriet had corresponded dur-ing the two years since Boudinot had left the Cornwall school, and in 1824 Harriet accepted his proposal. As her sister Mary later noted, Harriet's parents "had previously felt that marriages of this kind were not sinful, and now they had a severe trial in the case of their beloved daughter."[29] Their daughter's engagement challenged them to live up to their principles in the face of extreme social pressure; they considered their standing in the community and the furor this marriage would likely cause. The Golds had a higher social status than did the Northrups: Benjamin Gold was a min-ister's son, a successful merchant farmer, and a deacon; two of his brothers had gone to Yale; and his older daughters had married Congregationalist ministers and a general in the state militia. They also hoped to dissuade Harriet because they did not want her to move away to the Cherokee Nation.[30]

For all these reasons, in early autumn 1824 Benjamin Gold wrote to Boudinot forbidding the marriage. Soon after, Harriet fell seriously ill. As she grew weaker, her parents began to think that their decision had displeased God and that her sickness was a divine warning to them. Finally, they told Harriet that they would no longer oppose her marriage, and she began a slow but steady recovery. Throughout this difficult time, no one knew of the Golds' crisis of conscience—not even Harriet's sisters and brothers. Realizing that John Ridge's marriage had almost wrecked the mission school, the Golds dreaded the public revelation of Harriet's choice and their blessing.[31] They realized that there would be strong family and community objections owing to race prejudice and the fear of potential effects on the school.

But Harriet's engagement could not be kept a secret forever. When her brother-in-law General Daniel Brinsmade informed the school's Board of Agents of her plans, the agents issued her an ultimatum: break off the engagement or face humiliation by the publication of the banns.[32] Harriet remained determined to marry the man of her choice and become a missionary to the Cherokees, so the school agents published a special report on June 17, 1825. In this desperate attempt at damage control, the agents denied any responsibility for the engagement and condemned all parties involved: "We regard those who have engaged in or accessory to this transaction, as criminal; as offering insult to the known feelings of the christian community: and as sporting with the sacred interests of this charitable institution."[33]

The agents' report took the village by storm. For her own protection, Harriet went into hiding at a friend's house. That night an angry mob, led by her brother Stephen, burned her in effigy on the village green. Harriet witnessed this scene and described it in a letter to her sister Flora and brother-in-law Herman Vaill: "A painting had before been prepared representing a beautiful young lady and an Indian. . . . The church bell began to toll, one would certainly conclude speaking the departure of a soul. . . . Brother Stephen set fire to the barrel of tar, or rather the funeral pile. . . . My heart truly sung with anguish at the dreadful scene." And yet this "dreadful scene" did not shake Harriet's determination: "I still have the consolation of feeling that I have not acted contrary to duty and that what

I have done as respects forming a connection is not *adverse to divine approbation.* . . . I have done nothing but what I had a perfect and *lawful right*
to do." Harriet's engagement also forced Mrs. Northrup and her family to
leave Cornwall for their own safety, because many Cornwall residents
accused her of arranging the two Indian marriages.[34]

In the face of violent community opposition, Harriet privately argued
that her marriage was lawful in the eyes of God and the state. Her position
did get some support in the press. *Niles' Weekly Register*, a respected Baltimore newspaper, responded to the school's publication of the engagement
by wondering, "Why so much *sensibility* about an event of this sort?" The
article pointed out that many Americans brag about their Indian blood,
"but the rev. doctor . . . who is at the head of the school, rudely exposes
the name of the young lady who has found pleasure in the society of an
Indian youth, and makes the affair 'criminal.'"[35] The *Boston Recorder* also
criticized the school's "preemptive strike" against the Gold-Boudinot marriage and suggested that the union was evidence of missionary success:
friends of missions should "regard such connexions as indicative of the
smiles of heaven upon their exertions."[36] "A Friend to Missions" in the
Religious Intelligencer insisted that the school officials were wrong when
they claimed that the marriage insulted the Christian community. In contrast, "by such persons it is thought; all the nations of the earth are brethren, being made of one blood; and that whatever our personal preferences
or antipathies may be; we have no authority to make them rules for the
government of others." In fact, the writer goes on to say, intermarriages
may even be the means of "preserving the aboriginal tribes from that
destruction with which the cupidity of white men is threatening them."[37]
This echoed the statement made by the Congregationalist minister and
geographer Jedidiah Morse several years earlier in his report to the secretary
of war: "Let the Indians, therefore, be taught all branches of knowledge
pertaining to civilized man; then let intermarriage with them become
general, and the end which the Government has in view will be completely
attained. They would then be literally of one blood with us, be merged in
the nation, and saved from extinction."[38]

The Gold Family: A House Divided against Itself

Harriet's stance seems even more courageous when we consider that she
did not have the complete support of her family. As Harriet wrote: "There
is a great division of feeling among many, but especially in our family. It
appears as though a house divided against itself could not stand."[39] Many

Cornwall residents were also shocked by Stephen Gold's public denunciation of his sister: "Even the most unprincipled say, they never heard of anything so bad even among the heathen as that of burning a sister in effigy."[40]

The Gold family were divided on what they called "the Subject," and a series of fast and furious letters flew among them. The loudest protests came from Harriet's brother Stephen and her influential brothers-in-law, General Daniel Brinsmade, the Reverend Herman Vaill, and the Reverend Cornelius Everest. Brinsmade and Vaill spoke from an insider's perspective, since Brinsmade was one of the school agents, and Vaill had been an assistant teacher at the school.[41] Harriet's parents were particularly angered by these attacks on their youngest child; as Brinsmade wrote to Vaill: "I wish to tell you, your letter you sent to Cornwall made them *mad*. Mother said you had put up one of your old sermons but she was glad you had paid the postage for it was not worth reading."[42] Harriet's brothers-in-law seem to have felt particularly betrayed by the engagement; they thought they had connected themselves with a respectable family, only to be drawn into a public controversy.

Harriet's brother Stephen was one of the major opponents to her marriage. In an angry scrawl, he wrote to inform his brother-in-law Vaill of Harriet's surprise engagement: "The dye is cast. Harriet is gone, we have reason to fear. Yes. She has told [the school agent] that she was engaged to that Indian E. and that she is determined to marry him. O!! dear!!!"[43]

Brinsmade, married to Mary Gold, was enraged over the public embarrassment brought on the family by Harriet's engagement. He wrote to Vaill for support in stopping this "Cornwall business": "Our parents have long since given their written consent to the union thro Harrietts craftiness by making them believe she should die if she did not have her Indian last winter. I have not words to express my indignation at the whole proceeding—the whole family are to be sacrificed to gratify if I may so express it the animal feelings of one of its number."[44] A few weeks later he expressed his anxiety about the prospect of biracial children: "To have black young ones and a train of evils—O I am sick at heart."[45] Brinsmade seemed most concerned about the effects of a very public scandal, but he also harbored some objection on a racial level. In denouncing Harriet's "animal feelings," he eroticized the relationship and condemned the Indian-white marriage as neither Christian nor civilized. He was also one of the few family members to raise the issue of children; lumping Indians into a nonwhite category, he described the future offspring as "black."

Another of Harriet's brothers-in-law, the Reverend Cornelius Bradford

Everest, married to Abby Gold, shared this resistance to the marriage and denounced it as against the law of nature and the law of God. In a letter to Stephen he wondered why the family, the school, and the "cause of Christ" should be "so cruelly tormented":

> Ah, it is all to be summed up in this—*our sister loves an Indian*! Shame on such love. Sad was the day when the Mission school was planted in Cornwall. What wild enthusiasm has been cherished by some in that place! And how much wickedness has been committed under this cloak of religion and of a missionary spirit. But can this unnatural—this foolish—this wicked and mischievous connection be permitted to take place? . . . [W]e cannot give up. This contemplated marriage must not take place.

Like many others in Cornwall, he blamed the Foreign Mission School for instigating the marriage. His race-based objection was both biological and religious; that is, the marriage was both "unnatural" and "wicked." In a postscript, Everest described the community support he had in Windham: "The best people here, and neighboring clergymen say that they would oppose it to the last moments, & that if she was a friend of theirs they should much rather follow her to the grave. . . . Nineteen twentieths of New England view the subject just as we do."[46]

Another clerical brother-in-law, the Reverend Herman Vaill, married to Flora Gold, and now living in Millington, responded to Brinsmade's call to action with a lengthy letter to Harriet in which he exhorted her not to go through with the marriage: "*I do, most affectionately advise, that you give up all present intentions, and all thoughts of becoming united in marriage with an Indian.*" He had long admired Harriet's desire to be a missionary, he told her, and if she were called by God to the Cherokee Nation, he would bless her and wish her well. He was concerned, however, about whether her motivation was love for God or love for Boudinot: "There is a wide difference between going, because we love the cause of Christ, and have a single eye to his glory; and going because we love another object; and have a selfish inducement." Vaill assured her that he did not consider mixed marriages criminal and that he had no objection to Boudinot, although he would respect the man more had he not considered it "necessary that he should marry a white woman." Mixed marriage was a slippery slope. It might "give license to others of the scholars, to think they might follow the example of Ridge and Boudinott." But Vaill had another worry, one overriding any evidence of Harriet's true calling, legal betrothal, and worthy fiancé. For Vaill, Harriet's marriage would "annihilate" the Foreign Mission School. It would lessen support for missionary work in general.

And, alas, "more of the heathen will be lost." He trusted that somehow God would reach out to the lost heathen, but he prophesied that Harriet and her family would bear God's wrath: "Should you become the instrument of the school's destruction, God will cause the heathen to hear his word through some other channell—'Deliverance will arise to them from another place';—but remember the word, 'but thou, and thy father's house, shall be destroyed.'" He finally exhorted her, "Do not go away like Cain and Judas; but come back like Peter. . . . Will you go? If you are a hypocrite, and designed for a reprobate, doubtless you will. But if you are a Christian, it must be you will listen, and regard the advice of friends, and the call of God and his church."[47]

Several family members read the letter and reacted strongly to Vaill's harsh words. Harriet's sister Mary Gold Brinsmade wrote to Vaill to express her disappointment in the letter, and to inform him that he had offended his in-laws: "Permit me to tell you, my dear brother, that I was sorry to see some expressions which I saw in the latter part of the letter which H. received from you last week—Our parents thought you said very hard things and very unjustly."[48] A few weeks later another sister, Catherine Gold, wrote to Vaill regarding his suggestion that he would make public his letter to Harriet: "Mary says unless you wish to disgrace yourself you must not publish it. . . . Harriet said she thought your letter was a pretty candid one till nearly the close but she cannot put up with this."[49]

Vaill did get some support from his brother-in-law and fellow clergyman Cornelius Everest: "Depend on it we are *steadfast, immovable* and almost continually *abounding* in our efforts to break up the Indian wedding." Everest was writing to Boudinot, he said, in order to strike a "*death blow* to this business.[50] Harriet's siblings felt betrayed because they had been kept in the dark for so long; as Everest insisted, "The business concerns us all."[51] At the same time, however, as the scandal grew, they wished to vindicate themselves of the charge of prior knowledge.[52] The engagement, nevertheless, was not a complete surprise. The signs had been apparent all along, but only Harriet's mother was willing to read them. The rest had been "wilfully ignorant." Catherine wrote to the Vaills:

> How often ma used to tell Flora & me that she believed that Harriett loves Elias—& that she could not say, that she did not think it possible but that she might marry him—we thought that ma was criminal in saying as she did, & used to tell her so, we thought that it would give people occasion to talk—we were always offended when she introduced the subject [because?] she did tell

us she did not know . . . we heard and saw enough to convince us of the fact had we not been determined not to believe it."[53]

With the benefit of hindsight, family members also remembered that long before the Ridge-Northrop marriage, Stephen had feared that Harriet would marry an Indian.[54]

A clear gender gap emerges from the Gold family controversy: while most of the men vigorously objected to the marriage, Harriet's sisters began to change their minds. Perhaps the men felt that they had failed in their roles as protectors of white womanhood; this failure to restrict sexual access to white women undermined their gender and race privilege and perhaps even their sense of their own masculinity. This may have been especially true for Harriet's brothers-in-law: if Elias Boudinot could also marry a young woman from the Gold family, it placed him on the same level as them and made them feel that their own status was diminished. Perhaps the Gold sisters came around because they did not have as much to lose as the men did and because they wanted above all to maintain family ties. On a more speculative note, they may have seen marriage to an Indian as a means of thwarting patriarchal power and moving beyond the control of their male relatives. Developing ideals of romantic love in the early nineteenth century may also have played a role.[55]

The men of the family were dismayed by the "turn-overs" among the women. A letter from Mary to Herman Vaill offers evidence that, while Harriet's brothers-in-law continued their anti-marriage campaign, her sisters had begun to rally to her defense:

> I have had a multitude of conflicting emotions concerning our sister Harriet since we last saw each other, but my mind has at length become more calm. I opposed the thing until conscience repeatedly smote me, and now I must acknowledge that I feel it my duty to be still. My feelings are in unison with the multitude of my Christian friends who tell me to comfort Harriet. Some of the most conscientious and best informed christians . . . think that some great good is to be brought about in these latter days by means of this event.[56]

On the same day, Mary's husband, Brinsmade, sent his own message regretting his wife's "conversion" and asserting that his opposition to the marriage was "unalterable."[57]

Harriet's sister Catherine also described how many people were rethinking their initial opposition to the marriage. After a serious illness, the Golds' friend Eunice Bindsey had changed her mind: at first she had thought "that she had rather a friend would die, than to marry an Indian;

but she did not feel so now."[58] Although Catherine herself did not approve of Harriet's plans, she was becoming resigned to its inevitability: "Strange that she can love an Indian but it is so—And she will get him if she can."[59]

After a visit with her family at Cornwall, Flora Gold Vaill was still reluctant to have her sister move so far away, but she had become "satisfied and reconciled" to Harriet's decision. Flora also reported that Stephen still opposed "indian connections" but had given up his anti-marriage campaign. He planned to absent himself when Boudinot arrived, and Flora believed that he did not intend violence.[60] With Stephen, Mary, Catherine, and Flora willing to tolerate Harriet's marriage, only sister Abby Gold Everest remained a holdout and sided with her husband in his staunch opposition. This position divided the Everests from the rest of the family and led Benjamin Gold to forbid them even to visit. As Abby wrote, "I think of my dear friends in Cornwall almost constantly, not with pleasure as I have always been accustomed to do, but with pain inexpressible. O that their eyes might be opened to see the right way."[61] Everest, however, insisted that the parental ban did not bother them: "We may keep away from his house, if we please. We are neither *frightened* nor *angry.*"[62] Despite this stubborn hostility, Harriet wanted the chance to reconcile with her sister, and asked Vaill to urge Everest to bring Abby to Cornwall.[63]

This family matter was also a topic of public debate, and as the weeks passed, the rumors continued to fly. As sister Mary described, "A thousand false reports are abroad, envious and unprincipled people are watching for an opportunity to afflict—the lying tongue is heard with approbation, but it will all soon be over."[64] Some asserted that the Gold family had planned the marriage all along in order to overthrow the missionary school; others blamed the school for instigating Indian marriages. Other Gold family members and Cornwall residents came to admire Harriet for her firm convictions and felt it was their Christian duty to comfort her in a time of persecution, regardless of their thoughts on her marriage.[65]

In September 1825 Benjamin Gold wrote a response to Vaill and to the letter that had caused so much commotion: "I saw the long letter you wrote Harriet—in which you throw out many things against her and me and my wife—about the Indian connection—which are altogether uncandid—unjust—and untrue. . . . It is through pride and prejudice—that all this clamour has been raised *against Indians.*" Gold went on to tell him that other family members had united around Harriet: "Our whol family which have been together this summer have become very harmonious on this subject."[66] Harriet's sisters and parents claimed that objections to her marriage were based on prejudice and worldly vanity about social status. Some accepted the marriage as God's will; others at the very least felt the call to comfort the persecuted.

Vaill took this hint to come on board with the rest of the family. The Vaills had also been warned by Catherine that, if they were not more respectful to their parents, the Golds were ready to take back the carpet and furniture they had promised them.[67] In a later letter to his in-laws, Vaill offered a quasi-apology, explaining that he did not blame the Golds for the marriage, but that he had simply warned Harriet that her marriage would open her parents to public criticism. In a convoluted argument, Vaill insisted that he was not prejudiced but was merely concerned about the particular circumstances of the relationship in light of the recent controversy surrounding the Ridge-Northrup marriage:

> As to their being prejudice in my mind against indians, or indian matches, I certainly have none. Harriett knows I have none. She has my own declaration in *black* & *white* that I do not think a *red* connexion to be sinful in itself. She knows I have no particular objection to the *man*;—And if H. had married Boudinott in precisely the same circumstances in which Sarah Northrop married Ridge, (that is,) before the tendency of the thing upon the school & upon Missions had been proved;—likely or not I should have said "Let 'em mix." . . . [A]s I have no prejudice against Indian matches, when they are formed as they ought to be, I shall be wholly reconciled in this case, if it can be made to appear that the matter has been managed by Harriett, with a consistent regard to her character as a Christian, & a Missionary.[68]

While insisting that he was not prejudiced against Indians, Vaill suggested that the family should bow to public prejudices; he was most concerned about how the situation appeared to outside observers. We can assume that he was worried about what his congregation had to say about the family scandal. As Brinsmade wrote to him: "How does Millington people like the idea of having a clergymen who is brother to an Indian. . . . O, I am sick at heart."[69]

Almost a year passed between the publication of the banns and the marriage, a time that allowed for some degree of family reconciliation. Most of Harriet's sisters and their husbands were able to make peace with Harriet before her marriage. In addition, brother Stephen, who had burned his favorite sister in effigy and threatened Boudinot, reconciled with her and later became a close friend of Boudinot's. Reports suggest, nevertheless, that Stephen remained at work in the sawmill during the ceremony.[70] Vaill, whose letters to Harriet had caused so much controversy, wrote her a farewell letter in which he recapitulated their disagreement, reminded her that he had always thought "such connexions" were "correct and scriptural," and offered his "kind regards and best wishes, to Brother Boudinott."[71] The Everests, by contrast, did not join in the family reconciliation; Cornelius Everest refused even to see the Golds while on a visit to Cornwall—a fact not unnoticed by the townspeople, who wondered, "Is this a minister of the gospel?"[72]

Reactions from the Cherokee Nation

The uproar surrounding the Ridge and Boudinot marriages also set off a flurry of letters from the Cherokee Nation. The ABCFM ministers in the field wrote back to the home office in Boston warning of the effects of the scandal on missionary work among the Cherokee. Upon his arrival in the Cherokee Nation, the Reverend Samuel A. Worcester reported back to Boston "that affairs in Connecticut relative to Boudinot's marriage have very much excited the minds of the Cherokees."[73] Cherokees from the mixed-blood elite also wrote to the ABCFM home office to protest their treatment in this matter. They were not necessarily advocates of interracial marriage, but rather they objected to the double standard at work and the racism that placed them in an inferior caste, contrary to all that the missionaries had taught them about Christian brotherhood.

The Reverend Daniel S. Butrick was a frequent correspondent and advocate for the Cherokees in this matter. One of the first ABCFM missionaries to the Cherokee Nation, he had arrived in 1818 and remained with them the rest of his life. He had a genuine interest in Cherokee history and culture and learned the language.[74] Ten months after the Ridge-Northrup marriage, Butrick reported that John Ridge "is not altogether pleased with the treatment he received at the North, with regard to his wife . . . he thinks his marriage was not a crime, for which they need make apologies." Butrick added that the marriage seemed to be a success: "His wife appears quite contented, and pleased with her situation."[75]

A few weeks later Butrick wrote again to Boston, this time expressing his own conviction that there was "no evil" in the marriage and his disapproval of the way the Cornwall school directors had caved in to popular prejudice. He shrewdly analyzed the role of the amalgamation taboo as a means of enforcing white supremacy: "This is placing the Cherokee youth in a very delicate situation. . . . They must be viewed with suspicion and as a grade of inferior beings." He also understood that the scandal could undermine the ABCFM's commitment to the school and urged that the scandal not deprive the Cherokee youth of educational opportunities.[76]

After his engagement became public the next year, a clearly troubled Boudinot confided in Butrick about his difficult situation, and Butrick offered his encouragement and support. No longer making calm arguments, Butrick expressed outrage over the threatening letters Boudinot was receiving from the North, which warned that if he "should appear in Cornwall, half the state would rise against him; and that his life would be in danger!" He wondered why more people did not defend Boudinot on this clear matter of justice and observed that a white male missionary had married an Indian woman "without censure" from the ABCFM. Butrick also made a scriptural argument for the validity of the marriage: because they were both Christians, "there is nothing between the two lids of the Bible to forbid such marriages." In other words, for Butrick, faith, not race, was the determinant for marital eligibility. According to this standard, not only did the objectors lack biblical support for their position, but also they directly challenged God's authority.[77]

During the controversy, John Ridge's father, Major Ridge, also looked to the local ABCFM missionaries for advice and explanation. The Reverend William Chamberlain noted that in a conversation, "[Ridge] said he wanted to know if my northern friends had any grounds from scripture or any thing else to justify them in their violent opposition to inter marriages with the cherokees, I told him I knew nothing in the bible that would justify their violant opposition."[78] Chamberlain's experience in the Cherokee Nation led him, like Butrick, to disagree with the agents in New England, who were not willing to give public support to Indian-white marriages. In addition, there were no secular laws in Connecticut forbidding interracial marriages; the state never had passed such laws—and never would. As the Cornwall incident demonstrates, however, this shortage of legal impediments did not mean that Connecticut citizens embraced the prospect of interracial marriages; clearly, social taboos were as powerful as any law could be.

David Brown, a Cherokee who had attended the Foreign Mission School with Ridge and Boudinot and later spent a year at Andover Theological Seminary, also wrote to the ABCFM to express his feelings of betrayal and confusion regarding the opposition to the marriages:

> Respecting Brother Boudinot, it becomes me to speak with some delicacy as I also am an Indian. . . . These things are the common topics of conversation among us & we know not how to understand them. Your missionaries have told us that the people of New England were our firm friends & that we might

at all times lean on them for assistance; & we have felt particularly greatful for their kind offices. But you will not be supprized to hear that our confidence is now somewhat shaken. We are necessarily led to inquire, whether our friends in New England have always acted from love to us & a desire to do us good. If they loved us how could they treat us in this manner. They can not suppose it wicked for white people to marry Cherokees because members of Baptists, Methodist, and Presbeterian churches have married Cherokee ladies without censure. If white men may marry among us without offence, how can it be thought wicked for us to marry among them; especially if some of our white sisters are pleased with such connexions.

Do our beloved friends in Connecticut say that such marriages will cast an indelible stain on their characters & be a reproach to their state? But if they loved us, would they not be willing to stoop down & take a part of our reproach rather than add to the enormous weight under which we have so long been lying?[79]

As Brown observed, perhaps disingenuously, the failure of the ABCFM to defend its Cherokee students had repercussions far beyond Connecticut; this betrayal threatened the Christian missions in the Cherokee Nation as well, for when the Cornwall and Boston missionaries failed to rise to the occasion, the Cherokees learned that no white institution could be trusted to support them.[80]

There are some key voices missing in this series of protest letters from the Cherokee Nation. Specifically, there is little record of the reactions of John Ridge and Elias Boudinot to the controversy. A letter from Ridge published during the controversy over his engagement, however, does give some sense of his anger over white attitudes: "Prejudice is the ruling passion of the age, and an Indian is almost considered accursed. He is frowned on by the meanest peasant, and the scum of the earth are considered sacred in comparison to the son of nature."[81] Here Ridge draws on Enlightenment notions of the "noble savage" in order to protest his treatment. Another small piece of evidence is a letter Ridge wrote to the ABCFM after his marriage requesting that his father-in-law, John Northrup, be hired to run the farm at a new mission station: "You knew him in the character of a steward of the F. M. school, with credit and benefit to the institution untill the crime was committed in the act of marriage with his daughter and myself."[82] Ridge implies that his support for the mission depended on the hiring of his father-in-law; perhaps he felt that the fiasco at Cornwall entitled him to make demands.

Boudinot's attitude toward the scandal can be caught only in glimpses. A few weeks after his marriage, he asked his white audience in a fund-raising lecture: "What is an Indian? Is he not formed of the same materials with yourself? For 'of one blood God created all the nations that dwell on the face of the earth.'" A year after his marriage, he wrote to Vaill asking him to drum up subscribers for the *Cherokee Phoenix* "if any are to be had in Connecticut, the land of *intermarriages*."[83] He also emphasized his Indian identity in his letters: for example, in 1829 he boasted to his in-laws that his daughter Mary "has real Indian black eyes" and signed himself "your Indian brother."[84]

Although first-person accounts of Ridge's and Boudinot's reactions to the Cornwall scandal are sparse, scholars of Cherokee history agree that the reaction of whites to their marriages was a bitter lesson. As Theda Perdue observes, they "discovered that just beneath the philanthropic surface of American society lurked a virulent racism."[85] According to Thurman Wilkins, Ridge learned that race prejudice was all-pervasive, found in both "enlightened" and "ignorant" society.[86] This experience also had a profound influence on Boudinot, according to Perdue: "He had believed that conversion and education would erase all differences between Indians and whites, yet he found himself treated as an outcast by the very people he tried to emulate."[87]

Despite their feelings of betrayal and disillusionment, Boudinot and Ridge never broke their ties with the ABCFM. Boudinot worked closely with Samuel Worcester on Cherokee translations of the Bible and on the *Cherokee Phoenix*. John Ridge still valued the educational opportunities the ABCFM brought to the Cherokee Nation. As James Parins notes, "Despite his preoccupation with making a living and the bad feelings engendered by the reaction to his marriage, Ridge did not cease to champion the cause of the missionaries, especially their educational efforts."[88] Soon after his arrival in the Cherokee Nation with his new bride, Chamberlain reported that "young Mr. Ridge appears very friendly to the Missionary cause."[89] In addition, Ridge continued to see New Englanders as valuable allies in the battle against Georgia. In an 1832 speech at the Old South Church in Boston, Ridge described to his listeners how the Cherokee General Council had sent him to seek their help: "Go to the cities of the North, and let them know our distress. Go to the land of that great man who . . . nobly defended the Cherokees on the floor of Congress; go to the land of EDWARD EVERETT. . . . Go to the city of that man who struggled for our rights to the last, and died in the cause of the Cherokees; the city of Jeremiah Evarts."[90]

The Wedding and the Aftermath: Cornwall's Indian Removal

In December 1825 the Cherokee General Council sent Boudinot north on a tour to raise money for a Cherokee press and newspaper. This trip was very important for personal reasons as well: as Samuel Worcester observed, "He will visit Cornwall and I presume does not intend to leave it without a wife."[91] After lecture stops in Charleston and New York, Boudinot went on to Cornwall, where he and Harriet were married on May 1, 1826.[92] Because Boudinot had received threatening letters in Georgia, the Gold family took every safety precaution.[93] Harriet's parents accompanied the newlyweds as far as Washington, Connecticut, then from there the Boudinots traveled on their own. They made lecture stops in several cities and then headed for Cherokee country.[94] It is there as editor of the *Cherokee Phoenix* that Boudinot made a name for himself, but he and Harriet also left their mark on Connecticut.[95]

The directors of the ABCFM in Boston knew that the incidents at Cornwall would have an inevitable effect on their missionary work. The corresponding secretary, Jeremiah Evarts, insisted that there was nothing wrong with the marriages and attacked the school's committee for publishing letters denouncing them. Like Butrick, Evarts knew that the Cherokees would see the denunciations as "a declaration that they & their people are doomed to perpetual inferiority."[96] Butrick and Evarts did disagree, however, about the implications of this incident for the school. Evarts believed that the school could not survive this controversy and brought the matter before the board's Prudential Committee. The ABCFM waited until the fall to close the school officially in order to convince the public, especially mission contributors, "that policy considerations and not the Gold-Boudinot marriage had led to the school's closing."[97] Regardless of this charade, it is clear that the Foreign Mission School did indeed close its doors as a result of the intermarriage scandal.

Although the quarterly reports of the Foreign Mission School repeatedly addressed the controversy and acknowledged that it was hurting support for the school, the annual reports of the ABCFM and the official history by Joseph Tracy are silent on the intermarriage scandal, reflecting the ABCFM's desire to downplay the controversy. Nowhere do they say that the Cornwall school closed because of the Indian-white marriages, nor are these marriages even mentioned. Nevertheless, the language of the reports makes it clear that the marriages were not easily forgotten.

The reports of the Cornwall school for 1822–24 are overwhelmingly positive. Tracy's history, published in 1842, acknowledges that as late as 1823, "there seems to have been no suspicion that the School must ultimately be discontinued," but, trying to anticipate the closure in his narrative, he contends that the school's growing management difficulties were evident.[98] The evaluations of the school started to decline at the 1825 annual meeting, and a committee was appointed to decide whether the school should even remain open.

Why the radical shift? By the 1825 meeting, the Ridge-Northrup marriage was well known, and the banns for the forthcoming Boudinot-Gold marriage may already have been published. Although these events are not referred to directly, the scandal surrounding the school is hinted at: "Still every human institution has its defects, and is exposed to evils which cannot always be foreseen."[99] Romances between the students and the local young women could easily fall into the category of "unforeseen evils." The report goes on to suggest that it might be cheaper and more effective to send missionaries to the Indian nations and abroad rather than have a few young men come to eastern cities and towns. This plan also had the benefit of keeping the "foreigners" away from the local young women.

The next year, at the 1826 annual meeting, the board concluded "that the Providence of God appears to indicate, that the continuance of the Foreign Mission School in Cornwall is not expedient."[100] Again there is no direct mention of the Ridge-Northrup and Boudinot-Gold marriages, which had taken place earlier that year, but the alarm that these events caused can be read in the reasons given for the school's closure. The board first explains that "the design of giving a good education to young men of heathen birth and parentage, in order that they may aid in evangelizing their countrymen, can now be executed more favorably at several missionary stations, than at any place in a Christian country."[101] This decision also upholds the goal of segregation of the races. Second, the board discusses the difficulty of regulating the social interaction of the students with white society: "If permitted to visit at all . . . they are apt to receive more marked attentions from persons of all ages and both sexes, than any of our own young men receive, or than we should think it safe and proper that any young persons should receive."[102] Here the board reveals its concern with the popularity of the students among the local young women and even asserts that the students are sexual rivals for Cornwall's young men. Because this situation was neither "safe" nor "proper," the school could no longer function effectively.

To be fair to the board, the closing of the school did reflect other policy considerations; the Cornwall experiment had demonstrated that small schools that isolated potential converts from their people and culture were not "effective instrument[s] for cultural transformation."[103] Because acculturation techniques did not win many converts, in future missions such as the Whitman Mission in Oregon (1836–47) the ABCFM emphasized spiritual education over secular education, but without success.[104]

If the ABCFM records erase the intermarriage scandal, Theodore Gold's 1877 history of Cornwall is more frank about what happened: "The school was a decided success as far as its original plan was concerned, and was closed because the opportunities of educating the heathen on their own ground were opened, thus rendering it unnecessary and from the local opposition produced by the marriage of two Cherokee Indians with respectable white girls residing in the town."[105] Nevertheless, Theodore Gold (Harriet's cousin, who would have been eight years old when the school closed and whose father, Dr. Samuel Gold, treated Harriet during her illness) declares that the whole scenario should have been avoided: "Many things are lawful which are far from being expedient. Had such who wished this connection to take place, known more of human nature, and the prejudices of society in which they lived they would not have involved themselves and others in such evils as actually took place. This event greatly embarrassed the mission school, and led to great evil in the church and society."[106] Clearly, Gold belonged to a branch of the family that never accepted the marriage; his cousin's sin was not marrying an Indian but rather challenging deeply held prejudices before the family and the community were ready. Another town historian, Edward Starr, who downplays the scandal as a "tempest in a teapot," also acknowledges that the marriages had contributed to the school's closure.[107]

Cornwall was not the only Connecticut town where educational opportunities for people of color led to controversy. In 1833–34 the violent public opposition in Canterbury to Prudence Crandall's school for "colored females" forced her to close it down. As in Cornwall, fears of intermarriage played a large role in the opposition, although it seems that no marriages actually took place—and unlike in Cornwall, the Canterbury residents opposed the school from the start. At a town meeting, residents condemned the school as promoting "disgusting doctrines of amalgamation." Ironically, as Edwin and Miriam Small relate, many of these same critics claimed to be "true friends of the Negro in their capacity as members of the Friends of Colonization in Africa." As the ABCFM concluded about its Indian students, the advocates of colonization believed that blacks should be educated only in order to prepare them to return to Africa. Neither town could envision a permanent place for students of color in its community.[108]

Gender, Pride, and Prejudice

It is only fitting that this discussion of Indian-white marriage should begin with a missionary school. The government-sponsored work of the ABCFM and other organizations was part of a large-scale attempt at the cultural assimilation of Indians. The violent reaction to amalgamation shows that white support of missionary endeavors stopped short when they led to intermarriage, especially the intermarriage of Indian men and white women. The situation might have been different if female Indian students had married white men from Cornwall; the marriage of Indian women to white men was seen as a good method of "whitening" and "humanizing" the Indian race. But the marriage of Indian men to white women threatened white superiority and triggered masculine anxiety. In any case, the Enlightenment ideals of the Indians' potential for "civilization" soon gave way to the belief that "you can't change an Indian." With the election of President Andrew Jackson, the public officially rejected models of biological or cultural assimilation in favor of policies of removal and racial segregation.

The objections to Indian-white marriages raised in the Cornwall incident were rooted in prejudice (and "prejudice" is the word commonly used by parties in the controversy). For Cornwall's townspeople, as John Andrew observes, "civilizing savages meant extermination of their culture and instruction in Protestantism, not marriage to them."[109] Thus, no matter how well educated and devout the Cherokee suitors were, they could never become "white" and therefore were not acceptable husbands for white women. Interestingly, one of the Cornwall town histories notes the differences in the Cherokee cousins' appearance: Ridge "did not look the Indian," while Boudinot "looked the Indian."[110] Thurman Wilkins, in his history of the Ridge family, agrees that Ridge's complexion was light and that he might have "passed" for white as a child.[111] The greater controversy surrounding the Boudinot marriage may have been owing partially to the fact that Boudinot's otherness was marked on his face. And if "money whitens," the prosperity of his family may also have made Ridge seem a slightly more suitable husband.

Gold family members were keenly aware of public hostility and the loss of social status attendant on Harriet's marriage. Seen as both "wicked" and "unnatural," interracial marriages were said to violate God's will. In a few other New England states, Indian-white marriages were also illegal. Although such marriages were not illegal in Connecticut, the extreme social pressure may have served as an effective deterrent.

White defenders of the two marriages denounced the attackers for their "pride and prejudice." They observed that the taboo against Indian-white marriage was a means of enforcing an inferior status and also noted the double standard that allowed white men to marry Indian women without censure. They also argued that mixed marriages were not forbidden by the Bible and offered an alternative interpretation making faith the basis for marital eligibility.

The Cherokees made many of these arguments themselves and also recognized the scandal as a telling betrayal: it was a sign that the whites did not love them "as their neighbor" and that they would never be welcomed into white society. The scandal at Cornwall and the consequent closure of the Foreign Mission School made Boudinot and Ridge reconsider their beliefs in acculturation and peaceful coexistence; their exposure to prejudice among their "Northern friends" likely influenced their decision that removal was the best chance for Cherokee survival.

The intermarriage scandal disrupted the narrative of civilization and conversion at the Foreign Mission School. Established with the best missionary intentions, the school was threatened by the students' marriages to white women. After much conflict and struggle, equilibrium was restored only when the couples left town and the school was closed. The narrative of racial incompatibility thus triumphed over the disruptive narrative of intermarriage.

Intermarriage caused problems for white Americans on both sides of the removal debates: it pushed missionaries to the limits of their desire for assimilation, while at the same time it challenged the narratives of racial incompatibility that justified the ongoing removal of the Indians. As will be seen in the next chapter, colonial governments over a century earlier had recognized the disruptive potential of interracial marriage and tried to contain it within legal discourse.

2

A "Wicked and Mischievous Connection": The Origins and Development of Indian-White Miscegenation Law

But can this unnatural—this foolish—this wicked and mischievous connection be permitted to take place?
The REVEREND CORNELIUS B. EVEREST

The scandal at Cornwall raises some significant questions about early national society. Why would reformers, eager for the assimilation of Indians into the larger society, so definitively reject interracial marriage, which would seem to offer a commonsense avenue to assimilation? What was so threatening about these marriages that even radical reformers froze when they were proposed and panicked when they were realized?

Attitudes toward Indian-white marriages in the early nineteenth century depended in part on evolving beliefs about the relationship between religion/culture and heredity/"blood."[1] This new biological definition of "race"—that heredity determines culture—made racial identity the fundamental criterion for citizenship and land rights for both whites and Indians. As a consequence, the regulation of sex and reproduction through miscegenation laws became crucial. As the legal scholar Rachel F. Moran explains, miscegenation laws served the purposes of "defining racial identity, establishing racial inequality, and preserving moral propriety"; I would add that the desire for property underlay all these motivations.[2]

Through a chronological narrative of race prejudice and miscegenation law arising in the English colonial experience and extending into the new United States, I describe in this chapter the evolving and unstable meaning of "race" as the term changes over time, emphasizing the connections between religion and heredity in forming categories of difference. I then trace the origins of the social taboo and law back to their origins in colonial

34

times. Building on this background, I discuss the endorsement and rejection of Indian-white marriages in the era of Jeffersonian Indian policy. Finally, I broaden the discussion with an Indian perspective on intermarriage, comparing the substantial body of Cherokee miscegenation law with that of the American states. What becomes clear is that concerns about interracial marriage are closely linked to concerns about property.

Defining "Race"

Before I address the taboo against interracial marriages, it is important to realize that "race" has meant different things in different historical moments, for these historical shifts are a crucial component of the controversies over intermarriage. Current scholars see race as a social construction. As David Brion Davis observes, "Since responsible scientists have long discredited any biological or genetic definition of racial groups, historians have increasingly recognized that the so-called races of mankind" were invented to justify and expedite European colonialism. The fact that race does not have a biological basis, however, does not make it any less powerful as a concept in creating a social hierarchy. Scholars generally concur that racism, as we understand it in twentieth-century terms, did not develop until the nineteenth century. Although by this time race was seen as a set of biological traits, earlier notions of difference included cultural and religious factors as well.[3]

In Europe, the idea that heredity determined religious and cultural identity, a key concept in racial theory, developed in Spain during the fourteenth and fifteenth centuries.[4] Before this time, Christians, Muslims, and Jews lived together in a state of *convivencia*, at best an "uneasy coexistence." After the anti-Jewish riots of 1391, however, Spanish Jews were under increasing pressure to convert, and many of them did, using their new Christian identities to acquire wealth and political power. But while they were no longer Jews in religion, they still suffered from anti-Semitism. Some of the "old Christian" leadership began to challenge the religious identity of the *conversos*, charging them with being "secret Jews." To a considerable extent, this fear sparked the infamous Inquisition. The Inquisition of 1480 engendered a belief in "the hereditary nature of social status"; the argument was that *conversos* could not be true Christians because of the overpowering influence of their Jewish "blood." After the forced conversions of the Muslims in the early sixteenth century, the Inquisition investigated similar claims about the Moriscos, or Muslim converts to Christianity. Thus, being Christian by heredity and not by conversion became a highly important distinction. In order to avoid the stigma of conversion, many Spaniards sought a Limpieza de Sangre (purity of blood) certificate from the church, which guaranteed that the bearer was free of the "taint" of Jewish or Muslim blood.[5] In effect, notes Henry Kamen, "what had begun as social discrimination developed into social antagonism and racialism."[6] It is important to realize that the Limpieza statutes were not universally accepted and were hotly debated. Nevertheless, the legacy of the Spanish Inquisition for racial thought was a significant one: it rejected the possibility of conversion or assimilation and located cultural and religious identity in the blood.

The Spanish brought their Catholic religious enthusiasm with them to the New World; a corresponding Protestant zeal was also a fundamental aspect of English identity. In the new world of colonial expansion, "religious affiliation . . . was often the key to not only another person's identity, but also to how the person was to be treated."[7] Thus when the English encountered Indians in North America, Christianity was seen as the primary distinction between the peoples. The first English settlers did not see themselves as a "race" separate from the Indians in the way that the term would be used by the mid-nineteenth century; although the Indians did differ from the English in appearance, religion, and culture, they were not thought to belong to a distinct, inferior biological group: "Pilgrims and Puritans did not think that Indians were a race apart," write Charles Segal and David Stineback. "Adam and Eve were their parents, too."[8] Religion, however, was a significant barrier. As Ann Taves puts it, in the English colonies "the initial social distinctions between 'us' and 'them' were primarily, but not exclusively, religious." Taves also lists the English names for the native peoples compiled by Roger Williams: "*Natives, Savages, Indians, Wild-men . . . Abergeny men, Pagans, Barbarians, Heathen.*" Such names indicate that for the English, "the primary distinctions between the native peoples and the colonizers were *religious* (pagan, heathen), *cultural* (savage, wild-men, barbarian), and *geographical* (native, Indian, aborigine)."[9] The religious distinctions were particularly important because paganism could be grounds for exclusion from humanity in some circles; at the very least it was evidence of cultural inferiority.[10]

Whereas the first English settlers divided the world into Christian nations and heathen tribes, eighteenth-century Enlightenment thinkers were more likely to see climate as the cause of human difference. In other words, writes Reginald Horsman, "environment, not innate racial differences, accounted for the marked gaps in achievement between different peoples and different nations." This environmental view was coupled with a belief in the possibility of the improvement of "savage" peoples.[11]

In the early national period, the ideals of Enlightenment environmentalism conflicted with the experiences of European Americans with Indian and African populations. These peoples were not always eager to adopt "superior" Anglo-American ways. In addition, many Anglo-Americans were more interested in profiting from Indian land and African labor than in doing missionary work. In order to acquire land and hold slaves, they defined Indians and Africans as permanently inferior.[12] Rather than attributing differences to environmental causes, they defined these differences as biological, fixed, and unchangeable. Or, as Elise Lemire puts it, there was a "shift in the definition of race from a set of environmentally induced characteristics to [a set of] hereditary species traits."[13]

The Cornwall intermarriage scandal is a case in point. For most Cornwall residents, Indian "otherness" was reason enough to forbid the marriages; for a small minority, John Ridge and Elias Boudinot's Christian status made their marriages to white women acceptable. Evolving questions about the connections among religion, culture, and "blood" helped make these marriages so controversial. Could religion and culture be separated from "blood" or biological heredity? Attitudes toward Indian-white marriages depended on the answer to this question. Those few Cornwall residents who accepted the notion of "one blood" and held on to the Enlightenment connections among religion, culture, and environment were able to support the Ridge and Boudinot marriages. Those who opposed the marriages believed that religion and culture were a matter of blood and that assimilation was an impossible ideal. The ABCFM members who opposed the marriages walked a difficult line: their whole mission was based on a belief in the possibility of conversion, but they could not overcome the racial barrier between whites and Indians. Caught between changing ideas about race, they found themselves advocating both assimilation and separation, a contradictory position that could not hold.

This new understanding of race is succinctly explained by Hannah Franziska Augstein:

> Nineteenth-century racial theory combines several elements: the first is the notion that mankind is divisible into a certain number of "races" whose characteristics are fixed and defy the modifying influences of external circumstances. Secondly, it contains the idea that the intellectual and moral capacities may be unevenly spread within the various human races. Thirdly, it advocates the

notion that mental endowments are bound up with certain physiognomical specificities which, being defined as racial characteristics, are considered to reveal the inward nature of the individual or the population in question.[14]

Using this theory of Anglo-Saxon superiority, the English and the Anglo-Americans came to believe that "blood, not environment or accident, had led to their success." Thus "race was the key to historical explanation," Horsman notes, and "the basis of English and American nineteenth-century power."[15]

It is ironic that nineteenth-century racial theory focused so heavily on "race purity," since the English and the Americans themselves were an example of a "hybrid race." The English responded by "flaunting their hybridity as an English virtue" (here is also an example of the overlapping language of "race" and "nationality"). Opponents of amalgamation in the New World found themselves in the difficult position of attributing the achievements of the Anglo-Saxon race to its historical mix of peoples, but then arguing that further mixture would lead to the degeneration of this greatness.[16] Detractors from this racial schema countered that there was no "Anglo-Saxon race," noting that "England clearly contained a mixture of peoples, and the white population of the United States was even less homogeneous."[17] But despite these critiques, the growing belief that race was a matter of biology made sex and reproduction matters for government control.[18]

Indian-White Marriage in Colonial Tradition and Law

By the time of the Cornwall incident, British authorities had been struggling to control interracial contact in America for at least two hundred years. Several influences led to the taboo against intermarriage and to the development of Anglo-American miscegenation law, including the English experience with the Irish and the the Puritan typological view of history. As a result of these and other influences, the English refused to accept Indians, even Christianized ones, as equals.

Since the earliest days of settlement, English colonial authorities feared Indian-white liaisons, to a great extent because of their prior experience with "racial others"—notably the Irish. To a nation that had conquered the Gaelic Irish, the American Indians presented a comparable case and a comparable opportunity. Gaelic society, condemned as heathen (though nominally Catholic), violent, uncivilized, and savage, provided, as R. F.

Foster describes, "an index of comparison for observation of American Indians and Africans." Like the Irish, Nicholas Canny concurs, "both Indians and blacks . . . were accused of being idle, lazy, dirty, and licentious." Among other similarities, the Irish and the Indians did not make "proper use" of the land, a deficiency that justified an English takeover both in Ireland and in America.[19] At the same time the English conquerors felt a certain fascination with these primitive peoples. The "conundrum" of the Irish which R. F. Foster describes could easily be applied to the Indians: "How could the Irish be both savage and subtle? Both warlike and lazy? At once evidently 'inferior,' yet possessed of an ungovernable pride? Cowardly, yet of legendary fortitude in the face of death? Socially primitive, yet capable of complex litigation?"[20]

Despite—or because of—these supposed negative Irish qualities, the English colonization of Gaelic Ireland also demonstrated how readily Englishmen could be fascinated and seduced by contact with "savage" lifestyles and "savage" women. The Old English, or descendants of the first conquerors of Ireland, became Gaelicized at a rate that was alarming to English observers: they sent their children out to be fostered in Gaelic families, intermarried with the Gaelic population, and used Gaelic wet-nurses.[21] By 1366 the "degeneracy" of the Old English had reached such a crisis point that the Statutes of Kilkenny banned intimate relationships between the English and Irish, ordering that "no alliance by marriage, gossipred, fostering of children, concubinage or amour or in any other manner be henceforth made between the English and Irish."[22] The law also established restrictions "forbidding Englishmen to wear Irish dress or hairstyles, to speak the Irish language, . . . to trade with the Irish," or to take Irish names. Irish games, poetry, and music were also outlawed.[23] Three hundred years later, while the English were establishing settlements in North America, the government was still trying to protect Englishmen from succumbing to the Irish way of life. Commentators noted that assimilation was happening in reverse, as "English settlers in Ireland were lapsing from their former state of civility to become absorbed into native society."[24]

It was an easy step to equate the Irish with the Indian, and the anxiety that Englishmen would revert to savagery through biological intermingling with the "uncivilized" was extended to the Indians of North America.[25] Reference to the *Oxford English Dictionary* further illustrates the connections between "others" in the Old and New Worlds. Throughout the seventeenth and eighteenth centuries, the English used "savage," meaning "uncivilized; existing in the lowest state of culture," to describe Scottish

Highlanders, Irish Celts, and Indians. For example, entries include references to "the sauage Irish" (1600), "a savadge of America" (1605), and "the highlanders, whom more savage nations called Savage" (1772).

In contrast, although the Statutes of Kilkenny defined the English way of life as superior, the most disparaging term for the Irish used in the law is "Irish enemies." The fact that the "Irish enemies" had become "sauage Irish" by the time of the American settlements may reflect increasing frustration with Irish resistance, carrying serious implications for interactions with the "savadges of America." By the late sixteenth century, there were still a few Tudor officials who believed that the Irish could be civilized, but this relative benevolence was contradicted by the "scorched-earth policy" of the Elizabethan army. Officials talked about "removing" the Gaelic Irish to make room for an English state, and the literature now described the Irish not as "enemies" but as "a population of beasts and vermin." Pagan and uncivilized, the hopelessly savage state of the Irish justified the English takeover. This formula would be repeated in the New World.[26]

Protestant cultures invest Scripture with ultimate authority in questions of human behavior, so it is not surprising that colonial authorities turned to the Bible for guidance about intermarriage.[27] They found a wealth of scriptural prohibitions against it. The first Puritan settlers read the Geneva Bible of 1560, from which they could draw lessons from the experience of the Israelites; the 1611 King James Version contained identical injunctions against mixing with foreign peoples.[28] The Puritan reformers believed in a typological view of history, that is, they believed that their destiny was foreshadowed by prior events in the history of God's first chosen people, the Israelites. Thomas Davis writes, "The peculiar circumstances of the New England experiment—the New Exodus, the journey through the Wilderness, the establishment of a New Israel, and so on—provided the Puritan with a continuous analogy to the great biblical dramas."[29] For this reason, the Puritans believed that the injunctions given to the Israelites against intermarriage applied also to them. According to Jill Lepore, they feared that in the New World, "instead of becoming 'visible saints' for all of Europe to see, the English might expect to become more savage with each passing year, not only less religious but also less and less like Englishmen. And more and more like Indians."[30]

In the Old Testament, the Lord repeatedly warns the chosen people not to mix with the original inhabitants of the Promised Land. On the journey to Canaan, he admonishes the Israelites to stay apart from the Canaanites, Amorites, Hittites, and so on: "So acute is the danger of syncretism," observes *The Jerome Biblical Commentary*, "that the Israelites are to make no agreements with them."[31] In Exodus the Lord warns them to "make no compact with the inhabitants of the land . . . lest thou take of their daughters unto thy sonnes, and their daughters go a whoring after their gods, and make thy sonnes go a whoring after their gods" (Exod. 34:11–16). The real danger is that intermarriages would cause the Israelites to turn from their true God. As Moses commands in the book of Deuteronomy: "Nether shalt thou make marriages with them, nether give thy daughter unto his sonne nor take his daughter unto thy sonne. For they wil cause thy sonne to turn away from me, & to serve other gods: then will the wrath of the Lord waxe hote against you and destroy thee sodenly" (Deut. 7:3–4). The Puritans also emphasized exclusiveness, even earlier in England and Holland, "in order to protect themselves from the sinfulness of others."[32] In *Of Plymouth Plantation*, for example, William Bradford explains that the decision of the Separatists to leave the Netherlands for America was in part based on their fears for their children, who "were drawn away by evil examples into extravagant and dangerous courses."[33]

Despite these warnings from Moses, upon entering the Promised Land the Israelites fail to keep themselves separate, and they intermarry with the "people of the land." Several books of the Old Testament, including Sirach and Nehemiah, blame the fall of Jerusalem on the foreign wives taken by the priests and by King Solomon himself. These foreign women lead Solomon away from his fear of God; his violation of the law leads to a schism in the nation.[34] The results are catastrophic: the Babylonian army destroys Israel and sends the chosen people into exile. The Plymouth colony faced similar threats in the New World from Thomas Morton's Merrymount settlement, where Morton and his coterie maintained a "School of Atheism," sold guns to the Indians, and, significantly, drank and danced with "Indian women for their consorts." The colonial authorities clamped down on Merrymount for several reasons, but one was to avoid the catastrophe suffered by Israel.[35]

In the post-exilic period, the Israelites became increasingly isolated, though their obsessive "fear of pagan, religious infiltration" is somewhat understandable, considering that pagan influence is what "drove the Israelites headlong into the debacle of Exile."[36] In the post-exilic books of the Old Testament, there is a compelling desire not to repeat past errors. Back in Jerusalem, however, the Israelites fall into their old patterns and do not obey the injunction to keep themselves separate, as evidenced by the reprimands in the books of Malachi (2:11) and Nehemiah (10:30).

The priest Ezra takes the most extreme stance against the mixed marriages: "The people of Israel . . . are not separated from the people of the lands . . . for they have taken their daughters to them selves, and to their sonnes and they have mixed the holy sede with the people of the lands" (Ezra 9:1–2). Here Ezra conflates the language of religion and heredity; the Israelites' status as God's chosen people makes them "a race apart" from Canaan's original residents. This holy status, grounded in biological distinctiveness, requires that they separate themselves from all other peoples. In order to fulfill this mandate, Ezra leads the people to take a drastic step: "Now therefore let us make a covenant with our God to put away all the wives (and suche as are borne of them) according to the counsel of the Lord" (Ezra 10:3). This incident, in which the chosen people abandon "strange" wives and children, eerily foreshadows the practices of American miscegenation law. As the *Jerome Commentary* observes, "Natural law obligations of justice and decency toward spouses in good faith and utterly innocent children seem never to have entered the heads of these reformers, excited by a kind of mob psychosis for which Ezra cannot escape blame."[37] Like nineteenth-century Americans, the Israelites do not know what to do with the offspring of mixed marriages. Similarly, the children of these marriages are made illegitimate because the marriages were declared unlawful (Ezra 10:44 note n).

This horrific scene in the book of Ezra illustrates the complex, highly gendered nature of intermarriage bans. In different historical contexts, both "strange men" and "strange women" were perceived as threats to a society. In the Old Testament, "foreign women" are seen as the root of Israel's problems; these temptresses are dangerous threats in their ability to lure the Israelites away from their true God. The English attributed a similar power to the Irish women who "lured" their soldiers away from English "civilization" to a savage life. At the same time, in Anglo-American society it was the male other whose sexuality was most feared; black and Indian men were denied sexual access to white women in order to construct white masculinity as superior. In this construction women of color are not so dangerous, but they are stereotyped as passionate and sexually available to white men. In either case, whether women are perceived as threats or as available sex partners, bans on intermarriage strip them of any legal protections. Such marriages are either illegal or liable to retroactive nullification, leaving intermarried women and their mixed-blood children quite vulnerable.

The ban on intermarriages continues in the New Testament, but it is couched in the new terminology of Christianity. The apostle Paul separates religion from blood: the divide is no longer between "chosen people" and "people of the lands" but between "believers" and "unbelievers." As Paul writes to the Corinthians: "Be not unequally yoked with the infideles: for what felowship hathe righteousness with unrighteousness? and what communion hathe light with darknes? . . . Wherefore come out from among the[m] and separate your selves, saith the Lord: and touche none uncleane thing, & I will receive you" (2 Cor. 6:14–18).[38] He informs the Colossians that in this new faith the former divisions have passed away: "Where is nether Grecian nor Jewe, circumcision or uncircumcision, Barbarian, Scythian, bonde, fre: but Christ is all and in all things" (Col. 3:11). In Paul's letter to the Galatians, he echoes this statement and adds, "And if ye be Christs, then are ye Abrahams seed, and heires by promise" (Gal. 3:28–29). Paul continues to use images of heredity, but transforms the image to make metaphorical "heires" of all who believe in Jesus. Thus, the new measure of a marriage partner's suitability is not race or ethnicity but faith in Jesus Christ.[39]

It was not difficult for English colonists to apply the stories of the Old Testament to their situation in the New World. The Puritans already saw themselves as God's new chosen people, so to obey the injunction to stay clear of the "peoples of the land," the Indians in the role of Canaanites, was a logical step. The radical reframing of the issue in the New Testament posed more difficult interpretive problems: the prohibition was now between believers and unbelievers, more dynamic and fluid categories than the simple formula of chosen people versus people of the land.

The chosen people by definition are the people of God; it is their inheritance and it is in their blood. The New Testament says that the new people of God are the believers in Jesus Christ as the Messiah, regardless of whether they first were Jews or not. This separation of religion and blood has been a challenge to the church from the beginning. As we have seen, several New Testament letters deal with this issue, instructing the first Christian communities that there is no longer a division between Gentile or Jew, servant or free, woman or man.[40] Pope Nicholas V himself reminded Spanish Catholics of this teaching in response to a 1449 law banning *conversos* from public office in Toledo when he "denounced the ideas of excluding Christians from office simply because of their blood origins" and declared "that all Catholics are one body in Christ."[41] Despite the many voices echoing this argument, Spanish Catholic society ultimately rejected this separation of faith and heredity. The Puritans also rejected the New Testament separation of faith and blood. While they halfheartedly worked to convert the Indians, in their eyes the only true Christians were the English Puritan ones. "No matter how hard the Puritan tried to transform the Indian or how completely the Indian conformed," writes G. E. Thomas, "the cause was ultimately hopeless because the Indian could never become white."[42] Even into the nineteenth century, as the scandal at Cornwall demonstrated, praying Indians were treated as second-class Christians at best.[43]

Although Indian-white marriages were not illegal in most colonies, they were relatively rare. The Irish colonial experience, biblical injunctions, and the failure to accept even Christian Indians as equals, all factors reflecting a fear of cultural loss and degeneration ("going native"), discouraged New England colonists from intermarrying. In addition, demographic factors such as balanced sex ratios, family emigration, and a declining Indian population also prevented extensive intermarriage.[44]

By way of a regional comparison, the South also had a scarcity of Indian-white marriages. Virginia, the site of the famous marriage of Pocahontas and John Rolfe in 1614, did not produce a significant number of Indian-white connections during the seventeenth century. The Virginia settlement, though lacking the Puritan devotional fire, also heeded the advice against mixing with native people. Rolfe worried about the scriptural ban before his marriage to Pocahontas, but then rationalized an exception through his noble intentions: "for the good of this plantation, for the honour of our countrie, for the glory of God, for my owne salvation, and for converting to the true knowledge of God and Jesus Christ, an unbeleeving creature, namely Pokahuntas."[45] While Powhatan, as early as 1608, was willing to promote intermarriage to build a military alliance with the English, John Smith was distrustful and refused the offer. The peace created by the Pocahontas-Rolfe marriage lasted only until the Powhatan Uprising of 1622; from then on the English abandoned any moves toward a biracial society.[46] As in New England, David Smits contends, a host of historical and cultural forces contributed to the paucity of interracial marriages in early Virginia: "English anxieties, insecurities, and ethnocentrism, manifested in suspicion, discrimination, verbal abuse, exclusiveness, and violent aggression toward Indians, were the paramount deterrents to intermarriage." In addition, the Indians simply were not interested in English marriage partners: "Indian resentments, rebelliousness, marital customs, and female matrimonial preferences" all led to a low probability of Indian-white marriages.[47]

Since intermarriages were not very common in seventeenth-century Anglo-America, miscegenation laws therefore seem to have been more concerned with defining power relationships than controlling an upsurge of disturbing behavior. Controlling sexual access to white women was one means of asserting white male power over people of color and over white women. As Kathleen Brown writes about late-seventeenth-century Virginia, "legal sexual access to English women . . . [had] become a defining feature of white masculinity."[48]

The first miscegenation laws in British America had little precedent in English legal tradition. There is no statutory precedent in English common law governing interracial relationships in England, but there are a few examples in English colonial settings. The 1366 Statutes of Kilkenny, discussed earlier, regulated Anglo-Irish relationships in Ireland. In 1644 the Antigua Assembly passed a law forbidding "Carnall Coppullation between Christian and Heathen," the latter being defined as Negro or Indian.[49] Antigua was probably the only colony in the British West Indies to pass miscegenation laws in the seventeenth century, though Bermuda passed a law banning marriages between "his Maiesties ffree borne subjects" and "blacks" in 1663.[50] This is not to say that there was not a fear and rejection of various non-English "others" prior to the development of Anglo-American miscegenation law.[51] Nevertheless, the need to regulate interracial relationships seems to have originated in the British colonial experience.

Only two colonies, Virginia and North Carolina, expressly banned Indian-white marriage by law. In 1691 Virginia expanded its 1662 statute, which had prohibited fornication between "Christians" and "Negroes," to include Indians. This new law forbade interracial marriages between "English or other whites" and "Negroes, mulattoes, or Indians" and provided special punishments for interracial bastardy. (Virginia omitted its prohibition of Indian-white marriages in a revised intermarriage law in 1753.) North Carolina adapted provisions from Virginia's laws and in 1715 banned interracial marriages between "whites" and "Negroes, mulattoes, or Indians." The law also provided for harsher punishments for women bearing mixed-blood illegitimate children. In 1741 North Carolina reiterated the ban on Indian-white marriages and defined racial categories more stringently: "Indians, Negroes, mustees, or mulattoes, 'or any Person of Mixed Blood, to the Third Generation'" could not marry a white person. Consequently, a white person could marry a person with a maximum one-sixteenth Indian ancestry—a designation indicating an early concern with blood quantum and with the challenge of classifying mixed-race people in an absolute racial system that persists to this day. In all these laws the penalties fell mostly on white women who married outside their race, a fact supporting David Fowler's argument that these laws were a response to white women who challenged the patriarchal order by crossing the color line.[52]

In addition to the law's emphasis on gender, there are some interesting shifts in the terminology used to distinguish between different groups. As discussed earlier, Christianity was the mainstay of English identity, and this Christian identity was present in the earliest miscegenation laws. After the early eighteenth century, however, the English were distinguished from other residents by the label "white," a shift implying that racial objections now overrode religious concerns.

Virginia's first miscegenation statute in 1662 banned fornication between "Christians" and "Negroes." In the 1691 statute regarding marriage and bastardy, the term "Christian" dropped out and was replaced by "English" and "other whites." Religion does make a comeback in Virginia's 1705 statute. While interracial marriage and bastardy are discussed in racial terms—"English" and "free whites"—other provisions state that if a white master or mistress marries a "negro, mulatto, or Indian, Jew, Moor, Mahometan, or other infidel," his or her white, Christian servants are to be set free.[53] In other words, a white Christian cannot serve a master or mistress who marries outside either the white race or the Christian faith; both sins seem to be equally serious in this religion-race conflation. Byron Martyn argues that this provision cleverly disguises racist intent "clothed in the language of religion," pointing out that the law did not protect nonwhite Christian servants.[54] In 1705 Massachusetts passed its first miscegenation law, which banned marriage and fornication between Negroes or mulattoes and "English" subjects or subjects "of any other Christian nation."[55]

After the Massachusetts and Virginia statutes of 1705, however, lawmakers used "white" instead of "Christian" to designate the English in miscegenation law. The conversion of Indians and African slaves may have prompted this redesignation: once people of color became Christian, a new label was needed to separate them from those of European ancestry. Heathen status provided one of the primary justifications for the exploitation of people of color: the English could take Indian land because the Indians were not civilized and did not use it properly; the English could claim to enslave Africans for the purpose of conversion. Once Indians converted, the English needed a new justification to take their land. And once African slaves converted, the English needed a new justification to keep them in bondage. The shift from religious to racial language in miscegenation law reflects the developing ideology of racial inferiority.

Of course, this does not mean that religion disappeared from racial discourse. Ideas in the modern era about human differences have been based on intersections among religion, culture, and heredity. What we now call "scientific racism" developed later in the nineteenth century; consequently, religion as a basis for separation was not abandoned immediately. As Audrey Smedley explains, "'race' as a new and infallible truth had to await the development of a proper substitute for religion, and science became that substitute."[56] The new "race science" of the nineteenth century would define differences as a set of "hereditary species traits."[57] But the reformers of the early national period still believed in human improvement and trusted that Indians could be "civilized" and incorporated into white society.

Enlightenment Ideals and Racial Rejection in the Early Republic

The Revolutionary era marked the peak of acceptability for Indian-white marriages and for their mixed-blood offspring. This trend Joyce Chaplin attributes to "Enlightenment romanticization of savagery and the frontier, colonists' desire to contrast their country and people to the Old World, and a need to expand the number of supporters of the Revolution, which played to mestizo populations willing to bear arms against the British."[58] This peak of acceptability did not produce widespread acceptance, however, as several states expanded their bans on miscegenation to include Indians. At this time, nevertheless, several leading statesmen dared to advocate intermarriage as the solution to the "Indian problem." Thomas Jefferson and his followers in the early nineteenth century were among the last to speak of intermarriage as a real possibility.[59]

Jefferson believed that savagery could be destroyed by the acculturation of the Indians, a policy, writes Bernard Sheehan, supported by "every administration from Washington to John Quincy Adams and a variety of private philanthropic organizations."[60] Most advocates of acculturation understood culture as a matter of social environment rather than of racial heredity. When Jefferson spoke of acculturation, however, he also meant biological intermingling of the races. As he wrote to Creek agent Colonel

Benjamin Hawkins in 1803, "In truth, the ultimate point of rest and happiness for them is to let our settlements and theirs meet and blend together, to intermix, and become one people. Incorporating themselves with us as citizens of the United States."[61] In several speeches to the Indians, he encouraged them to adopt the white way of life: "We shall all be Americans; you will mix with us by marriage, your blood will run in our veins, and will spread over this great island."[62] As Winthrop Jordan remarks, "Confronted by three races in America he determinedly turned three into two by transforming the Indian into a degraded yet basically noble brand of white man."[63] Jefferson, however, saw the white absorption of Indian blood as part of a future historical progression, and so he did not promote intermarriage in the present.[64]

Disagreeing with Jefferson's time frame, Patrick Henry believed that intermarriage could help race relations in the present and should be actively promoted. After the Revolutionary War, Virginia struggled to eliminate the constant warfare between Indians and frontier whites on the state's western border. Considering intermarriage the best means to promote peace between the races, in 1784 Henry introduced a bill in the state legislature offering financial incentives "for the encouragement of marriages with the Indians." Although the benefits varied, both white men and women are included in the bill.[65]

The most significant portion of the bill comes at the end: "That the offspring of the intermarriages aforesaid, shall be entitled, in all respects, to the same rights and privileges, under the laws of this commonwealth, as if they had proceeded from intermarriages among free white inhabitants thereof." In other words, mixed-blood descendants would have the same rights as all-white citizens: intermarriage would "whiten" the Indians.[66] At the time of Henry's proposal, Indian-white intermarriage was legal in Virginia, the prohibition of such marriages having been omitted from the 1753 marriage law, but for the government to offer incentives for intermarriage was quite unheard of.[67] The bill made its way through the legislative process owing to the sheer force of Henry's personality, but after he was elected governor, it quickly failed.

William H. Crawford, the old-school Jeffersonian statesman from Georgia, like his Virginian colleagues, proposed interracial marriage as the solution to the Indian problem. Crawford played a major role constructing the government's civilization policy: as secretary of war in the Madison administration, he established significant government support for the missionary organizations. His commentary on Indian-white marriages, however, ignited a controversy that would follow him for the rest of his political career.[68]

As secretary of war, Crawford was responsible for Indian affairs. In his March 1816 report to the Senate on "Indian Trade and Intercourse," he highlighted the importance of introducing ideas of private property among the Indians. The controversy stemmed from his almost tangential final paragraph. There he proposes that "when every effort to introduce among them ideas of separate property . . . shall fail, let intermarriages between them and the whites be encouraged by the Government. This cannot fail to preserve the race, with the modifications necessary to the enjoyment of civil liberty and social happiness."[69] Like Henry and Jefferson before him, Crawford believed that the Indians could "become white" and that this was the honorable—and probably exclusive—alternative to the extinction of a noble race.

The controversial report was soon met by a series of scathing, satirical replies in the Democratic press. The authorship of the series, *Strictures Addressed to James Madison on the Celebrated Report of William H. Crawford, Recommending the Intermarriage of Americans with the Indian Tribes*, is not clear, being attributed to "Judge Cooper," "John Binns," and "Americanus." In vicious language, the author takes issue with Crawford's plan and claims that the Indians cannot be civilized and are unfit to be American citizens. The tract insists that, for whatever cause, the white youth on the Indian frontier should not be tempted to "prostitute their persons . . . to filthy ferocious half naked savages."[70]

Crawford's report came back to haunt him when he ran for president in 1824. The series was resurrected by his opponents as a pamphlet in order to reveal "the real character of the man" running for president. In a new preface, the anonymous author asserts that Crawford's position on interracial marriage made him unfit to be president.[71] The year after the election, Crawford did receive some indirect support in *Niles' Weekly Register*. The newspaper noted the public denunciation of the Boudinot-Gold marriage by the Reverend Lyman Beecher and wondered what all the fuss was about. The writer goes on to link the Boudinot-Gold and Crawford scandals, reminding readers that "a gentleman who was thought fit, by many thousands of the people, for the office of president, openly and frankly recommended an incorporation of the Indian race with the citizens of the United States, by intermarriages,—and we could never see any reason why, on account of *that* recommendation, his claims to the office should have been lessened."[72]

Jeffersonian ideas about Indian acculturation were not just the beliefs of one man; Jefferson was merely the most articulate and prominent advocate of the "philanthropic" approach to the Indian problem which dominated federal policy during the early national period. This approach demanded that Indians adopt the white way of life.[73] The more radical extension of this policy proposed by Southern statesmen, the advocacy of intermarriage, gained support among some Northern intellectuals and would be explored in some of the leading historical fiction of the 1820s and 1830s. Nevertheless, Indian-white marriages never occurred on a large scale because of the gap in beliefs between philanthropic idealists and frontier whites, because the marriages that did take place between frontier men and Indian women did not succeed in promoting white ways, and because the Indians were not willing to give up their tribal identities.[74]

Despite the relative acceptance of Jeffersonian Indian policy in the early national period, during this time three Northern states—Massachusetts, Rhode Island, and Maine—passed laws banning Indian-white marriages. It is difficult to say why their neighboring states did not also enact such laws. It is clear, however, that the absence of a legal ban did not mean the absence of a social taboo, as is demonstrated by the scandal at Cornwall and the low incidence of such marriages. In addition, it is important to recognize that although many Northern states did not pass miscegenation legislation, from colonial times they had passed a series of laws that kept Indians and blacks in an inferior position. For example, New Jersey, New Hampshire, and Connecticut tried to avoid "the miscegenous headaches" that were troubling their neighbors in the eighteenth century by a "preventative program of keeping Negroes and Indians out of their respective colonies." In 1715 Connecticut passed "An Act for Prohibiting the Importation or Bringing into this Colony, any Indian Servants or Slaves," which declared that the Indians were "of a malicious and revengeful spirit, rude and insolent in their behavior and very ungovernable." Authorities also feared that a large Indian population would be a threat to the colony.[75]

Massachusetts passed the first miscegenation law in New England in 1705. In this law, "An Act for the Better Preventing of A Spurious and Mixt Issue, Etc.," banning fornication and marriage between "negroes or molattos" and "English" or people "of any other Christian nation," legislators intended to include Indians in the prohibition.[76] The law as passed, however, did not include them. Justice Samuel Sewall, who led the opposition to the bill, also tried to exclude "negroes" from it, but did not succeed. As Sewall wrote in his diary for December 1, 1705: "If it be pass'd,

I fear twill be an Oppression provoking to God. . . . I have got the Indians out of the Bill, and some mitigation for them [the Negroes] left in it."[77] Massachusetts revised this law in 1786 with an "Act for the orderly Solemnization of Marriage" providing that "no person authorized . . . to marry shall join in marriage any white person with any Negro, Indian, or Mulatto, under penalty of fifty pounds; and all such marriages shall be absolutely null and void."[78] Indians were now added to the group forbidden to marry whites. This may have been prompted by the prevalence of Indian-black intermixture. Intermarriage with African American men was a common occurrence in the Indian struggle to survive in southern New England, and "there was extensive miscegenation of the two races after the middle of the seventeenth century."[79] Under this new law, no special penalties for interracial fornication or adultery obtained, and the only person punished was the one who solemnized the marriage.[80] Since all interracial marriages were null and void, however, the children of these relationships were punished by illegitimate status. The Pequot William Apess called this law a "disgraceful act" and, like the Cherokees, argued that prejudice against marriage with Indians revealed white hypocrisy: "I would ask if this corresponds with your sayings—that you think as much of the Indians as you do of the whites."[81] Massachusetts's miscegenation law was repealed in 1843, ten years after Apess's critique.[82]

In 1798 Rhode Island added the 1786 Massachusetts provision almost verbatim to its existing "Act to prevent clandestine Marriages." The addition banned the marriage of "any white person with any Negro, Indian, or mulatto" and declared these marriages "absolutely null and void."[83] David Fowler suggests that the motivation for this law was not clear and that the legislature may have passed the entire marriage law without debating the component parts.[84] There is reason to believe, however, that the miscegenation component of the law was quite deliberate. Ruth Wallis Herndon and Ella Wilcox Sekatau describe a process by which Indians were redesignated as blacks in town records in eighteenth-century Rhode Island; in being written out of the records, Indians were denied political status and land claims. The separation of whites from the other races dictated by the 1798 law became even more important in order to keep "nonwhite society" on "the economic, political, and social margins of white society."[85] The law would not be repealed until 1881.

When Maine, previously a part of Massachusetts, became a separate state in 1820 under the provisions of the Missouri Compromise, it kept all Massachusetts law that did not conflict with the new Maine state constitution. The following year Maine revised the 1786 Massachusetts law with "An Act for regulating Marriage, and for the orderly solemnization thereof." This was a "bare bones" prohibition; it simply said that "all marriages between any white person and any Negro, Indian or Mulatto . . . shall be absolutely void." Maine had few free blacks at the time but had numerous Indians, especially on the frontiers, so this law was probably aimed at them.[86] The law was repealed in 1883.

The early national period is marked by extremes regarding Indian-white intermarriage. Advocates of intermarriage believed that white culture could be acquired: Indians could be Christianized and civilized. The many opponents of intermarriage believed that culture and religion were a matter of heredity and that Indians, by virtue of their race, were inescapably different. Consequently, by their very nature, Indians could never be American citizens. This racial rejection would dominate U.S. Indian policy by 1830.

The Cherokee Law of Intermarriage

Intermarriage was a controversial issue among Indians as well, even among the Cherokees, who are said to have intermarried with whites more than any other Indian tribe. Like the U.S. government, the Cherokees used race as a measure of citizenship, and therefore they needed to regulate sex and reproduction. As Fergus M. Bordewich reminds us, "The concept of 'Indianness' has long been rooted at least partly in the belief that blood is fundamental to identity."[87] The control of citizenship was also a sovereignty issue. In order to have treaty rights upheld in the U.S. courts, the Cherokees could not afford—as no tribal nation could afford—to have any questions raised about the nation's status as a sovereign political entity. Any incursion onto that sense of separate "Indianness" was diplomatically perilous. In part, this was a defensive reaction to what Maureen Konkle describes as the white "logic of identity-thinking," which "*always* has as its ultimate objective the destruction of Native political organization for the purpose of gaining Native land."[88] At the same time, Cherokee miscegenation law rejected white definitions of "Indianness" and claimed the right of self-definition. Other southeastern tribes followed the Cherokee model and incorporated the regulation of intermarriage into their code of law. In addition, there were similar regulatory trends among some New England Indian nations in response to concerns about property and the control of resources.[89]

According to Rennard Strickland's comprehensive study of the development of the Cherokee legal system, both the British and U.S. governments encouraged the development of the Cherokee nation-state. Government officials believed that "by transforming Indian institutions into copies of white institutions, the Indian problem, if not the Indian, would disappear." Contrary to these expectations, however, with their adoption of an American-style system of government, "the Cherokees emerged as worthy adversaries who demanded that their institutions be respected."[90] The most important factor in their legal transition was the belief of the Cherokees that new laws would save their nation and preserve their lands; it is also important to note, writes Konkle, that the new system "emerged not from a single act but by a gradual acculturation process fusing tribal law ways and Anglo-American legal institutions." The development of a written code of law was also accelerated by pressures for removal: "In the early nineteenth century the Cherokee took up writing as central to their political survival; they argued before the Supreme Court that, based on the treaty record, it was clear that Europeans had recognized their existence as a sovereign nation."[91] The new Cherokee government developed quickly during the early national period: the first written law was passed in 1808, the Cherokees became the first tribe to publish its laws in 1821, and the Cherokee Constitution was established in 1827. It made all land the "common property of the Nation," although citizens did own any improvements they made on the land.[92]

The regulation of marriages between Cherokee women and white men was one of the earliest concerns of the new Cherokee legal system. Unlike in the American states, where Indian-white marriages were banned or otherwise frowned upon, in the Cherokee Nation white spouses were accepted and granted the privileges of citizenship. These laws were chiefly designed to maintain Cherokee lands and to regulate citizenship, protecting Cherokee women and the nation from white fortune hunters. In November 1819 John Ross, president of the Cherokee Nation, signed into law a measure designed to prevent such abuses. The law said that a white man must marry a Cherokee woman according to white laws (with a minister or judge and a license) before he could be admitted to citizenship; that he could have only one wife; that the husband could not dispose of his wife's property; and that if he were to leave his wife, he must pay damages and forfeit citizenship.[93] The Choctaw Nation passed a similar law in 1840.[94]

The regulation of these marriages and the citizenship status of the parties involved, including that of the mixed-blood children, remained a con-

ST CHARLES COMMUNITY COLLEGE
LIBRARY
WITHDRAWN

cern of the Cherokees until the end of the nineteenth century, when the Cherokee court system was dismantled by the U.S. government. White citizens were a small but growing minority in the Cherokee Nation: according to the 1825 Cherokee census, there were 13,563 Indian citizens, including 147 white men and 73 white women married into the nation.[95] An 1825 law clarified a disputed point: that the children of a married Cherokee man and white woman were citizens of the Cherokee Nation, just as mixed descendants of Cherokee women were.[96] In 1829 the National Council addressed the citizenship status of a white citizen after the death of a Cherokee spouse: the law said that if the marriage had produced children, then the white widow or widower could remain a Cherokee citizen as long as he or she remained single or remarried a Cherokee. If the marriage was childless, then the widow or widower was "deprived of citizenship." This was one of the rare regulations that applied to white men and women equally. Its harsher elements were repealed by an 1843 act which said that childless white widows or widowers could remain citizens as long as they did not marry a white spouse.[97]

Despite this regulation of Indian-white marriages, there was still concern that it was too easy for white men of low character to marry Cherokee women. An 1828 article signed "Socrates" in the *Cherokee Phoenix* argued that a stricter law was needed "to exclude the thief, the robber, the vagabond and the tipler and adulterer, from the privilege of intermarrying with Cherokee women." "Socrates" suggested that an office be established in which white men would bring recommendations testifying to their good character and would post bond for their honorable behavior; if they did not live up to their testimonials, the marriage would be nullified, and they would be expelled from the nation.[98] Making respectable moral stature a requirement for white citizenship suggested an implicit definition of Cherokee national character as virtuous.

Over the years, the Cherokee government adopted the "Socrates" plan. The 1839 "Act to legalize Intermarriage with White Men" reiterates the provisions of the 1819 law and adds that if "the fact should afterwards be established that he [the white husband] left a wife elsewhere, he shall be subject to removal as an intruder." A revised version of this act in 1843 made the provisions even stricter: instead of getting a license from the clerk of a district court, the prospective husband had to apply to the National Council. He also had to take an oath of allegiance to the Cherokee Nation and "freely alienate himself from the protection of all other governments."[99] In like manner, the Choctaw Nation was also increasingly concerned with white exploitation of Indian women. In 1849 the Choctaw passed "AN ACT compelling a white man living with an Indian woman to marry her lawfully" or leave the nation for good; the man also had to be of good character in order for the marriage to be allowed.[100] The Cherokee laws became progressively more strict. In addition to the license and loyalty oath, by 1855 a white groom had to have a certificate of "good moral character" from seven Cherokee citizens. By 1866 the law referred to the "intermarriage of white men and foreigners" and required the signature of ten Cherokees "by blood" who had known the groom for six months. (This is one of the rare mentions of "blood" in Cherokee intermarriage law. White Cherokee citizens who had married into the nation were not acceptable character witnesses. Only Cherokees by birth were permitted to vouch for a white hopeful husband.) Similar versions of these laws were passed in 1880 and 1890, and the Choctaws used these as models for their 1888 law.[101] While the marriage of white men to Cherokee women was strictly regulated, there seems to have been no similar procedure for the marriage of white women to Cherokee men. White women were not perceived as threats; for example, the presence of Harriet Gold Boudinot and Sarah Northrup Ridge did not cause controversy among the Cherokees.

At the same time that it became more difficult for white men to marry into the Cherokee Nation, the law codified the customary practice of accepting marriages between Cherokees and other Indians. An act titled "Intermarriage of Cherokees with Other Indians" reaffirmed that Indians from the tribes in Indian Territory who married into the Cherokee Nation were Cherokee citizens.[102] This law affirmed "Indianness" as a unique identity, a gesture of cultural and political solidarity.

While Cherokee intermarriage laws regulated Cherokee-white marriages, another strain of Cherokee miscegenation law banned Cherokee-black marriages, revealing the influence of white racial thought. This ban emerged within the context of a developing slavery code. As the Cherokee elite took up white farming methods, the need for labor led to the development of plantation slavery. Traditionally, Cherokee slaves were other Indians taken captive in war; their slave status was marked by their lack of kinship ties. By the 1820s, however, the Cherokee view of slavery resembled that of Southern whites. The Cherokees saw themselves as radically different from Africans, who were now considered suitable as slaves by virtue of their race. As Theda Perdue notes, "Kinship became less crucial in a per-

son's claim to humanity and freedom than his skin color." Although many
Cherokees did adapt the white system of African slavery, it is important
to realize that Cherokee slave codes prior to removal, unlike the antebellum slave codes of Southern whites, say-little about the behavior of masters
and slaves. Most notably, "the hysteria which usually accompanied any
suggestion of sexual relationships between white women and blacks is
missing."[103]

Five years after the 1819 law regulating marriages with white men, the
Cherokee National Council resolved "that intermarriages between negro
slaves and indians, or whites, shall not be lawful." Slaveowners who permitted their slaves to intermarry with "Indians or whites" would be fined
fifty dollars. Male Indians and whites who married a "negro woman slave"
would be punished with fifty-nine stripes, while female Indians and whites
who married a "negro man slave" would receive twenty-five stripes.[104]
The law bans marriage only to "negro slaves"; free blacks are not mentioned. Unlike the law regulating Cherokee-white marriages, which focused mainly on the actions of white men and seemed unconcerned with
white women who married into the nation, this ban affected all white and
Cherokee men and women who crossed the black color line (the women
did get a slightly more lenient punishment). The available records show
that in 1888 the Choctaws similarly banned intermarriage between "Choctaws" and "negroes"; it is difficult to say, however, whether this was the
first law of this nature.[105]

The 1827 Cherokee Constitution addressed the citizenship status of
mixed-race descendants of intermarriages. The constitution declared that
"the descendents [sic] of Cherokee men by all free women, except the
African race" and "the posterity of Cherokee women by all free men" were
citizens. The use of the term "all free men" allowed for the citizenship of
the children of a Cherokee mother and a free black father. (It is not clear
whether this was a holdover from the traditional matrilineal society or the
adoption of the Southern white policy of the child following the "condition of the mother.") The male descendants of a Cherokee mother and a
free black father were allowed to vote, a right extended to "all free male
citizens, (excepting negroes and descendants of white and Indian men by
negro women who may have been set free)." These descendants, however,
were ineligible for public office: "No person who is of negro or mulatlo
[sic] parentage, either by the father or the mother side, shall be able to
hold any office of profit, honor, or trust under this Government." The
children of Cherokee mothers and free black fathers were thus eligible

for a form of second-class citizenship—they could vote but not hold office—while the children of black mothers had none of the rights of citizenship.[106]

Following removal to Indian Territory (present-day Oklahoma), the laws became increasingly severe, and the status of slaves and free blacks under Cherokee law consequently declined. In the 1840s and 1850s it became illegal for slaves and free blacks "not of Cherokee blood" to own property, sell liquor, and carry a weapon; it was also illegal for a Cherokee citizen to teach them to read or write. Fears of revolt and collusion between free blacks and slaves led to slave patrols and a crackdown on free blacks who aided in escapes; after an 1842 revolt, all free blacks (except those freed by Cherokee citizens) were ordered to leave the nation by January 1, 1843.[107]

Cherokee miscegenation law developed in this context of increasing severity. The 1839 Tahlequah Constitution repeated the provisions of the first constitution, providing that mixed-blood descendants were citizens (but ineligible to hold public office), except if their mothers were African. In the same year the National Council passed "An Act to prevent Amalgamation with Colored Persons." This law echoed the earlier 1824 ban, but it moved closer to the language of white racism, especially in its use of "amalgamation," which was the term used to describe "race mixing" during the antebellum period. The law banned intermarriage between "a free male or female citizen with any slave or person of color not entitled to the rights of citizenship." This confusing law expanded the terms of the 1824 ban on marriage with slaves to include free "colored persons." In effect, a free citizen (who had to be Cherokee, white, Cherokee-white, or Cherokee-black with the black inheritance on the paternal side) could marry someone of African descent under one condition only: that the intended spouse was a Cherokee-black citizen whose African inheritance came from his or her father. The penalty for most participants in Cherokee-black marriages was not to exceed fifty lashes, but the penalty for "any colored male who may be convicted under this act" was one hundred lashes. It is clear that black male transgressions were feared the most; the hysteria about black male sexuality that Perdue claims is absent from the law prior to removal is clearly visible in this new ban.[108]

Also clear in this intermarriage ban is the desire of the Cherokee to resist being lumped into the category of "colored persons" by the white society. This process was institutionalized by the U.S. Census, which between 1800 and 1840 used the category "free person of color" for most nonwhites,

including Indians.[109] William G. McLoughlin writing about the Cherokees, and James H. Merrell about the Catawbas, explain how the various
southeastern tribes learned racism from their white neighbors; prejudice
against blacks was an act of self-preservation. McLoughlin does not wish
to excuse the Cherokees, but he contends that they "could not hope to
remain in the heart of the deep South and at the same time advocate
abolition or racial equality."[110] Governor Joseph McMinn of Tennessee
wanted the government to end tribal ownership of lands, which would
accelerate the removal process. Under McMinn's plan, the Indians would
not become full citizens, but would be given "all the rights of a free citizen
of color of the United States."[111] By 1800, Merrell notes, there was a
"propensity to lump native Americans with Afro-Americans in a great
'colored' underclass."[112] The Catawbas were quite sensitive to being classified as black. For the southeastern tribes, "faced with cultural extinction,
hating black people was one way to avoid being considered black themselves," writes Merrell.[113] To be relegated to a colored underclass would be
political suicide for Indian nations. It was to sacrifice nationhood for no
status at all.

This process of redesignation was also happening in New England,
hastening the "disappearance" of people who were supposed to have vanished after King Philip's War. The intermarriage of Indians with blacks,
notes Colin Calloway, "made it difficult for outsiders who employed categories of racial purity to identify Indians. . . . [T]hey seemed to 'vanish' as
Indians among 'people of color.'"[114] Also contributing to this process, says
Thomas Doughton, was the new "race science" that "codified notions of
red, black, and white 'races' in such a way that the only real Natives were
racially distinct" and "full-blooded."[115] As explained earlier in my discussion of Rhode Island miscegenation law, Herndon and Sekatau see a sinister motivation behind this process: New England officials by 1800 had
transformed "Indians" into "Negroes" in town records, a "deliberate redesignation of native people as Negro or black, as officials replaced cultural
description with physical description." This erasure of "Indians" from the
records ensured that they would not be able to reclaim tribal lands.[116]
Given the inferior status of blacks in white society, it is not surprising that
Indians resisted this redesignation. Cherokee miscegenation law, with its
goal of excluding "African blood," was one way of asserting a separate
identity from the black underclass.

So what impact did Cherokee miscegenation laws actually have? The
record is unclear. Rennard Strickland argues that the laws banning inter-

marriage were generally followed but not enforced, and that there was little Cherokee-black intermarriage. The Cherokee David Brown reassured his white audience in 1825 that "there is hardly any intermixture of Cherokee and African blood."[117] Perdue agrees that the laws were rarely enforced, but insists that "illegal sexual liaisons and marriages between Cherokees and blacks continued to occur as they had before removal. . . . 'Amalgamation' did not cease with the more stringent law which was passed after removal."[118]

What we do know is that the regulation of "tribal blood" through miscegenation laws was part of a policy of keeping Cherokee property in the hands of Cherokee citizens and protecting sovereignty through the preservation of "Indianness." For example, although Cherokee-white marriages were allowed, a white man could not inherit property from a deceased Cherokee wife unless they had living children. The ban on Cherokee-black marriages was meant to preserve "tribal blood" and to limit the inheritance of property by mixed-blood children.[119] Like white officials, Cherokee officials struggled with the measurement of blood quantum as the definition of citizenship became increasingly complicated. These complications over intermarriage and inheritance continued into the twentieth century: once Oklahoma became a state, residents were defined as either "of African descent" or "not of African descent." In other words, Indians were legally "white" and therefore eligible to marry other whites but not people "of African descent."[120]

Gender, "Blood," and the Politics of Exclusion

While Jeffersonian ideals of Indian assimilation shaped the government policy of the early national period, Jefferson's Louisiana Purchase of 1803 ironically led to the policy of removal. These newly acquired lands were seen as an alternative home for eastern Indians who were feeling white pressure for their land. For Jefferson, any such move would be voluntary. Segal and Stineback observe that by the Jackson administration (1828–36), however, "coercion became official policy." Furthermore, both Indians and frontier whites had demonstrated their opposition to assimilation plans, and the Indian Removal Bill of 1830 was "the first articulate expression of a growing sentiment among Americans that Indians were racially incapable of changing their way of life and assimilating into white American society."[122] In other words, Americans increasingly believed that race was an uncrossable barrier and that religion and culture were fundamentally matters of biology. The narrative of disruption created by interracial marriage was contained by legal narratives positing that racial mixture was impossible.

The Jeffersonian ideal of biological assimilation was also unworkable, owing to the American cultural context. Anglo-American domination of Indian lands depended on the labeling of Indians as inferior and vanishing; it also depended on the easy recognition of racial status. In turn, resistance to whites' land encroachment required a strong and united Indian citizenry. Thus, the Cherokee Nation fought back against "the colonial politics of exclusion," exercising sovereignty and designating for themselves "who could become a citizen rather than a subject" and "which children were legitimate progeny and which were not." The miscegenation laws written by the states and by the Cherokee Nation thus attempted to "construct and enforce legal and social classifications for who was *white* and who was *native*."[123] As Circe Sturm observes, "The blood legislation of both the Cherokee Nation and the U.S. federal government" usually had the "same underlying motivations: either to control access to economic resources or to maintain racial purity as the basis of a national identity."[124] From each point of view, it was racial status that conferred the right to the land: Cherokee tribal identity and citizenship established a share in the collective tribal lands, while the attributes of "civilization" and "proper land use" implied by whiteness formed the basis of Anglo-American claims to the land.

The equation of race and citizenship made by both the Cherokee and state governments put people who defied these categories in an impossible situation (although the Cherokee Nation did allow whites who married Cherokees to become citizens). For example, in 1829, as the removal crisis grew more intense, the local Indian agent in Georgia, with the support of the secretary of war, ordered that any white man with a Cherokee family who opposed removal would be chased out of the Cherokee Nation (and if he did not oppose removal, he would lose his home anyway).[125] The white Indian agents tolerated interracial family structures if and only if the families stayed loyal to white policy and thus denied their Cherokee citizenship. Of course, this extorted "loyalty" to the government of Georgia would be treason to the Cherokee Nation: those who challenged the equation of race and citizenship were left between a rock and a hard place.

In addition, this system of "regulating social relationships through racial metaphors necessitate[d] control over women" and sexual behavior.[126] For whites, this meant that marriage to white women was defined as normative and that the children of all-white marriages were the only legitimate ones. Sexual relationships with Indian or black women were condemned by law, and any resulting children were illegitimate. Sexual access to white women was also something to be denied to nonwhite men, even while white men would often pursue sex with nonwhite women without legal, financial, or social consequences. It is this white exploitation of Cherokee women that the Cherokee miscegenation laws were designed to prevent; it was the desire to reserve sexual access to white women for white men that led to the controversy in Cornwall.

Although the separation of Indians and Anglo-Americans had its origins in religious injunctions and uncertainties about the "other," the taboo against intermarriage intensified as race became a matter of biology and heredity. Both the U.S. government and the Cherokee Nation used racial descent or "blood" as qualifications for citizenship, and so the inheritance of "blood" became intertwined with inheritance of land. The controversy at Cornwall is a microcosm of the larger debates over the "Indian problem" and race in the 1820s; the issue of intermarriage forced people to articulate their beliefs about the relationships among race, religion, and culture. These controversies made powerful stories, and as we shall see in the next chapter, contemporary novelists dramatized the disruptive narrative of intermarriage from a range of perspectives.

3

Remembering and Removing the Indian: Indian-White Marriages in Sedgwick, Cooper, and Child

> The Indian and the white man can no more mingle, and become one, than day and night.
>
> MAGAWISCA in Catharine Maria Sedgwick's *Hope Leslie*

The interracial marriages described in scandals and statutes feature competing narratives of social disruption and social control. Although similar conflicts are found in fiction as well, the genre provides an important alternative. Not being encumbered by absolute fidelity to the facts, the literary artist can dramatize a general societal conflict in a plausible way and thereby get to the core of underlying issues. Rather than taking a simple pro- or anti-intermarriage stance, the fiction of Catharine Maria Sedgwick, James Fenimore Cooper, and Lydia Maria Child narrates the controversy about intermarriage from a range of perspectives. Because opposing views are given some consideration, the novelists offer more thoughtful, complex, and nuanced estimations of the issues than we have seen manifested in legislatures and in the Cornwall affair.

Written in the challenging context of the Indian removal crisis, the narratives of Indian-white marriages by Sedgwick, Cooper, and Child reveal the link between intermarriage and land in American culture. Their writing explores the relationship between race and culture and uses past Indian-white conflicts to address contemporary questions. Typical readings group the authors by gender, since Sedgwick and Child seem more open to exploring the possibility of interracial marriage. More significantly, they advocate racial equality on some level and believe that justice toward the Indians is still possible, while Cooper argues that the Indians' racial inferiority makes their extinction tragic but inevitable.[1] Although reading the fiction of Sedgwick and Child against that of Cooper is a useful approach, Cooper and Sedgwick have more in common than has been noted by literary critics. Both share a troubled family history of Indian land dispossession, and their attitudes toward Indians and intermarriage are shaped by their response to this legacy. Child's activism, significantly freer of family agendas, allows her to think of intermarriage as a lost opportunity of the past, leading toward her later advocacy of intermarriage as a solution to the race problem in the United States.

But despite these authors' different approaches to the intermarriage question, Indian-white marriage functions as a powerful narrative of disruption in all their work. In these stories, the social equilibrium is disrupted by land disputes or warfare as well as by intermarriage. Order is ultimately restored by the removal of Indians from the land and the suppression of intermarriages. Despite the authors' varying degrees of experimentation with social equality, at the end of their stories the outcome is remarkably similar.

Revising the Puritan Legacy:
Sedgwick's Indian "Connections"

Present-day readers of Catharine Maria Sedgwick's novel *Hope Leslie; or, Early Times in the Massachusetts* (1827) are fascinated by Sedgwick's portrayal of an Indian-white marriage and her retelling of the 1637 Pequot War from the Indian perspective. The novel treats two Indian removals: one, involving the Pequots in the seventeenth century, is integral to the plot; the other, concerning the Stockbridge Indians in the eighteenth century, is foreshadowed. Yet another Indian removal, I am convinced, one not present in the text, is crucial to the writing of *Hope Leslie*—and therefore to our reading of it. The nineteenth-century removal of the Cherokees was a topic of great national moment just as Sedgwick was composing her text. In her account of these removals, Indian-white romance emerges as a possible alternative to race war. Including Indians in the "American" family was more than an imaginative projection for Sedgwick, though: she sought out and embraced the Indian connections in her own family.[2]

Hope Leslie presents an alternative history to the traditional Puritan accounts of the victories of God's new chosen people over the "savages" of New England. Using seventeenth-century Puritan histories by John Winthrop, William Bradford, and William Hubbard as primary sources, Sedgwick's story of 1630s Massachusetts features two strong heroines and re-counts the Pequot War from the Pequots' point of view.[3] The story centers on the young people of the Fletcher household: Everell Fletcher, the hand-some hero; Hope and Faith Leslie, the orphan wards of Everell's father; and Magawisca and Oneco, slaves in the Fletcher household who were taken prisoner in the Pequot War. The last two are the daughter and son of the Pequot chief Mononotto, who seeks to rescue his children and take his revenge upon the colonists. He attacks the Fletcher household, killing Mrs. Fletcher and several of her children while taking Magawisca, Oneco, Faith, and Everell away with him. Mononotto plans to kill Everell to avenge the death of his older son at the hands of the Puritans. Here Sedgwick retells the Pocahontas–John Smith myth: Magawisca, out of love for Everell, throws herself between him and her father's hatchet. She loses her arm but saves Everell's life, saying: "I have bought his life with my own. Fly, Everell . . . to the east!"[4]

The narrative breaks off at Everell's escape and resumes seven years later. A "love quadrangle" develops as Hope, Magawisca, and Esther Downing (the ideal Puritan woman) are all in love with Everell. Everell admits that he once had romantic feelings for Magawisca until Hope came into his life: "I might have loved her—might have forgotten that nature had put barriers between us" (214). The love quadrangle is thus reduced to an all-white love triangle. Then, true to the conventions of the marriage plot, after a series of misunderstandings, Hope and Everell are rightfully united. The couple ask Magawisca to remain with them as their sister. Everell insists that "the present difference of the English with the Indians, is but a vapour that has, even now, nearly passed away" (330). This ethereal "va-pour" hardens into a "barrier" when questions of interracial marriage are involved, perhaps reflecting Sedgwick's profound ambivalence over the nature of racial difference. Nevertheless, Magawisca rejects Everell's appeal: " 'It cannot be—it cannot be,' replied Magawisca, the persuasions of those she loved not . . . overcoming her deep invincible sense of the wrongs her injured race had sustained . . . 'the Indian and the white man can no more mingle, and become one, than day and night' " (330).[5] Despite her feelings for Hope and Everell, Magawisca denies the possibility of joining the "white family" as a fictive "sister." Everell marries the spirited Hope (a better wife for him than the passive Esther would have been), and Maga-wisca and her people disappear into the wilderness.

Even as Sedgwick seems to pull back from the intermarriage alternative, she does allow another Indian-white relationship to succeed. In the second intermarriage plot of the novel, Hope's sister, Faith Leslie, has been Mon-onotto's captive since the attack seven years earlier. Hope is horrified to hear that Faith has adopted Indian ways and is married to Oneco: "'God forbid!' exclaimed Hope, shuddering as if a knife had been plunged into her bosom. 'My sister married to an Indian!'" (188). Magawisca replies with "proud contempt": "Yes—an Indian, in whose veins runs the blood of the strongest, the fleetest of the children of the forest, . . . and whose souls have returned to the Great Spirit, stainless as they came from him. Think ye that your blood will be corrupted by mingling with this stream?" (188).

Despite Hope's reaction, Faith and Oneco are very happy together; this is not, however, an unqualified endorsement of intermarriage as an alternative to Indian-white conflict. Captured by Indians while still a child, Faith has become culturally Indian and is unwilling to rejoin white society. Her marriage to Oneco, therefore, is not a true "marriage of cultures." Here Sedgwick challenges the facile equation of race and culture, using Faith's experience to demonstrate that culture is a matter of physical and social environment. Despite the sorrow of Faith's white family at losing her, they acknowledge that it would be "unnatural" to force her back into a white way of life. This point would be more compelling if Faith were not portrayed as lacking intelligence and competence: "[Her] face, pale and spiritless, was only redeemed from absolute vacancy by an expression of gentleness and modesty" (229).

Underlying the ambivalent messages about Indian-white marriage in *Hope Leslie* are the competing understandings of race in the 1820s, mostly involving the connections between culture and biology. In the preface Sedgwick explicitly states her beliefs about race: "The liberal philanthropist will not be offended by a representation which supposes that the elements of virtue and intellect are not withheld from any branch of the human family; and the enlightened and accurate observer of human nature, will admit that the difference of character among the various races of the earth, arises mainly from difference of condition" (6). In other words, Sedgwick makes the classic Enlightenment statement that racial differences are a matter of environment. She reinforces the idea of Indian equality, using as her epigraph to volume 1, chapter 2, a quotation from *A Key into the Language of America* by Roger Williams: "For the temper of the brain in quick apprehensions and acute judgments, to say no more, the most High and Sovereign God hath not made the Indian inferior to the European" (15). And for those who base their superiority on their Christian identity,

Sedgwick uses Williams again to argue for the spiritual character of the Indians: "He that questions whether God made the world, the Indian will teach him. I must acknowledge I have received in my converse with them, many confirmations of those two great points; first, that 'God is;' second, 'that he is a rewarder of all them that diligently seek him'" (247). The experience of Faith shows that culture is a matter of physical and social environment, but the heroic Magawisca insists that the races must live separately, perhaps because the cultural divide is so wide. Still, Sedgwick's exploration of Indian-white marriages and her insistence on Indian equality is quite radical for its time; her novel is a major contribution to the cultural conversation about the problem of Indian-white relations during the time when the removal crisis intensified.

Hope Leslie received positive reviews in the *American Ladies Magazine* and the *North American Review*. The latter loved Magawisca, reprinting in the article the entire scene of her rescue of Everell. Invoking Pocahontas, the reviewer contended that "the escape is almost too wonderful, but it is countenanced by the best authority in numerous instances, and also by a few such marvellous occurrences in the history of real life."[6] The *American Ladies Magazine* acknowledged the controversial nature of the novel: "Perhaps public opinion is more divided concerning 'Hope Leslie.' . . . All think it a work of great merit; but all do not prefer it."[7] The *New York Evening Post* praised Sedgwick's historical research: "The writer of Hope Leslie has, we are happy to see, diligently studied the spirit of this extraordinary period, & we believe her delineation of it is as accurate as it certainly is striking." The reviewer partially blamed the Puritans' typological worldview for their treatment of the Indians: the "superstition which likened their condition to that of the Hebrews among the Canaanites, probably made them less observant of the dictates of natural justice towards the savage tribes around them."[8]

The literary critic and historian Mary Kelley has suggested the captivity of Eunice Williams as an important source for the Faith Leslie plot.[9] Williams was a distant relation of Sedgwick's through the latter's maternal grandmother, Abigail Williams Sergeant Dwight. The experience of Sedgwick's Williams ancestors was the subject of local folklore as well as a best-selling captivity narrative, *The Redeemed Captive Returning to Zion* (1707). John Demos has told Eunice's story in his book *The Unredeemed Captive: A Family Story from Early America*.[10] In 1704 a French and Indian war party attacked the town of Deerfield, Massachusetts, killing 39 residents and capturing 112. The Reverend John Williams's family was a special target: two of his youngest children were killed at the house, Mrs. Williams was killed shortly into the march to Canada, and the five remaining Williams children became captives with their father. Eunice Williams, age seven at the time of her captivity, was the only Williams child who was not redeemed; she adopted Indian culture and married Francois Xavier Arosen in 1713, a Kahnawake Mohawk and Roman Catholic from the Montreal area.[11] Eunice visited her Williams relatives four times after her capture, the first meeting taking place after a thirty-six-year separation. Despite the best efforts of her family to "redeem" her back to the white way of life, Eunice chose to remain loyal to her Indian family and her Catholic faith. She lived until 1785, just four years before Catharine Sedgwick's birth. Contact between the English and Indian Williamses continued. In 1785 Eunice's grandson Thomas Thorakwaneken Williams visited his Williams relatives in Longmeadow; in 1800 he sent his son (Eunice's great-grandson) Eleazar Williams to school in Longmeadow for five years.[12]

Sedgwick was intrigued by this Indian branch of her family. In the summer of 1821 she traveled to upstate New York and Canada, and in the travel journal she kept for her friends at home, she expresses her disappointment that she was not able to visit the clergyman at Oneida who ministered to "the spiritual interests of the poor natives." This clergyman was the same Eleazar Williams, "a far-away cousin of ours." A deacon in the Episcopal Church, Williams had been appointed to do missionary work among the Oneidas. And so Sedgwick claimed a "mixed-blood" cousin among her distant relations:

> Do not be startled, my dear girls, though some Indian blood is mingled in his veins with a fairer current. He is descended from a daughter of a Parson Williams, of Deerfield. She was taken by the savages during one of their incursions into the newly-formed settlement of our pious ancestors. She was so young that she soon lost all recollection of her parents. Many years after, when peace was established with our wild neighbors . . . , her friends made a fruitless effort to recover her. She had married an Indian, and chosen his country for her country, and his God for her God; and, like the tender and true-hearted Ruth, she has been the mother of a servant of the Lord. Mr. Williams (for he bears the name of his maternal ancestor) is said to labor with great zeal and some success among the remnant of his tribe.[13]

A few years after her attempt to meet her "far-away" Indian cousin, Sedgwick wrote the novel that conflates events from the 1637 Pequot War with the 1704 captivity of Eunice Williams. As Sedgwick most certainly knew from her study of the Puritan histories, after the burning of the

Pequot village at Mystic, many Pequots fled westward seeking refuge among the Mohawks—as does the Pequot chief Mononotto in her novel. On the way, he stops to liberate his children and captures Everell Fletcher and Faith Leslie for revenge. Even more fascinating, the Pequot-Mohawk group visits an Indian village in "the lower valley of the Housatonick"— the future setting of Sedgwick's Stockbridge home (85). Indeed, the scene of Magawisca's sacrifice takes place in present-day Stockbridge.[14] It seems that, for Sedgwick, the story of the Pequots also has much to do with the story of the Stockbridge Indians.

To make sense of Sedgwick's references to the Housatonic Valley, we need to explore the history of the mission town of Stockbridge and the role of Sedgwick's Williams and Dwight relatives in its destruction. In 1734–35 the Reverend Stephen Williams joined in proposing an Indian mission at Stockbridge to the Housatonic Indians.[15] Williams had been captured along with his family in 1704, but he had been ransomed by the French governor. The experience led to his interest in Stockbridge, which, according to Hilary Wyss, allowed him to "rhetorically redefine" his own captivity "through his paternalistic actions as a minister willing to save the 'heathens' from their own religious captivity." But the mission could not erase Eunice's marriage. "This relationship haunts the early years of the Stockbridge mission," writes Wyss. The first missionary, John Sergeant, joked about English fears of intermarriage and "going Native." As he wrote to an unidentified friend in 1736, "Perhaps we shall be so taken with them and their way of living, that we shall take each of us a wife from amongst, & sadly disappoint all other fair ones that may have any expectations from us."[16]

The negotiations for the proposed mission were successful, and a mission town of thirty-six square miles was laid out in 1736. The group that eventually became known as the Stockbridge Indians was a composite community of Mahican bands from New York, Connecticut, and Massachusetts.[17] The four English families who joined the town to serve as models of Christianity and "civilization" included that headed by Ephraim Williams, a cousin of Stephen Williams and Catharine Sedgwick's great-grandfather.[18] His daughter (Catharine's grandmother) Abigail Williams married the missionary John Sergeant. Despite this alliance, the Williams family did not share Sergeant's dedication to the Indians' welfare.

After Sergeant's death, the English residents increased steadily in number and divided into factions over the appointment of his successor, Jonathan Edwards, in August 1751. The Williams family had previously led the opposition to Edwards's ministry in Northampton.[19] Another controversy surrounded the establishment of a boarding school for Indians, which had been a dream of Sergeant's. By 1751, ninety-five boys from Six Nations tribes (Mohawks, Oneidas, and Tuscaroras), as well as Stockbridge Indians, attended the school, a project that, as Patrick Frazier describes, blended "Christian charity . . . perfectly with colonial security," since the "Iroquois presence considerably strengthened the area against French and Indian attack." The school also provided an opportunity for the Williams family to profit, creating jobs and contracts that the family exploited. Ephraim Williams promoted his daughter Abigail as headmistress of a new girls' school, and the widowed Abigail married Brigadier General Joseph Dwight (Abigail and Joseph would become Catharine's grandparents), who was appointed by the Massachusetts General Court to oversee the schools. Edwards, supported by the Indians and many English residents, wrote multiple letters of protest to mission officials in Boston and London, detailing the Williams clan's misuse of public funds for family profit and contending that "it is enough to make one sick." Edwards also reported that the Iroquois had left town because of the Williamses, and the Stockbridges were threatening to disband and leave as well.[20]

At the same time, the Williams faction was also profiting by extensive land acquisitions from the Stockbridges, a process traced by Lion G. Miles.[21] The Stockbridges repeatedly protested to the General Court, observing, "Your Memorialists in Justice to themselves and posterity must put in Caviat against their Lands being taken away and disposed of without their consent."[22] Nevertheless, the town of Stockbridge was soon the only land remaining to the Stockbridge Indians in Massachusetts. The General Court decision in 1765, which allowed the Indians to sell land to settle debt, was "the final death blow" to the Indian presence in Stockbridge. It was common practice to encourage individual Indians to take on debts for goods and alcohol and then demand payment in land. By 1774, only 1,200 acres remained in Indian hands.[23]

The Indians were losing their places in the Stockbridge church as well. The Reverend Stephen West (married to Ephraim Williams's daughter Elizabeth) replaced Jonathan Edwards and began enforcing strict Calvinist discipline in the church. By the time the mission commissioners appointed John Sergeant Jr. to take over ministering to the Indians in 1773, West had excommunicated all of the Indians.[24]

Despite the betrayal of the Stockbridge mission, the Stockbridge Indians enlisted in support of the American Revolution. According to Colin Calloway, "no Indian community gave the patriot cause more dedicated service than the town of Stockbridge." During the war, the home community suffered deprivation as war widows sold land and the whites took over the local government. Ultimately, "the Revolution brought the final separation of the Indians from both their American neighbors and their Stockbridge lands."[25]

In 1783 the Stockbridge Indians, frustrated and betrayed by the depletion of their land bank, decided to accept the invitation of the Oneidas to join them in upstate New York. They informed the General Court: "In this late War we have suffered much, our Blood has been spilled with yours and many of our young men have fallen by the Side of your Warriors. . . . Now we who remain are become very poor. Now Brothers, We will let you know we have been invited by our Brothers the Oniadas, to go and live with them. We have accepted their Invitation." They also sought the government's help in settling their affairs in Stockbridge:

> Brothers, We will now tell you what we desire of you. We wish you in your wisdom, to make some Laws that will protect and gard us while we may remain or hereafter have occation to come into your Government. We wish you to appoint a few of our Neighbors, whom we believe to be our Friends to have Power to take care of the little Interest of Land we have in this Town. . . . We wish to have them directed, carefully to examine into all our Bargains for Land that the white people have made with us and see that we havt been cheated . . . that when we are ready to remove, we may feel well towards all our Neighbors.[26]

In other words, the Stockbridges asked that white friends of the Indians examine and certify land sales to make sure they were legal, as well as investigate any past deals in which they had been cheated.

In spring 1784 the young men of the tribe went to New York to plant corn and make provisions for the removal that began later that year. The main body of the tribe moved to New Stockbridge that year, but forty Indians (including some widows) stayed behind until April 1788, when they also left after the upheaval of Shay's Rebellion. By the time of Catharine Sedgwick's birth in 1789, the Indians were mostly gone, but there remained a seasonal Indian presence in Stockbridge as thirty or forty Indians would return to the town each winter to visit ancestral graves.[27]

There is, then, a direct connection between the arrival of the Sedgwicks in town and the departure of the Stockbridge Indians. Pamela Dwight, daughter of Joseph Dwight and Abigail Williams Sergeant Dwight, married Theodore Sedgwick of Cornwall, Connecticut. These were Catharine

Sedgwick's parents. The couple moved to Stockbridge after Theodore Sedgwick participated in the final land grab as the Indians left town. No doubt he received tips from his Dwight-Williams in-laws in Stockbridge.

Theodore Sedgwick made at least four small land purchases from Indians in the 1780s.[28] The first purchase was from Elisabeth Wauwaumpequunaunt, the widow of Daniel, who was killed during the Revolution. The Wauwaumpequunaunt family were leaders in the Mahican nation; Daniel's father, John, had been a translator for Jonathan Edwards.[29] This sale took place soon after the Stockbridges announced their intention to leave the town; it formed the nucleus of the present Sedgwick property on Main Street. The second and third sales were from another widow, Elisabeth Oneweemeene. Not much is known about her, although she belonged to the small faction that was slower to leave Stockbridge. Her second sale to Sedgwick bordered his property and was described by her as land "on which I now live." According to this evidence, she lived next door to Sedgwick for two years and must have had some contact with the family. The Mtohksin family, who sold Sedgwick his fourth piece of Indian land, was also slower to leave Stockbridge. Jehoiakim Mtohksin was the son of an original settler, a captain in the Revolution, and a hero of the siege of Boston in 1775.[30] Sedgwick was buying land from Indian patriots—Revolutionary War widows and veterans whose sacrifices helped make the new nation possible—and thus was actively participating in their final dispossession.

This complex town and family history forms a crucial backdrop to *Hope Leslie*. The fact that the Pequot-Mohawk party and its English captives join the pre-mission Housatonic Indians becomes significant for readers of the novel. Sedgwick sketches the Housatonic River Valley and the Indians who lived there in the seventeenth century. She creates an idyllic portrait of the "children of the forest," who obey the laws of nature and live untouched by "the aggressions and hostility of the English strangers" (83, 85).[31]

Sedgwick then contrasts the landscape and the population of the Housatonic Valley in the pre-mission past and her post-mission present. She notes how white settlers profoundly changed the landscape and the "gentle Housatonick" River: "Thus it flows now—but not as then in the sylvan freedom of nature, when no clattering mills and bustling factories, threw their prosaic shadows over the silver waters. . . . The axman's stroke, that music to the *settler's* ear, never then violated the peace of nature, or made discord in her music" (83). Sedgwick also uses this twist in the plot to leap forward in time to describe the late-eighteenth-century removal of the Housatonic Mahicans from Stockbridge: "This village, as we have described it . . . remained the residence of the savages long after they had vanished from the surrounding country. Within the memory of the present generation the remnant of the tribe migrated to the west; and even now some of their families make a summer pilgrimage to this, their Jerusalem, and are regarded with a melancholy interest by the present occupants of the soil" (86). Sedgwick was born a few years after the first removal of the Stockbridge Indians in 1784, but she could remember the secondary removals of the same Indians from upstate New York to the White River country of Indiana in 1818 and to the Wisconsin Territory in 1822.[32] In any case, she likely witnessed their summer pilgrimages back to their original home.

Although Stockbridge residents, Sedgwick included, regarded the "remnants" of the Housatonic Mahicans of Stockbridge with "melancholy interest," the narrator notes bitterly that they are "not permitted" to remember and honor the Indians' better days: "Imagination may be indulged in lingering for a moment in those dusky regions of the past; but it is not permitted to reasonable instructed man, to admire or regret tribes of human beings, who lived and died, leaving scarcely a more enduring memorial, than the forsaken nest that vanishes before one winter's storms" (83). Sedgwick thus challenges the collective amnesia about the Indian presence in Stockbridge and elsewhere. She reminds readers that the Indians were "tribes of human beings" whose lives had meaning, even though they did not develop the land according to Anglo-American values.

These direct references to Stockbridge in the novel suggest that the "unmarriage" of Magawisca and Everell can be read as a commentary on the failed mission. Their relationship represents the optimistic early days of the mission, when the English and the Indians could come together on the colonial frontier. Everell's rejection of Magawisca represents the collapse of the mission's ideals. During these years, men like John Sergeant and Timothy Woodbridge were the Indians' friends and advocates. Petitions from the Stockbridge Indians typically begin by rehearsing this history of friendship: "We were then happy in each other, your enemies were my enemies, your friends were my friends."[33] Sedgwick wants to remember such an idealized time and place, a time of true friendship and loyalty between the races.

The affinity between Everell and Magawisca (in the midst of interracial hostility) develops soon after her arrival in the Fletcher household. Everell's respect and kind treatment win her love and friendship, which everyone notices. As Mrs. Fletcher writes to her husband: "Innocent and safe as the intercourse of these children now is, it is for thee to decide whether it be not most wise to remove the maiden from our dwelling. Two young plants that have sprung up in close neighbourhood, may be separated while young; but if disjoined after their fibers are all intertwined, one, or per-chance both, may perish" (33).

Sedgwick's reverential portrayal of the missionary John Eliot invokes the memory of John Sergeant, a frequent advocate for the Stockbridges. Eliot speaks on Magawisca's behalf when she is accused of conspiracy against the colony; his "expression of love, compassion, and benevolence, seemed like the seal of his Creator affixed to declare him a minister of mercy to His creatures" (282). He reminds the court that the "Lord's chosen people" were not "selected to exterminate the heathen, but to enlarge the bounds of God's heritage" (283).

Like the Stockbridge Indians, Magawisca makes enormous sacrifices for her white friends, losing her arm, quite tellingly, on a mountain in the future town of Stockbridge. She risks her life despite the fact that the English have destroyed her people and enslaved her. Her sacrifice repre-sents the enormous sacrifice made by the Stockbridge Indians in the Amer-ican Revolution. They fought for the colonists, although the colonists frequently took their land, which was as essential to their nationhood as Magawisca's arm is to her body.[34]

But despite these massive sacrifices, an Indian remained an unwelcome marriage partner in the novel and in the new nation. In a telling exchange, the Fletchers' former servant Digby tells Everell that at one time "I viewed you as good as mated with Magawisca; forgive me for speaking so, Mr. Everell, seeing she was but a tawny Indian after all." In reply, Everell acknowledges that a loving marriage with Magawisca had been a real pos-sibility: "Forgive you, Digby! You do me honour, by implying that I rightly estimated that noble creature; and before she had done the heroic deed, to which I owe my life—Yes, Digby, I might have loved her—might have forgotten that nature had put barriers between us." Digby disagrees: "Things would naturally have taken another course after Miss Hope came among us. . . . Now all is as it should be" (214). Similarly, the English settlers superseded the Stockbridge Indians who were off fighting in the Revolution. Despite the "heroic deeds" to which the new nation owed its life, there was no room for the Indians among the all-white citizenry of the new republic. For the white settlers of Stockbridge, all was "as it should be."

Like the later Stockbridges, Magawisca recognizes the impossibility of remaining in Massachusetts and decides to move west. She resents the loss of her land and the betrayal of her trust; she also makes it clear that white perfidy makes it impossible for the races to live together: "We cannot take as a gift that which is our own . . . the Indian and the white man can no more mingle, and become one, than day and night" (330). Similarly, in a last-ditch attempt to get some land back after the Revolution, the Stockbridges insisted that their land was given to them by the "great Spirit" and remained theirs "by the custom and laws of all nations."[35] Their white friends offer some needed assistance: the fictional Hope and Everell help Magawisca escape from jail, as in Stockbridge, John Sergeant Jr. and his committee supervised the remaining land sales. But these acts are too little, too late, and ultimately serve to expedite the removal of the Indians. As the narrator records: "This little remnant of the Pequod race . . . began their pilgrimage to the far western forests. That which remains untold of their story, is lost in the deep, voiceless obscurity of those unknown regions" (339). According to Sedgwick's novel, a similar fate met the "remnants" of the Stockbridge Indians.

In the 1850s, when Sedgwick began her autobiography, she glossed over this time in her family history. Her beloved niece Kate's husband, William Minot, prompted her reminiscences of Stockbridge when he requested that she write her autobiography for her great-niece Alice. This new project required her to reflect on both family history and Stockbridge history, which were so closely intertwined.

In her autobiography Sedgwick flatters the Dwight grandparents she never knew. Her maternal grandmother, Abigail Williams Sergeant Dwight, was "a woman much celebrated in her day for her intelligence and character." Her grandfather, Joseph Dwight, displays "most delicately beautiful hands" in his portrait, perhaps "to prove to his descendants that he had kept 'clean hands,' a commendable virtue, physically or morally speaking." Historians and contemporary reports agree, however, that the Dwights made large profits from the Indian school, and that their hands were certainly not clean.[36]

The family stories about Indians which survived were not about the mission Indians but about the violent threats of hostile Indians, "for in my youth, dear Alice, the dark shadows of the Indians had hardly passed off our valleys, and tales about them made the stock terrors of our nurseries."

One family legend recounts how the Irish servant Lynch carried the two-year-old Pamela Dwight, Sedgwick's mother, to safety during an Indian alarm after another servant had abandoned her.[37] Larry Lynch, the hero of this legend, became one of the leading landowners of Stockbridge.[38]

Sedgwick also writes about the lackluster performance of the mission. She notes that John Sergeant Jr., her grandmother's son from her first marriage, served as missionary to the Indians: "I believe he worked faithfully in the field, but I never could hear that the poor man reaped any harvest. His Indians had lost the masculine savage quality, the wild flavor, and had imbibed the dreg-vices of civilization, without in the least profiting by its advantages."[39]

But by 1855, Sedgwick took a more romanticized view of the mission and its legacy. She wrote to Nathan Appleton, the husband of her cousin Maria Gold, requesting that he sell an old barn, formerly "the Missionary Church in Brainard, Sargent, and Jonathan Edwards' time—they all preached in it." She went on to explain the plans for creating a monument to the mission:

> The design, I believe, is to remove it to the old Indian burying ground . . . to restore it as far as possible to its original appearance, and to erect beside it a monument on which is to be inscribed a record of the friendship that existed between the English people, and the tribe of Indians resident in these parts and of their extraordinary fidelity to their pledges. . . .
>
> The title to the Indian burying ground still remains in the Indians [possession?] and our people have *recently* come to a sense of its sacredness.[40]

It is possible to read the unmarriage of Magawisca and Everell as evidence of Sedgwick's timidity, prejudice, or inherent conservatism. But if we read the story as a commentary on the Stockbridge mission and the fate of the Stockbridge Indians (and there are too many references in the text to ignore), matters become much more complicated. Sedgwick views the aborted marriage of cultures at the Stockbridge mission as a lost opportunity. Furthermore, in light of her embrace of her Indian connections, a simple verdict of prejudice on Sedgwick's part does not make any sense. In her autobiographical and personal writing, however, we catch Sedgwick in the act of reflecting on a history that she perceives as compromising her own privilege, and so there are limits to what she can express.

There are no explicit references in *Hope Leslie* to the Cherokees, as there are to the Stockbridges and Pequots. But like many of her contemporaries, Sedgwick explored colonial history to make sense of the Indian removal crisis.[41] When she writes about the removal of the Pequots and the Stock-bridges, she not only writes about lost opportunities but also creates a usable past, telling this story to promote change. In the case of the Cher-okees, concerned citizens might still shape the future outcome. In addi-tion, since Harriet Gold, who married the Cherokee Elias Boudinot, was Sedgwick's cousin, the marriage created a personal connection to the na-tional question of Indian removal.

The Sedgwicks had many close ties to the Foreign Mission School in Cornwall. Sedgwick's first cousin, Edwin Welles Dwight, served as the first principal of the school in 1817–18. The grandson of Joseph Dwight and Abigail Williams Sergeant Dwight, Edwin Dwight carried on the family tradition of missionary work.[42] Sedgwick even mentions the school in two of her other novels. In *A New-England Tale* (1822), a character uses her patronage of the Foreign Mission School as an excuse not to care for her orphan niece: "Mr. Daggett and herself *calculated* to do a great deal for the Foreign Missionary Society; . . . no longer ago than that morning, Mr. D. and she had agreed to pay the expense of one of the young Cherokees at the School at———"; and in *Redwood* (1824), one of the characters joins "the knitting society, which has lately been established in aid of the pious youth at the Cornwall school."[43]

Catharine Sedgwick was also linked to the school and the scandal on her father's side of the family. Her father's eldest sister, Sarah Sedgwick, had married the Reverend Hezekiah Gold, minister of the Congregation-alist church in Cornwall. Their son, Benjamin Gold, was the father of Harriet Ruggles Gold, whose marriage caused such an uproar. Harriet was a generation younger than Catharine Sedgwick: Benjamin Gold and Sedg-wick were first cousins, and so Harriet was Sedgwick's first cousin once removed.[44]

Because Stockbridge and Cornwall are less than thirty miles apart, the Sedgwicks were close to the scandal surrounding Harriet's 1826 marriage to the Cherokee Boudinot. It cannot be mere coincidence that Sedgwick's novel published the very next year featured an Indian-white marriage. Although there is no direct evidence of the Sedgwicks of Stockbridge writing about the scandal, there was occasional correspondence and visits between the relatives in Stockbridge and Cornwall.[45]

Whatever Catharine Sedgwick may have thought of her younger cousin's marriage, in time she reached out to her new Indian relations, just as she had sought out her Indian Williams cousin in 1821. On her 1831 trip to Washington, D.C., she planned a visit with the Cherokee leader John

Ridge, cousin to Boudinot, and claimed him as a relative, writing to her niece, "Mr. Ridge, the Cherokee, and our connection, is coming to see us at ten this morning."[46] Apparently they exchanged calls, because Sedgwick wrote that her brother Robert "is going out to call on Ridge and Vann the Cherokees."[47] Sedgwick gave her brother Harry a very favorable report on Ridge: "I saw Ridge at Washington one of the Cherokee Chiefs, a most gentlemanly intelligent man. I will send you a letter . . . which I think proves his soul worth Jackson's and all his Cabinet. The impression among the dispassionate and respectable people is very much against the President."[48]

Perhaps this familial connection intensified her interest in the Cherokee removal crisis. After reading Jeremiah Evarts's celebrated defense of the Cherokees, she commented: "I have been reading Evarts pamphlets on the Indian rights and I do not see that a plainer case can be made out than that of the Cherokees. They can it seems to me only be removed on the avowed Georgian principle that 'might makes right.'"[49] When the Cherokees lost their battle with the state of Georgia, the Sedgwick family was also deeply involved: their cousins by marriage Ridge and Boudinot signed the Treaty of New Echota, while cousin John Sedgwick (later a famous major general in the Civil War) served under General Winfield Scott during the Trail of Tears.[50]

The connections among the Sedgwicks, Cornwall, and the Cherokees have significant implications for the interpretation of *Hope Leslie*. First, the timing is important. Sedgwick created her novel during the controversy over Sarah Northrup's and Harriet Gold's marriages. In an 1825 letter to her brother Harry she mentions William Hubbard's history and her search for additional source material: "I have had a very kind letter from Howe . . . offering to obtain for me some rare books on the pilgrim subject. . . . He mentions Winthrop's journal and the collections of the historical society, which he says he can obtain from Hale. I shall write to beg that he will."[51] In the midst of this research, the Cornwall scandal and the escalating Cherokee crisis likely brought the question of intermarriage and removal into sharp contemporary focus.

Second, Harriet Gold's story both parallels and complicates the story of Eunice/Faith. The most obvious and important difference, of course, is that Harriet was not a captive and Elias adopted *her* culture. Eunice/Faith chooses an Indian husband, but she has also become culturally Indian and fully converted to the Indian way of life. In contrast, Harriet chose Elias in part because he was Christian and educated in Anglo-American schools.

She also joined an Indian nation, not only as an adopted family member but also as a "missionary." Elias and Harriet left New England, just as Oneco and Faith do, but they planned to bring elements of New England culture with them. In the Gold-Boudinot marriage, Sedgwick sees a viable alternative to the absolutist rhetoric of civilization or extinction: a familial and political bond that values Cherokee nationalism and discusses Cherokee claims in the language of republican rights, Christian love, and the rule of law.[52]

Finally, in both the scandal and the novel, family members initially reject the marriage but ultimately accept it. A clear gender gap emerged in the Gold family: at first, Harriet's sisters reacted with horror to her engagement but then came around to accepting Elias. Similarly, Hope shudders when she learns of her sister's marriage. But she too comes around: "Hope took a more youthful, romantic, and, perhaps, natural view of the affair; and the suggestions of Magawisca, combining with the dictates of her own heart, produced the conclusion that this was a case where 'God had joined together, and man might not put asunder'" (338–39).

The Sedgwick family history of Indian marriages, missions, and land expands the critical reading of *Hope Leslie*. In Sedgwick's literary and historical imagination, the disruptive narrative of intermarriage perhaps offered a chance for familial and national redemption.

"Racial Gifts" and Indian Land: Cooper's Indian Romances

Like Theodore Sedgwick, William Cooper, the father of the famous author James Fenimore Cooper, benefited from the displacement of Indians in the aftermath of the Revolution, but on a much grander scale. After the Iroquois were abandoned by their British allies, William Cooper became a powerful land speculator and politician in upstate New York. Like Catharine Sedgwick, James Fenimore Cooper grappled with this family legacy in his fiction.

Cooper's Indian novels from the 1820s explore two interlocking problems: the rightful ownership of the land and the nature of racial identity. In all of these novels, white characters quickly reject Indian marriage proposals either with outrage or with Natty Bumppo's head-shaking observation that kind must marry kind. Cooper never refers to miscegenation law in his novels; in fact, his persistent legal concern was property law. Nevertheless, the issues of racial identity and property rights were closely related. The racial anxiety that is central to Cooper's fiction also has political motivations: Cooper denies the possibility of intermarriage because it would ultimately threaten white claims to the land. Both racial separation and white land possession are in keeping with the "law of nature" in Cooper's fiction. Alan Taylor, in *William Cooper's Town*, traces the rise and fall of the Cooper estate in upstate New York and James Fenimore Cooper's attempt to "imaginatively reclaim the estate he had lost."[53] I would add that Cooper's concern over land has everything to do with his concern about intermarriage.

Set in upstate New York in 1793, *The Pioneers, or the Sources of the Susquehanna, A Descriptive Tale*, was the first Leather-stocking novel published and the fourth installment in the series (if read according to the chronology of Natty Bumppo's life). The novel features Judge Temple, a frontier landowner, and his daughter Elizabeth; a minister, Mr. Grant; and an unlikely trio of woodsmen—Natty Bumppo, now an old hunter; Indian John, formerly known as Chingachgook; and Oliver Edwards, a young "halfbreed." The central struggle of the novel is over the rightful ownership of the land.

A related controversy in the novel is the possibility of Indian conversion and the nature of the "half-blood." The local minister, Mr. Grant, like many of the American Board missionaries involved in the Cornwall scandal, is quite earnest about including the Indians in his ministry: "The Redeemer died for all, for the poor Indian, as well as for the white man. Heaven knows no difference in colour; nor must earth witness a separation of the church."[54] Also denying the equation of religion with skin color, the servant Benjamin tells Indian John, "The parson says the word that is true, John. If-so-be, that they took count of the colour of the skin in heaven, why, they might refuse to muster on their books, a christian-born, like myself, just for the matter of a little tan, from cruising in warm latitudes" (95). This kindly intended, convoluted statement speaks to the confused relationship between race and religion. At first, the servant separates religion and biology in his insistence that skin color is irrelevant, but he then goes on to draw a distinction between himself, "a christian-born," and John, an Indian convert, suggesting there may be some difference "in the blood" after all. By discussing his "little tan, from cruising in warm latitudes" he also seems to endorse the Enlightenment view of racial differences as a result of climate. His reference to the "muster books" of heaven calls to mind the categorization of the races by the law, in a system in which citizenship and belonging *does* depend on the color of the skin.[55]

Complicating the question of Indian conversion is Oliver Edwards, a man *with*, as Natty Bumppo would put it, "a cross in his blood," or so it seems. After Edwards furiously denounces Judge Temple for stealing his people's lands, Mr. Grant explains to his daughter: "It is the hereditary violence of a native's passion, my child. . . . He is mixed with the blood of the Indians, you have heard; and neither the refinements of education, nor the advantages of our excellent liturgy, have been able entirely to eradicate the evil" (143). Mr. Grant is also confident that Edwards will not "relapse" into "the worship of his ancestors," for "his white blood would prevent it" (144). This statement is an interesting challenge to the typical nineteenth-century characterization of biracial people, who are usually portrayed as having all of the vices and none of the virtues of both races. A local landlady believes that conversion will break down racial barriers: "It's to be hoped that the missionaries will, in his own time, make a convarsion of the poor divils; and then it will matter little of what colour is the skin, or wedder there be wool or hair on the head" (150). Like the residents of Cornwall and the missionaries who supported the Ridge and Boudinot marriages, these characters believe that religion and not race is the major distinction between Indians and whites.

Despite all the white enthusiasm for Indian conversion, Natty Bumppo doubts that conversion has been to the Indians' benefit. He notes that Indian John was "christianized by the Moravians" and hints that missionary meddling led to the dispossession of the Indians (156). In fact, Chingachgook/John's fate makes an argument for cultural separation. He has only been hurt by his contact with whites: stripped of his land, addicted to alcohol, nominally Christian but never embraced by the Christian community, on his deathbed he returns to his native religion.

Cooper elides the problem of Edwards's mixed-blood identity by revealing at the end of the novel that he is *not* biologically Indian after all. His grandfather, Major Effingham, had been adopted as the son of a Mohican, and so Edwards's connection to the Delawares is merely honorary: "I have no other Indian blood or breeding; though I have seen the hour, Judge Temple, when I could wish that such had been my lineage and education" (441). Edwards, who was really Edward Oliver Effingham in disguise, had come to New York to claim his Tory family's lands, which had been held in trust by Judge Temple during the Revolution, and which he thought Judge Temple had stolen. The happy ending is marked by the return of his property and his marriage to Elizabeth Temple.

Issues of land ownership and identity are central to the novel. Throughout the plot, the rights to the land shift from the Indians and frontiersmen such as Natty Bumppo to the Tory Effinghams, then to the American Temples, and back to the Effingham-Temple Anglo-American marital alliance. It is clear that young Effingham retrieves his land only because he is an English heir; had he truly been half Indian, his claims would have had no legitimacy under the American legal system. Despite his honorary ties to the Indians, Effingham does not restore any land to the Indians or to men of the woods such as Natty Bumppo; in this tale, the Indians die or disappear, the white hunters who bridge the cultures are forced out, and a white couple inherits the land of the new nation. As Natty heads west, he looks forward to "the great day when the whites shall meet the redskins in judgment, and justice shall be the law, and not power" (455).

The Leather-stocking series continues with a "prequel" to *The Pioneers. The Last of the Mohicans; A Narrative of 1757* (1826), Cooper's most famous novel, "has perhaps done more to give shape to our basic images of the Indian," writes Fergus Bordewich, "than any other single book in American history."[56] The epigraph on the title page foreshadows its theme of racial interaction: "Mislike me not, for my complexion, / The shadowed livery of the burnished sun" (*The Merchant of Venice*, 2.1.1–2). Indian-white marriage is suggested but never allowed to happen. Two sisters, Alice and Cora Munro, find romance in their search for their father during the French and Indian War. The fair (and helpless) Alice is appropriately paired off with the earnest (but often useless) Major Duncan Heyward. In contrast, her dark sister, Cora, attracts the admiration of the Indians, an attraction explained by her mixed racial heritage. Her dark beauty and passionate nature come from her mother, who was "descended, remotely, from that unfortunate class, who are so basely enslaved."[57]

Two Indians desire Cora: the "good Indian" Uncas loves her and protects her, while the "bad Indian" Magua wants to get revenge against her father by blackmailing her into marriage. Alice and Duncan refuse to be ransomed at such a price. As Duncan exclaims, "Name not the horrid alternative again; the thought itself is worse than a thousand deaths" (109). Cooper does not think that marriage to the noble Uncas would be any less horrid: both Uncas and Cora are killed during the attempted rescue. Their Indian funeral is also a marriage ceremony as the Indian girls sing of their union in the "blessed hunting grounds" (343). Natty Bumppo explicitly denies that this mixed marriage could take place in heaven. For a man who insists dozens of times that he is "without a cross" in his blood, such a marriage is against the law of nature in this world and in the next.[58]

In *Mohicans*, Cooper continues to develop Natty's notion of "racial gifts," which makes character and behavior a matter of racial heredity. Although skin color determines proper behavior in this schema, as Geoffrey Rans observes, there are times when white men must go against their "gifts."[59] As Natty advises Duncan when he leaves on a rescue mission: "Remember, that to outwit the knaves it is lawful to practise things, that may not be naturally the gift of a white skin" (229). In order to maintain this schema of racial gifts, Cooper ignored many historical realities about his fictional Indians, including the fact that many of them shared the "white gift" of Christianity.

Contemporary reviewers criticized Cooper for his inaccurate portrayal of Indians; one reviewer suggested that he would write better books if, instead of going to Europe, he met some actual American Indians.[60] The *North American Review* disapproved of the relationship between Cora and Uncas: "Cora is quite a bold young woman, and makes rather free, we think, with the savages. This, probably, she felt the better title to do, in respect of the dark blood which flowed in her own veins." The reviewers also objected to this decision to make Cora a mixed-blood character: "We acknowledge it to be a vile and abominable prejudice; but still we have (and we cannot help it) a particular dislike to the richness of the negro blood in a heroine."[61]

Leaving behind the forests of upstate New York, the fifth and last novel in the Natty Bumppo life cycle (but the third novel published), *The Prairie* (1827), features the former warrior and hunter as an old man, reduced to trapping on the prairies west of the Mississippi, and his interaction with the Ishmael Bush family, a caravan of squatters heading west in search of a place ruled only by natural law. As in *Mohicans*, the plot features light and dark ladies in distress, a useless man of book learning, men of action, Indian rivalries, chases, captures, escapes, and recaptures. Perhaps sensitive to charges of inaccuracy, Cooper assured a correspondent that the Indians in the novel were based on personal acquaintances.[62]

This story is written against the backdrop of Indian removal, as Cooper writes in the later 1832 introduction: "The remnants of the Mohicans, and the Delawares, of the Creeks, Choctaws, and Cherokees, are destined to fulfil their time on these vast plains."[63] As even Cooper acknowledges in his story, however, these "vast plains" are already occupied by Indian nations, such as the Sioux and the Pawnees his characters encounter. And these various Indian nations will not be alone for long. The story is set just after the Louisiana Purchase, and so a deluge of white settlement is soon to come. Of course, the Indian residents were not party to these white political dealings, as a Pawnee warrior denounces: "And where were the chiefs of the Pawnee Loups, when this bargain was made! Is a nation to be sold like the skin of a beaver!" Natty responds that if the law of the Great Spirit were followed, the Indian "right to the Prairies would be as good as that of the greatest chief in the settlements, to the house which covers his head" (188). *The Prairie*, writes Susan M. Ryan, "call[s] into question the foundational logic of benevolent removal. What we see in this novel is a vision of a complicated West whose geography and existing animosities dictate that it simply cannot be shaped and reshaped to fit every removalist proposal."[64]

In this context of cultural clashes and land disputes, the possibilities and threats of intermarriage are an important factor. As the United States took over the Louisiana Territory and governed its new citizens of Spanish and French descent, Cooper notes, the transition was eased by romance among the various European peoples: "The barriers of Prejudice and religion were broken through by the irresistible power of the Master Passion, and family unions, ere long, began to cement the political tie which had made a forced conjunction, between people so opposite in their habits, their educations, and their opinions" (156). This logic of the salutary effect of intermarriages, however, is not extended to white-Indian contact on the prairie. While the Indians offer marriage in several instances, the whites emphatically reject the possibility. Ellen will not even let Natty translate Mahtoree's proposal to Inez: "Spare your breath, all that a savage says is not to be repeated before a Christian Lady" (291). All the whites are shocked when Mahtoree advises Ishmael to leave his old wife, Esther, and offers him his youngest wife, Tachechana, in her place; he also promises to find Indian wives for Ishmael's sons. Esther is the most furious and launches a tirade against her husband: "Who set an Indian up for a maker and breaker of the rights of wedded wives! . . . And you, Ishmael Bush, . . . Would ye disgrace colour, and family, and nation, by mixing white blood with red, and would ye be the parent of a race of mules" (298).

Dr. Battius, a naturalist accompanying Ishmael's party, reacts with horror to the suggestion of an Indian marriage, especially because of the uncertain identity of any resulting children. When Natty asks him if he would enjoy life "among the savages . . . with perhaps a couple of wives and five or six children, of the half-breed to call you father?" he responds that such a situation would be unnatural: "'Impossible!' exclaimed the startled naturalist, 'I am indisposed to matrimony, in general, and more especially to all admixture of the varieties of *species*, which only tend to tarnish the beauty and to interrupt the harmony of nature. Moreover, it is a painful innovation on the order of all nomenclatures!'" (221).

Natty agrees that "half-breeds" are problematic, "altogether more barbarous than the real savage" (29). As Cooper explains in a note, "half-breeds" are "men born of Indian women by white fathers. This race has much of the depravity of civilization without the virtues of the savage." (Note that Cooper's definition does not include the children of white mothers and Indian fathers.) Dr. Battius sees such marriages as unnatural; as a scientist, he is most troubled by the threat half-bloods pose to prevailing racial categories ("the order of all nomenclatures"), defying definition and requiring different parameters of thought. It is important to note that Cooper's attitude toward Battius is never approving: he's a fool, and what he says is foolish. Cooper seems to be mocking the developing field of race science and its growing obsession with categorizing people.

Natty's dual identity causes both whites and Indians to question which group he belongs to. Ishmael wonders that "you have the colour and speech of a Christian, while it seems that your heart is with the red-skins" (76). Natty himself seems to defy the system of racial gifts he so forcefully endorses. A Pawnee warrior, accustomed to reading political allegiance through race, questions, "The skin of the traveller is white . . . does his heart say one thing and his tongue another?" (188). While Natty is a liminal figure, like the half-blood, he is always careful to note that his Indianness is only cultural, that he can take on Indian gifts at will without losing his essential whiteness: "Still am I a man, without the cross of Indian blood" (76).

Even more significantly, Natty dies without leaving a son to carry on his position between cultures. As he says soon before his death, "When I am gone there will be an end of my race" (383). The ending of *The Prairie* suggests that the amalgamation of the best of the Indian and Christian white cultures can exist only in romance. Once Natty dies, the possibility of this marriage of cultures dies with him.

After Natty's death in *The Prairie*, Cooper abandoned the Leatherstocking saga for over a decade. In *The Wept of Wish-ton-Wish* (1829), Cooper, in a response to Child and Sedgwick's Puritan novels, turned to the exploration of the Puritan character.[65] It is no accident that part of the novel is set during King Philip's War. Stories about King Philip played an important role in the removal debates. Jill Lepore writes, "Both advocates and opponents of Indian removal looked to earlier Indian conflicts—

especially the much memorialized conflicts of the seventeenth-century colonies—to bolster their arguments."[66] The novel features the trials of the Heathcote family, headed by Captain Mark Heathcote, "a stern, fanatical soldier" in Cromwell's army who becomes a farmer in the New World (3).[67] After twenty years in the Massachusetts Bay Colony, he takes his family into the wilderness of Connecticut, where they face the constant threat of Indian attack. There are many similarities to Sedgwick's *Hope Leslie*: like Magawisca, the young Indian prisoner in their household, Miantonimoh, saves one of the white children; like Faith Leslie, little Ruth Heathcote, the captain's granddaughter, is captured and adopted by the Indians. These plot parallels led to charges of plagiarism, to which Cooper responded, quite unbelievably, that he had never read the novel or heard of its story. This is particularly unlikely because the same firm, Carey and Lea, published both books, and the publisher kept Cooper informed about Sedgwick's novel.[68]

The intermarriage plot is not raised until the final third of the novel, during the crisis of King Philip's War. The captive Ruth Heathcote is now a young woman and the wife of the great chief Conanchet. Her new name is Narra-mattah ("the Driven-Snow"), and she proclaims her allegiance to her Indian family: "If the Great Spirit made her skin of a different colour, he made her heart the same" (315). Nevertheless, Conanchet believes that she belongs with her white family, and reunites Narra-mattah/Ruth with her mother. He also brings their half-blood son to stay with his white in-laws. There may be some degree of white male fantasy here: that Indian men who married white women would realize the error of their ways. A neighbor offers to add the baby to a newborn group of triplets to avoid local gossip, but Ruth's father refuses: "It is his will that one sprung of a heathen lineage shall come beneath my roof, . . . My child, and all that are hers, are welcome" (355).

Meanwhile, Conanchet has met up with Submission (a regicide in hiding) as they travel through the war-torn woods. In a shorthand version of the famous Natty Bumppo–Chingachgook relationship, they bond, and Submission proclaims, "Though of white blood and of Christian origin, I can almost say that my heart is Indian" (368). While fleeing from the allied Pequots, Mohicans, and English, Conanchet sacrifices himself so that his white friend can escape. Like Child's Hobomok and Sedgwick's Magawisca, in Conanchet, Cooper creates an idealized Indian lover/friend who nobly sacrifices himself before disappearing forever.

While in the clutches of his archenemy, Uncas, Conanchet asks for one day before his execution to see his wife. Conanchet goes to the white village and leads Narra-mattah/Ruth and their baby into the woods for a final meeting. He tells her that the Great Spirit is angry at their marriage and their half-blood son, who is "neither red nor pale" (381). He explains to her that he is a prisoner of the Mohicans, and she suggests in her sadness that he join her white family instead of going to his death: "The Great Spirit sees that the man and his wife are of different tribes. . . . He wishes them to become the same people. Let Conanchet quit the woods, and go into the clearings with the mother of his boy" (383). But Conanchet refuses this breach of honor and returns to his enemies. Before he dies, he again declares that his son belongs with the whites: "It is a blossom of the clearings. It will not live in the shade" (388). Even though he speaks in racial terms, his motivation for sending his wife and son to their white relatives may be mixed. He may foresee the defeat of his people and want to ensure they are protected after his death. Narra-mattah/Ruth dies of grief the same day, and their child is erased from the narrative.

The dedication of the novel, however, suggests that the boy lived to have his own family and descendants:

To The Rev. J.R.C. of ****** Pennsylvania
The kind and disinterested manner in which you have furnished the materials of the following tale, merits a public acknowledgment. . . .
. . . You have every reason to exult in your descent, for, surely, if any man may claim to be a citizen and a proprietor in the Union, it is one, that, like yourself, can point to a line of ancestors whose origin is lost in the obscurity of time. You are truly an American. In your eyes, we of a brief century or two, must appear as little more than denizens quite recently admitted to the privilege of a residence. That you may continue to enjoy peace and happiness, in that land where your fathers so long flourished, is the sincere wish of your obliged friend,

THE AUTHOR

This dedication provides a frame for the story in the "tale of truth" tradition of early American fiction: the narrative was given to the author by a friend who is telling the story of his family history and wishes to remain anonymous. (Child uses a similar narrative approach in *Hobomok*.) It suggests that the friend is a descendant of Conanchet and Ruth/Narra-mattah through the child who disappears at the end of the novel. Cooper proclaims that this is a proud heritage: "You have every reason to exult in your descent." In fact, his Indianness makes him the most American of all, for "if any man may claim to be a citizen and a proprietor in the Union, it is one, that, like yourself, can point to a line of ancestors whose origin is lost in the obscurity of time." Cooper then acknowledges that the Anglo-Americans are relative newcomers: "In your eyes, we of a brief century or two, must appear as little more than denizens quite recently admitted to the privilege of a residence." He ends by saying, "That you may continue to enjoy peace and happiness, in that land where your fathers so long flourished, is the sincere wish of your obliged friend." This is a particularly amazing statement when we consider that Cooper's fiction mourns but generally defends Indian land dispossession. Is "The Rev. J.R.C." acceptable because his Indianness is rather distant? Because he seems to live an Anglo-American lifestyle? Does the goodwill message of the dedication match the message of the book, in which the last significant Indian military resistance in New England is defeated?

Cooper's Indian novels of the 1820s were written at a time when Indian removal was an important issue for intellectuals and lawmakers alike. In his Indian novels, Cooper struggled to justify removal in the face of Indian land claims. Supreme Court Chief Justice John Marshall dealt with similar issues in the judicial arena. Marshall would later rule in favor of the Cherokees, but in an 1823 case he laid the groundwork for the Indian Removal Act of 1830. His logic is amazingly similar to Cooper's—and reveals how closely linked the taboo against intermarriage was to land possession.

Cooper was particularly sensitive to issues of land dispossession and the legitimacy of land claims. When he began *The Pioneers*, his first Leatherstocking novel, he was heir to his late father's significant landholdings in upstate New York; by the time the novel was published, he had been "stripped of his properties and [was] responsible, as a man of honor, for thousands of dollars of debts accrued on behalf of his father's unsettled estate."[69] William Cooper had made his fortune by speculating in the land lost by the Iroquois in retaliation for their British sympathies during the Revolution. Although *The Pioneers* considers the "flawed foundation of his family's fortune," as Alan Taylor observes, the novel in the end philosophically establishes the Coopers as the rightful landowners, just as the series establishes the Anglo-Americans as the rightful inheritors of the nation.[70] In fact, Cooper would deny in his writings that the Indians had any lawful claim to the land at all, and, as Susan Scheckel argues, mourned the last members of a noble race "as a means of expiating guilt."[71] Scheckel draws important parallels between the narratives constructed by Cooper and by Chief Justice Marshall to justify white claims to the land.

The Supreme Court established legal grounds for the denial of Indian sovereignty and land rights in *Johnson v. McIntosh* (1823). In what David E. Wilkins calls this "foundational case addressing aboriginal possessory rights" (even though no Indians were party to the lawsuit), the court ruled that Indians could not sell their occupied lands to whomever they wanted because they lacked full title to them. This land dispute between two white men, each of whom claimed to have bought land from the Indians, established far-reaching principles affecting Indian tribes: "the discovery doctrine, the inferior status of Indian property rights, the notion of conquest, the allegedly inferior cultural standing of tribes, the impaired ability of tribes to sell their 'incomplete' title, and the 'so-called' diminished political status of the tribes." In this case, the court ruled that the Indian right of occupancy or possession of the land was superseded by the European right of "discovery" or conquest. This right of discovery "created a 'landlord-tenant' relationship between the federal government and the Indian tribes" and gave the Europeans the right to extinguish Indian land titles. This ruling was a political compromise, giving the Indian residents limited rights while preserving state and federal lands that had been acquired by treaty.[72]

It is the particular elements of Chief Justice Marshall's reasoning in the case that make the connection between land rights and amalgamation explicit. While Marshall acknowledges the weaknesses of the legal fiction of "discovery," he grants the Europeans title to the land in part because it is impossible for Indians and whites to be "one people":

> The title by conquest is acquired and maintained by force. The conqueror prescribes its limits. Humanity, however, acting on public opinion, has established, as a general rule, that the conquered shall not be wantonly oppressed, and that their condition shall remain as eligible as is compatible with the objects of the conquest. Most usually, they are incorporated with the victorious nation, and become subjects or citizens of the government with which they are connected. The new and old members of the society mingle with each other; *the distinction between them is gradually lost, and they make one people. . . .*
> But the tribes of Indians inhabiting this country were fierce savages, whose occupation was war, and whose subsistence was drawn chiefly from the forest. To leave them in possession of their country, was to leave the country a wilderness; to govern them as a distinct people, was impossible, because they were as brave and as high spirited as they were fierce, and were ready to repel by arms every attempt on their independence.
> What was the inevitable consequence of this state of things? The Europeans were under the necessity either of abandoning the country, and relinquishing

their pompous claims to it, or of enforcing those claims by the sword, and by the adoption of principles adapted to the condition of a people *with whom it was impossible to mix*, and who could not be governed as a distinct society, or of remaining in their neighborhood, and exposing themselves to the perpetual hazard of being massacred.[73]

Thus the European right of discovery was upheld because it was "impossible to mix" with the savage Indians. The ruling also justified European land rights on the basis of the superiority of European culture: "The character and religion of its inhabitants afforded an apology for considering them as a people over whom the superior genius of Europe might claim an ascendancy."[74]

Clearly, the contention that it was "impossible" for Europeans to mix with the Indians was an unconvincing legal fiction, undermined by the very existence of biracial offspring. Cooper solved the "half-blood problem" in different ways in his Indian romances of the 1820s: Oliver Edwards turns out to be an adopted Indian, and he claims his inheritance as a white man; Cora Munro, with her stain of African blood, is killed off; the son of Conanchet and Ruth Heathcote is returned to his white family; and Natty Bumppo, despite the fact that his heart often feels Indian, is "without a cross" in his blood. In all cases, "white blood" dominates, and the Europeans or Euro-Americans are the rightful inheritors of the land.

Compared to many of his contemporaries, Cooper demonstrated some respect and admiration for the Indians, yet his system of "racial gifts" relegated Indians to an inferior position. This understanding of "racial gifts," which locates cultural and moral traits "in the blood," makes it only consistent for Cooper to reject intermarriage as a possibility. Indian-white relationships—real or imagined, past or present—would undermine white claims to the land, especially because white claims were based on the impossibility of such relationships. As Susanne Opfermann notes: "When Cooper in his historical novels maintains that amalgamation of red and white had never been a viable way . . . he is also saying that the land, his land, could not have been acquired by interracial marriage. . . . Alliances between whites and Indians would have established Indian hereditary claims to land that had already been taken away from Indians."[75] In his fiction, therefore, Cooper can allow only "metaphoric kinship" with Indians.[76] Nineteenth-century notions of race separation and miscegenation bans were likewise politically motivated: Indians were defined as inferior and unchangeably different in order to justify white possession of the land.

Reviewers noted Cooper's advocacy of manifest destiny through the character of Leather-stocking: "[The tales] depict, with singular clearness and force, the superiority of the white blood in its simple strength enamored of forest life, and struggling alike with the wilderness and the savage—forcing away for the advance of the more industrious, and less adventurous settler—while the less enduing nature of nations of the forest perishes by the way."[77] However ambivalent and complicated Cooper's personal views on race may have been, in the end, the perspective of Natty Bumppo, the "man without a cross," prevails, dominates, and survives.

What Might Have Been: Child's Colonial History

Born in 1802, Lydia Maria Child was thirteen years younger than Cooper and Sedgwick, but she began her literary career at about the same time. Child looked to Sedgwick, the older and more established writer, for inspiration and literary guidance, and the two struck up a regular correspondence. Child's early letters are full of gushing admiration: "It is one perpetual wish to *think*, and *write*, and *be* like you. If ever I devote what intellectual faculties I have to a lofty and useful purpose, much, much, my dear Miss Sedgwick, will be owing to your salutary influence."[78] Sedgwick seemed to enjoy this effusive young writer, and she consulted her as a literary confidante: "I shall send you my little Hope Leslie in a few days—I have been a good deal troubled about one half of my title, 'Early times' etc., lest it should be deemed *pretensionary*."[79] Later in her career Child would criticize Sedgwick for her conservatism and lack of political engagement, but as a new writer she looked to Sedgwick as a model of female authorship.

Lydia Maria Child's earliest writings were inspired by the "Indian problem," which she learned about firsthand while living as a teenager in the frontier town of Norridgewock, Maine. Child, the most radical of the "miscegenation fiction" writers, challenged the racial discourses of the 1820s. Her novel *Hobomok, A Tale of Early Times, By an American* (1824) and her short story "The Indian Wife" (1828) shocked readers with their exploration of interracial marriages, the theme that would dominate her fiction for the rest of her career. Inspired by the Cherokee removal crisis, she went on to endorse Indian-white marriages in her revisionist history *The First Settlers of New England* (1829).[80]

In *Hobomok* and "The Indian Wife," Child portrays Indian-white marriages in contrasting colonial settings. *Hobomok* takes place in Puritan

Massachusetts in 1629, and "The Indian Wife" portrays Sioux-French interaction by the Falls of St. Anthony (present-day Minnesota) in 1765. There is also a different gender-race configuration in the two stories: *Hobomok* features a marriage between a Narragansett man and an English woman; "The Indian Wife" portrays a marriage between a Sioux (Lakota) woman and a Frenchman.[81] As seen in the Cornwall scandal, New Englanders worried most about white women crossing the color line in their relationships. *Hobomok* was thus the more controversial story because of the white woman's choice.

Although it is generally understood that the French were more open to intermarriage with the Indians than were New Englanders, in "The Indian Wife," Child cautions that French-Indian marriages, in the context of colonialism, could also be exploitive.[82] The first French fur traders sought assimilation and saw "racial intermixing as an instrument of empire," as Olive Patricia Dickason describes. In the seventeenth century, intermarriages were encouraged by the French government as part of a colonial policy to create French nationals in the New France setting. Intermarriages never reached a high level of social acceptance, however, especially outside of frontier society. By the early eighteenth century, as the number of white women increased, there was growing opposition to intermarriages, and officials no longer encouraged the practice.[83] Ironically, just as the French began to move away from intermarriage as a political strategy, English officials in Nova Scotia were suggesting that the best way to compete with the French was to encourage intermarriage.[84] French-Indian marriages remained very common in the Great Lakes region; the pattern was continued by the English after they took over the fur trade.[85]

Despite the different colonial settings, however, Child's stories intersect at several points. Both emphasize family and community reaction to intermarriages, the cultural identities of biracial children, and conceptions of race.

In *Hobomok*, Mary Conant elopes in the middle of the night with the Indian Hobomok, after learning that her English lover, Charles Brown, has been lost at sea. The news of her marriage is a "deadly blow" to her elderly father, who admits that he would rather have his daughter dead than married to a "savage": "I find I could more readily have covered her sweet face with the clods, than bear this." [86] This "better off dead" reaction is a common motif in intermarriage narratives. In the novel, the English community overwhelmingly condemns Mary's marriage. Mary "knew that her own nation looked upon her as lost and degraded; and, what was far worse, her own heart echoed back the charge" (135). The only English person who does not neglect her is her friend Mrs. Collier, who "firmly and boldly stemmed the tide" of social rejection (136).

In "The Indian Wife," the young French fur trader Florimond de Rance is a "universal favorite" who has been adopted by the Sioux tribe; nevertheless, the Sioux chieftain reacts with "rage" and "a still and terrible wrath" when Florimond asks to marry his daughter Tahmiroo. The chief says that the marriage is beneath his family since a king's daughter must marry a king's son.[87] It is important to note that his objection is not racial, as he points out that "there are Sioux girls enough for the poor pale-faces that come among us" (165–66). When her father forbids the marriage, Tahmiroo becomes seriously ill. At the sight of his heartbroken daughter dying, the chief relents and permits the marriage, just as the Gold family permitted Harriet's marriage after she became ill. As was common in the fur trade, Tahmiroo and Florimond marry *à la façon du pays*.[88]

In both stories it is the Indian characters who are hopelessly in love and must win over their white beloved. As Werner Sollors observes, in the early nineteenth century, fictional Indians "were portrayed as perfect practitioners of chivalric courtly love."[89] Hobomok succeeds to some extent in winning Mary's love, and so they have a reasonably happy marriage. After two years, Mary has a son by Hobomok, and she tells her friend Sally "that every day I live with that kind, noble-hearted creature, the better I love him" (137). In contrast, the marriage between Tahmiroo and Florimond is a disaster for Tahmiroo. Florimond woos Tahmiroo only to gain access to her father's lands; after they are married, he treats her with indifference and neglect despite her conversion to Catholicism and adoption of French language and fashion. Child clearly contrasts the courtly Indian lover with the mercenary Frenchman.

Despite their contentment, the marriage of Hobomok and Mary does not last. After three years, Mary's first love, Charles Brown, surprises the colony with his reappearance; it turns out he was not dead after all but had been shipwrecked and held captive. Hobomok, out of love for Mary, decides to divorce her by Indian law and ritual. He then "forever passed away from New England," so that she could be with her true love (141).

Legal rhetoric and procedure are central to the breakup of Hobomok and Mary's marriage. Although there was no miscegenation law in Massachusetts in 1629, common law principles are subtly used to undermine the legitimacy of the marriage. The novel repeatedly emphasizes Mary's weakened state of mind when she married Hobomok, for example, her "frightful expression of one walking in his sleep" and the fact that "her reason was obscured" (125, 148). This is not simply an explanation for why a white woman would "lower herself" to marry an Indian; it establishes an important point of law. In a letter, her father "conjured her not to consider a marriage lawful, which had been performed in a moment of derangement" (136). According to common law, marriage is a civil contract, and so the parties must be willing and able to contract. One of the legal incapacities which would make a marriage void is "want of reason"; Mary's "deplorable state of mind" suggests that this may be true in her case.[90] To her credit, she still takes her marriage vow to Hobomok seriously, and she refuses to leave him. The questionable legitimacy of the union, however, may have made it easier for readers to accept the dissolution of her marriage and her hasty remarriage.

After Hobomok's departure, Charles and Mary wed, and little "Charles Hobomok Conant" is raised by his English family. The biracial boy assimilates as he grows up; he studies at Harvard and then goes to England to complete his education. The Indian half of his identity is quietly erased: "His father was seldom spoken of; and by degrees his Indian appellation was silently omitted" (150).

The cultural identity of biracial children is also a major issue in "The Indian Wife." Florimond wants his children to be French; this desire leads him to abandon his Indian wife. By the time his daughter Victoire is thirteen, Florimond realizes that it would be "impossible to gratify his ambitious views for his daughter without removing her from the attractions of her savage home" (172). He charms his wife into letting him sell tracts of her valuable land and then sends the money to Quebec, "whither he had the purpose of conveying his children, on pretence of a visit; but in reality with the firm intent of never again beholding his deserted wife" (173). After devastating Tahmiroo by telling her that he married her only for her father's land, Florimond takes Victoire with him to Quebec. With the revelation of this betrayal, Tahmiroo is permanently changed. She focuses her new fierceness on her son Louis: "Her only care seemed to be to make him like his grandfather, and to instil a deadly hatred of white men" (175). When Florimond returns for the boy three years later, Tahmiroo takes desperate action rather than lose another child to the French: she puts Louis in her canoe, and together they sail off to the "Spirit-Land" by going over the Falls of St. Anthony. Although this melodramatic ending may be the stuff of fiction, Sylvia Van Kirk, a historian of the fur trade, notes that many Indian women found themselves abandoned by their French or English husbands. Although many Indian-European marriages were long-lasting, some men did not include their country wives in their life plans after they made their fortunes; the practice of "turning off" Indian wives easily evolved into abandonment. Similarly, many white fathers wished their biracial children to be raised as white. Van Kirk observes that, by the late eighteenth century, biracial daughters were being "weaned" from their Indian heritage and educated as European ladies.[91]

Both stories demonstrate how the understanding of "racial difference" influenced attitudes toward Indian-white marriages. For Mary's father, religion is the main barrier between Mary and Hobomok. Upon hearing the news of her marriage, he laments that "to have her lie in the bosom of a savage, and mingle her prayers with a heathen, who knoweth not God, is hard for a father's heart to endure" (133). His use of "savage" and "heathen" implies that the differences are cultural and religious; there is no mention of skin color or biological difference. Mr. Conant's neighbor, Mr. Oldham, takes a different view of Indian marriages: "A pretty piece of business it would be of a truth, to have a parcel of tawny grandchildren at your heels, squeaking *powaw*, and *sheshikwee*, and the devil knoweth what all" (127). Oldham raises the specter of biracial grandchildren and in his description of their different skin color and language links biology and culture.

In "The Indian Wife," Florimond, too, understands cultural difference as a matter of racial difference. For financial gain, he puts aside any qualms he might have about an Indian family, but he is willing to live with his wife only in Sioux country. Since Florimond sees Tahmiroo's race as the determinant of her cultural identity, her conversion to Catholicism and adoption of French language and customs do not erase his contempt for her. Nevertheless, his attitudes toward his children demonstrate this bizarre equation of race and culture in action. Victoire and Louis have half "Indian blood" and half "French blood," and thus are divided between cultures. Which side "wins" is determined by their environment. Their Indian childhood was allowing their "Indian blood" to dominate. But in Florimond's eyes, his children are not yet lost, since their "French blood" makes it possible for them to become French, but only if they are in a French environment. Life in Quebec would not transform Tahmiroo, however, since her appearance marks her race, and she lacks the requisite blood for Frenchness.

Child tentatively portrays Indian-white marriages only to undermine them with "back from the dead" white lovers and white avarice for land. By the end of the 1820s, however, she had moved from her tentative exploration of interracial marriages to an endorsement of loving, mutually rewarding relationships between equals.

Hobomok received a rather severe critique in the *North American Review*. While acknowledging that the tale "displays considerable talent," the reviewers objected to the resolution of Mary's story:

> To our minds there is a very considerable objection to the catastrophe of this story. A high born and delicate female, on the supposed death of her lover, has, in a fit of insane despondency, offered herself as the wife of an Indian chief, . . . she lives with him three years, and an infant semisavage is the offspring of the union. At the end of that time, her white lover returns; her copper one with great magnanimity relinquishes her and departs, and she is married to the former. Now this is a train of events not only unnatural, but revolting, we conceive, to every feeling of delicacy in man or woman.[92]

As Carolyn Karcher has observed, the reviewers were upset by the sexual freedom Child granted her female heroine; her crossing of the color line goes unpunished.[93]

The ambitious Child was not going to let this remain the last word on her novel. After hearing that the "literary kingmaker" George Ticknor had praised her work, she asked him for help in promoting *Hobomok*. He responded by influencing the *North American Review* editor to include it in a mass review of ten American novels.[94] Here she was vindicated: "We think this book has suffered much from the general prejudice against the catastrophe of the story. . . . But we doubt not, that it will one day be regarded with greater favor."[95]

Any ambivalence about Indian-white marriages Child exhibited in her early fiction is gone by her 1829 history *The First Settlers of New England*.[96] Written as a dialogue between "Mother" and her two daughters, the book offers a "protofeminist" revisionist history of the Puritan-Indian wars.[97] Countering the cultural narrative of tragic Indian decline, promoted so vividly in Cooper's novels, Child argues that it is "decidedly wrong, to speak of the removal, or extinction of the Indians as inevitable" (281). The treatment of the Indians demonstrates for her the destructiveness of the misguided Puritan typological vision: the Puritans were "possessed with the notion that they, like the Israelites of old, were the peculiar favourites of heaven, and like them commissioned to drive out and destroy the heathen inhabitants of this land" (137). She argues that in place of violent Anglo-Indian confrontation, both groups would have gained from peaceful interaction and intermarriage.

Through her advocacy of Indian-white marriages (safely in the Puritan past), Child challenges the developing racial theory that equated biology with culture. In her vision, intermarriage would have been a cultural exchange from which a new American culture free of Puritan intolerance would have evolved:

> The primitive simplicity, hospitality, and generosity of the Indians would grad-ually have improved and softened the stern and morose feelings resulting from the false views of religion. . . . Our arts and sciences would have imparted to the Indians new light and vigour. The pure religion of Jesus would have strengthened and confirmed their innate convictions of the character and at-tributes of the Almighty, and the example of our divine master and instructer would have taught them to subdue their wayward passions, and evil propensi-ties. (65)

And yet we see here traces of the "racial gifts" concept seen in racial theory (and made famous by Cooper's Natty Bumppo): the Indians have an "in-nate" understanding of God but a "propensity" for evil. As Child chal-lenges the link between race and culture, she cannot completely relinquish the concept of inborn "race traits." She is also influenced by contemporary race rhetoric in that she holds on to the civilized/primitive dichotomy. Even though she frequently inverts the typical meanings of this rhetoric— in her history the "civilized English" are often "barbarous and wicked" and the "primitive Indians" are "great and noble"—the greater value placed on true Christianity and English mores remains. The contribution of the "children of nature" to this imagined American culture is to "subdue the wayward and sordid passions which are nourished in civilized society" (254). As Carolyn Karcher remarks: "If Child subscribed to a broader and more tolerant ideal of assimilation, she nevertheless shared with other progressive thinkers of her day a theory of historical evolution that mea-sured cultures on an ascending scale and described them as rising from savagery through barbarism and pastoralism to civilization."[98]

Responding to amalgamation anxiety, Child counters objections to in-termarriage by challenging notions of white superiority and by quoting Scripture. Through a discussion of the scientific achievements of the "Asi-atics," "Hindoos," and Egyptians, she debunks pretensions of white supe-riority (66–69). She also reminds readers that God "has made of one blood all the nations of men, that they may dwell together" (66). She notes ironically that the typologically inclined Puritans ignored this most impor-tant teaching of the Bible (159).

Child's New England history is framed by advocacy for the Cherokees;

the connection is relevant, she explains, because the people of Georgia used the same rationales to exterminate Indians that the Puritans did.[99] She describes the removal crisis as a chance for the nation to change its tradition of race war: by speaking out against oppression of the Cherokees, New Englanders and all Americans have an opportunity for redemption and reconciliation. Interestingly, there is no discussion of Cherokee-white marriages as a solution to the struggle over land in Georgia. Perhaps intermarriage was more of a lost opportunity than a viable contemporary strategy. Child certainly was aware of the strong public opposition to intermarriage, and because her husband, David Lee Child, as editor of the *Massachusetts Journal,* exchanged papers with the *Cherokee Phoenix,* she likely would have known about the scandal surrounding the Boudinot marriage.[100] Later in her career, she would advocate interracial marriage as a way of reconciling the nation's current racial conflicts.

There are many striking parallels between the Cornwall scandal and the controversies over Indian-white marriages in fiction. The fictional Indians in all the novels, like the real-life Cherokees, are open to sincere marriages between Indians and whites. For the majority of the white community, however, Indians are not suitable marriage partners. It does not matter that Tahmiroo, in "The Indian Wife," converts to Catholicism and speaks French, or in the Cornwall case that Ridge and Boudinot were Christian and well educated. Religion and culture are seen as hereditary features of race, making the barrier between the Europeans and the Indians uncrossable. Just as the Puritans in *Hobomok* worried about the anomalous position of "tawny grandchildren," General Brinsmade, Harriet Gold's brother-in-law, worried about "black young ones" arising from the Cherokee-white marriage. Fears of amalgamation also led to some radical statements: many characters proclaimed that a white woman would be better off dead than married to an Indian. Opponents to Harriet Gold's marriage adopted this extreme rhetoric: "They should much rather follow her to the grave."[101]

This extreme rhetoric also demonstrates that while Indian-white marriages were not common, their occurrence was a serious concern in early national America. In this context, fiction provided a venue for exploring the possibilities of intermarriage. The stakes were high in these explorations, as interracial marriages formed a powerful narrative of disruption: if the races were equal and Indians were worthy marriage partners, then the policy of removal was morally bankrupt and the Indians had a legal claim to their land. These works of fiction were also alternative histories, where writers could mourn Indian extinction, justify white possession of Indian lands, denounce the past, and explore alternative legacies to race war (often simultaneously). Sedgwick, Cooper, and Child made their artistic and rhetorical decisions in the context of the urgent "Indian problem"; they were also influenced by changing understandings of race. The inconsistencies and shifting ideas present in their work reveal their very human struggle with one of the major issues of their day.

All three novelists present different attitudes toward race and Indian-white marriage, but in the end, all their Indians fade into the forest, clearing the land for the settlement of the new nation. The bonds of interracial love or friendship are suppressed by the political agendas of race and land rights. These bonds were also suppressed in real life, as the Cornwall couples moved west to Indian Territory. For signing the removal treaty with the U.S. government, Boudinot and Ridge were assassinated by other Cherokees. Tragically, even the Cornwall marriages, whose story challenged contentions about the separateness of the races and the Indian capacity for "civilization," were not enough to override the legal and fictional narratives condemning intermarriage and advocating Indian removal.

While the taboo against Indian-white marriage was intertwined with the desire for Indian lands, the taboo takes on a different dimension when the parties involved were black and white. In part II I show how miscegenation laws were also designed to keep down the permanently landless labor force, the enslaved Africans.

II

BLACK-WHITE MARRIAGES

4

"Amalgamation College": Intermarriage and Abolitionism at New York Central College

Is it true or not, that a colored man has all the rights of a white man?

REVEREND TIMOTHY STOWE

In October 1852, Professor William G. Allen wrote a glowing report about the first-anniversary celebration of the "Jerry Rescue." This event commemorated the rescue of the fugitive slave Jerry McHenry from a Syracuse jail on October 1, 1851. An antislavery army of several thousand, including Liberty Party conventioneers and local sympathizers, had stormed the jail and sent McHenry to safety in Canada.

This "spontaneous" uprising against the tyranny of the Fugitive Slave Law was no surprise to Syracuse residents. In fact, Senator Daniel Webster had dared the local vigilance committee to try to prevent the enforcement of this hated law. The Fillmore administration saw Syracuse as an important test for the Fugitive Slave Law, owing to the vigorous opposition to the law in the city. During a lecture tour in support of the Compromise of 1850, Webster denounced the Syracuse vigilance committee as treasonous and issued this challenge to abolitionists in May 1851: "Depend upon it, the law will be executed in its spirit, and to its letter. It will be executed in all the great cities; here in Syracuse; in the midst of the next Anti-slavery Convention, if the occasion shall arise; then we shall see what becomes of their lives and their sacred honor."[1] To abolitionists, the arrest of McHenry during the Liberty Party convention fulfilled Webster's threat. But as the historian Donald Yacavone observes, "Despite appearances, McHenry's capture and the meeting of the Liberty Party were coincidental. Three weeks earlier, James Lear . . . attempted a seizure but was rebuffed by the slave law commissioner, who found Lear's evidence of ownership inadequate. The required evidence arrived on 30 September and the marshals arrested McHenry the next day."[2] The coincidental timing remained symbolically powerful for Syracuse residents, nevertheless, and both black and white abolitionists were ready for the challenge.[3]

As Allen reported the following year, an even larger crowd attended the first-anniversary celebration of this triumph over the Fugitive Slave Law, including such abolitionist luminaries as William Lloyd Garrison, Gerrit Smith, Frederick Douglass, Lucy Stone, Lucretia Mott, Samuel J. May, and local minister Lyndon King. A business committee defiantly resolved that "those who rescued Jerry on the first of October, 1851, were not a mob, but on the contrary were law-abiding citizens rescuing Jerry from a mob."[4] Just a few months later, many of these "Jerry Rescue" celebrants, most notably Allen himself, would be swept up in its proslavery counterpart: the "Mary Rescue."

In 1853 the engagement and marriage of the African American Allen and the white Mary King created an uproar in upstate New York. Allen was a professor and King was a student at New York Central College, one of the only colleges in the country that accepted students and professors of all races and genders. Even this utopian reformist college was shaken by the scandal, however, and its commitment to racial equality was sorely tested by the question of interracial marriage.

The scandal over the Allen-King marriage exposes the links between abolitionism and fears of intermarriage in the antebellum period. Using these fears as a red herring, the proslavery press dubbed abolitionists "amalgamationists," equating support for emancipation with the endorsement of intermarriage. Actual intermarriages also tested the commitment of abolitionists to racial equality. Some abolitionists, for instance, tried to reassure nervous supporters with a "live and let live" position, arguing that if there was in fact a "natural antipathy" between the races, they need not worry that emancipation would lead to widespread amalgamation. They also tried to reduce the heated rhetoric around the issue; while opponents decried amalgamation as a sin against God and nature, abolitionists defined intermarriage as a question of "personal taste." A radical few, such as Garrison and Allen, took a bolder stand, arguing that intermarriage was part of God's plan and an essential component of a strong national character.

The story of New York Central College, the scandal over the Allen-King marriage, and Allen's own analysis of the controversy highlight the relationship among racial thought, the taboo against intermarriage, and the slavery debate. Allen's first-person accounts of the scandal indict Northern racism and dramatize how the taboo against intermarriage functioned to uphold slavery.

New York Central College

New York Central College was a radical but short-lived institution (1849–1860) founded by abolitionist Baptists in upstate New York, not far from Syracuse. The first college in the nation established specifically for educating students regardless of race or gender, it was also the first college in the United States to appoint African American professors to its faculty. In the state of New York, it was the first to offer women the same course of study as men and to have both men and women on its faculty.[5] After about a decade of operation, financial difficulties and its unpopular abolitionist character caused it to flounder. In 1853, when the African American professor William Allen married the white former student Mary King, the fears of critics that integrated education would lead to "race-mixing" seemed confirmed.

New York Central College had its genesis in controversies within Baptist congregations over slavery and abolitionism. In the 1830s, calls for immediate abolition caused many divisions in the Baptist Church, the largest denomination in America at the time. The Baptist movement was particularly strong in the South: by 1820 it was growing faster there than in the Northern states. Early abolitionists had targeted the nation's churches, believing that if the churches were to condemn the sin of slavery and refuse fellowship with slaveholders, then slaveholders would be persuaded to free their slaves. But the Baptist leadership wished to prevent a showdown: "Fearing the disruptive effect of the slavery question, conservative Baptists took strong steps to quiet antislavery agitation in the missionary and publication societies that united the denomination."[6]

Disenchanted by church leaders' refusal to take an antislavery position, abolitionist Northern Baptists soon began to form groups of their own. In 1840 an abolitionist faction formed the American Baptist Anti-Slavery Society. After the Board of Home Missions, which organized Baptist missionary endeavors, declared that "abolitionist ministers, missionaries, and laymen" had no right to interfere with the slavery question, this faction turned its "efforts to the cause of 'free' missions." In 1843 they established the American and Foreign Baptist Board of Foreign Missions, and in 1846 they changed their name to the American Baptist Free Mission Society (ABFMS).[7] The famous sectional division of the Baptist missionary societies, in which the Southern states withdrew and formed the Southern Baptist Convention, had already taken place in 1845; but, as John McKivigan argues, abolitionists were still not satisfied by this split. Many "charged that most Northern Baptists continued to condone slavery by their church practices." For this reason, abolitionists broke away to join the ABFMS and to work for change within the denomination.[8]

The ABFMS was part of a larger phenomenon in the 1840s: the "antislavery comeouter sect." The term "comeouters" designates a separatist movement within Christian denominations that took as its inspiration the biblical injunction "Come out from her, my people, that ye receive not of her plagues" (Rev. 18:4). After failing to persuade their churches to embrace abolitionism, these antislavery Christians "came out" to form their own churches: "By the mid-1850s," writes McKivigan, "there were at least six major comeouter sects: the Wesleyan Methodist Connection, the American Baptist Free Mission Society, the Free Presbyterian Church, the Franckean Evangelical Lutheran Synod, the Indiana Yearly Meeting of Anti-Slavery Friends, and the Progressive Friends." The "comeouter" sect was not just a white Christian phenomenon. African Americans also created their own "comeouter" churches. Protesting the prejudice of the major denominations, they established the African Methodist Episcopal Church and the African Methodist Episcopal Zion Church. These sects constituted "a dramatic protest against the churches' failure to correct their proslavery and racist practices."[9]

The rallying cry of the abolitionist comeouter Christian was "No fellowship with slaveholders." In the constitution of the ABFMS, the organizers pledged to support a Baptist missionary society "that shall be distinctly and thoroughly separated from all connection with the known avails of slavery, in the support of any of its benevolent purposes." An 1846 ABFMS pamphlet explains the "free missionary principle" and specifies why a separate missionary organization was necessary: "The Free Missionary Principle does not recognise slaveholders as the representatives of a pure Christianity, or hold them in fellowship as the followers of Christ." True Christians, therefore, could not take the tainted money of slaveholders in order to spread the Gospel: "The Free Missionary Principle does not admit the reception of the known avails of slavery with which to support and carry forward the work of a just and holy God." As written in the Book of Isaiah, "I hate robbery for burnt offering."[10] Another ABFMS publication,

Facts for Baptist Churches, also insists on the necessity of a free mission society. The book reprints hundreds of documents exposing the collusion of Northern Baptist churches with the "slave power."[11]

The ABFMS sent missionaries to Haiti, Jamaica, Burma, and Japan and to congregations in the United States from New Hampshire to Kansas; the board also published newspapers, Bibles, and other religious texts.[12] The society, believing that African Americans must have access to education in order to achieve freedom and equality, soon also became involved in educational projects.[13]

An incident at Madison University, a Baptist college in Hamilton, New York (renamed Colgate in 1890), sparked interest in founding an abolitionist college. Madison permitted abolitionist discussion, but it did not allow formal antislavery organizations. In January 1847, after student George Gavin Ritchie published strong antislavery opinions in the *Hamilton Student,* a newspaper he published, he was expelled. The Ritchie case became a rallying point for antislavery supporters and inspired the ABFMS to found a college based on the principles of free speech.[14]

In May 1847, at the fourth annual meeting of the ABFMS, Cyrus Pitt Grosvenor, Baptist minister and abolitionist activist, advocated a "Free Seminary for the Literary, Scientific, and moral education of such youth of both sexes as may be placed under its influences."[15] The planning and fund-raising for Free Central College, renamed New York Central College, were soon under way.[16] As Grosvenor's *Christian Contributor and Free Missionary* newspaper reported, the school was located in McGrawville, about thirty-seven miles south of Syracuse. McGrawville outbid other potential sites with a $12,000 donation to the school. The article explained that New York Central College, unlike other schools, would "educate the physical and moral at the same time with the intellectual capacities." The Free Gospel principle was central to this mission: "God has given to Free Missionists a vantage ground where they may . . . by means of such an Institution, accomplish untold direct good and exert a corrective influence on the disastrous systems of education now generally in vogue."[17] The ABFMS solicited funds throughout the North and gained the support of many prominent abolitionists, including William Lloyd Garrison, Frederick Douglass, Wendell Phillips, Henry Ward Beecher, Horace Greeley, Gerrit Smith, and Senator John P. Hale of New Hampshire. The college opened in the fall of 1849, with Grosvenor serving as president.[18]

Referred to as the "Oberlin of the East" in recognition of the pioneering policy of Oberlin College to admit students regardless of race or gender,

New York Central College exceeded Oberlin's policies by hiring African American professors.[19] Integrated education was a controversial issue in the 1830s and 1840s as abolitionists worked for black equality. In 1831, for example, a proposed integrated manual labor school in New Haven was defeated by mob action in the aftermath of Nat Turner's slave rebellion. The next year, President Beriah Green opened Oneida Institute in upstate New York to interracial admission. Prudence Crandall's school for young ladies of color in Canterbury, Connecticut, met with violent town opposition in 1833; the state legislature even passed a "Black Law" making it illegal to operate a school for nonresident African Americans. In 1834 the Baptist Noyes Academy in Canaan, New Hampshire, had a similar experience: "The interracial and coeducation character of the school incensed local whites, . . . and they destroyed it the following year, using ninety teams of oxen to drag the building into a swamp a half mile from its original site." In 1835 abolitionist students who had withdrawn from Lane Seminary in Ohio agreed to enter Oberlin on the condition that black students be admitted as well. By 1835 abolitionists reported that there were six integrated colleges or high schools in the United States. The establishment of New York Central College, therefore, was seen as an important advancement in the movement for black education.[20] Other Free Mission Baptists opened a similar school, Eleutherian College, in Lancaster, Indiana, the same year.[21] The series of protests against integrated education revealed the strength of white prejudice; fears of amalgamation and links to abolitionism also played a part in each controversy. In Connecticut, the *Norwich Republican*, for instance, contended that the Crandall school "threatened 'to break down the barriers which God has placed between blacks and whites—to manufacture *Young Ladies of color*' who would go forth to entice 'our white bachelors.' "[22]

New York Central College was to be guided by four governing principles, as described in its prospectus:

> It is unchangeably pledged to the morality of Anti-Slavery, and will strive to sustain the doctrine of the unity, common origin, equality and brotherhood of the human race.
>
> 2nd. To contribute to the settlement of the equality of the sexes, and to bring woman to occupy her true position in moulding the public sentiment and actions of the world, it advocates and labors to secure for her, equal advantages in literary, scientific, moral and physical education.
>
> 3d. To form in the rising generation habits of industry—to make every kind of useful industry respectable; indeed to give honorable character to physical as well as mental labor, health to the body as well as vigor to the intellect, it is a principle of the incorporation to encourage and elevate honest toil, by provid-

ing that as early as practicable the means of labor shall be as extensive, proportionately, as the school privileges.

4th. The Bible is regarded as the text book in morals, and is placed among the Classics, to be studied in our own and the original languages, without regard to distinctive denominational creeds or preferences.[23]

At a time when polygenetic theories of human creation were gaining credence, Central College's commitment to the "unity, common origin, equality and brotherhood of the human race" was an important stance. In addition to these four principles, the school followed temperance practices: "[The students] will not be poisoned by either tea, coffee or alcohol, while the polluting use of that disgusting, filthy, slave-grown weed, tobacco, is carefully excluded from the College life."[24]

The college reflected the determination of abolitionists to work not only for the abolition of slavery but also for the equality of the races. As an early report proudly proclaims:

> The doctrine of exclusiveness and caste is here utterly repudiated, and New York Central College has been the first in the United States, to set the example of appointing a colored man to a Professorship. Here is no distinction on account of color, but the various shades of African blood, from the jet black to the bright mulatto, the copper tinge of the Aborigines of the forest, and the clear complexion of the vain-glorious Anglo-Saxon, are all seen mingled together; and those wearing these different hues associate on terms of the most intimate companionship and equality, nor does anyone at the College whisper a single complaint at this state of things.[25]

The 1853–54 college catalogue declares an ongoing commitment to these ideals: "All, rich and poor, black and white, male and female, may stand on one common platform, with the fixed belief of the equality and brotherhood of the whole human family. The Institution is earnestly and untiringly devoted to the great reforms of the day."[26]

The Career and Politics of William G. Allen

William G. Allen was born a free black in Virginia in 1820. He described his background in the racial parlance of his time: "My father was a white man, my mother a mulatress, so that I am what is generally termed a quadroon." His parents died when he was very young, and he was adopted by a "coloured family." He attended school for a short time in Norfolk until the Nat Turner Rebellion in 1831 led to the closure of schools for free blacks. Allen then sought his education among the "highly educated foreigners" and political refugees who served in the U.S. Army at Fort Monroe.[27]

At the age of eighteen Allen had the unexpected opportunity to leave the South and escape the social and legal no-man's-land that the free black faced in Virginia. A visiting minister from New York took great interest in Allen and informed Gerrit Smith, the wealthy philanthropist and abolitionist from upstate New York, of Allen's potential. Smith invited Allen to attend the Oneida Institute in Whitesboro, New York, at his expense.[28] Allen spent five years at Oneida, graduating in 1844. After graduation, he worked with Henry Highland Garnet on the reformist *National Watchman*, a short-lived newspaper in Troy, New York. The professorial appointment he dreamed about, however, was simply out of the question: "That any man having the slightest tinge of color," he later wrote, "should aspire to such a position, I soon found was the very madness of madness." In 1847 he went to Boston and studied law for two years with Ellis Gray Loring, who was Lydia Maria Child's close friend and frequent financial backer. Active in abolitionist circles, Allen also lectured on African cultural achievements and the future of the race. In his 1849 book *Wheatley, Banneker, and Horton*, published to accompany his lectures, he used historical examples to challenge the notion of African inferiority.[29] In December 1850 he was finally offered a professorship at New York Central College, "the only College in America that has ever called a colored man to a Professorship, and one of the very few that receive colored and white students on terms of perfect equality."[30]

Allen describes the college as being founded "by a few noble-minded men" who "sought to illustrate the doctrine of Human Equality, or brotherhood of the races." The college was thus persecuted by the public; the state legislature gave the school a charter but no financial support. The debates in the State House were marked by "vulgar flings at 'negroes'" and "cries of 'amalgamation.'"[31] Many state senators objected to the "common intermingling of the sexes" and the lack of "distinction between the colors"; the fact that the two sexes were seated together in class was also a matter of controversy.[32] The *Syracuse Daily Star*, hostile to abolitionist efforts, connected abolitionism and amalgamation and reported approvingly that "the Legislature refused to grant any assistance to this school because of its color corrupting tendency."[33]

Regardless of the public disdain for the college, however, Allen taught there successfully for several years. At the same time, he maintained a strong public presence in New York abolitionist circles and represented

Central College at antislavery meetings. Letters "from Professor Allen" appear frequently in abolitionist papers such as *Voice of the Fugitive* and *Frederick Douglass' Paper*, in which he urges self-sufficiency for African Americans.[34] Douglass praised a speech given by Allen at a county anti-slavery convention in Ithaca: "Mr. Allen made one of the best anti-colonization speeches I ever heard . . . well fitted to convince the audience that the presence of the colored people in this country is important to the progress of civilization, and to the highest elevation of the whole American people. . . . The colored people present looked delighted as they saw their champion scattering one after another, the barricades of their enemies."[35]

Allen was at his best, however, when he was able to merge his classical education with his political activism. In a speech before the Dialexian Society, a college oratorical club, titled "Orators and Oratory," he argued that great oratory always originates in the cause of freedom: "Orators worthy the name must necessarily originate in the nation which is on the eve of passing from a state of slavery into freedom." He began his speech with Demosthenes and Cicero and concluded with the great abolitionist orators, both black and white, thus placing them in the historical context of the worldwide struggle for human freedom. He urged the society's members to choose the spirit of freedom and to use their oratorical gifts wisely: "Members of this society, as ye cultivate the oratorical, do it diligently, and with purpose; remembering that it is by exercise of this weapon, perhaps more than any other, that America is to be made a free land, not in name only, but in deed and in truth."[36]

Allen was also able to translate his words into action. In a radical political act, he voted in the presidential election of 1852. This action is remarkable because, according to the New York State Constitution of 1821, "men of colour" had to meet a $250 property requirement in order to vote. This law effectively disenfranchised the vast majority of African American men in the state. At mid-century there still remained widespread support for the law: an 1846 statewide referendum on the question of this discriminatory clause defeated the cause of equal suffrage by almost three to one.[37]

Allen gave an immediate account of his success in *Frederick Douglass' Paper*: "It was a victory on my part, and such a one as makes me feel that were the colored people of this country more spirited and determined, more bold in the assertion of their rights, . . . they would accomplish more for themselves and for the cause of our common humanity." Allen was triumphant as he claimed the rights of citizenship and "common humanity," declaring, "I feel an enviable degree of self respect in view of the transaction." The 1852 election was a three-way race among Democrat Franklin Pierce, Whig Winfield Scott, and Free-Soiler John P. Hale. Because Allen delighted in the defeat of the Whig Party and claimed to have voted "of course for freedom," we may assume he voted for Hale.[38]

Allen's personal civil rights success became a standard feature of his abolitionist lectures. In 1854, he told a British audience how he had faced down his interrogator at the polls: "I demand my vote this day, not because I have or have not 250 dollars worth of real estate, but on the simple ground of my manhood."[39] Unfortunately, Allen's triumph did not have any immediate effect on the voting rights of other African American men: later referenda on equal suffrage were also voted down in 1860 and 1869, though by smaller margins each time.[40] Just as interracial marriage was used as an argument against integrated education, black suffrage and intermarriage were also linked in political debates. As one participant in the 1821 state constitutional convention argued, black men should vote only when public sentiment changes, for example, "when the colours shall intermarry."[41]

For Allen, this day of social equality could not come too soon: to him, intermarriage was essential to a strong national character. In a series of letters to *Frederick Douglass' Paper*, Allen lays out his views on race, nation, and "amalgamation." First of all, he makes an important distinction between race (biological identity) and nation (political entity). He goes on to contend that great nations result from a mixture of races and that American prejudice turns a source of national strength into a national taboo:

> Nations worthy of the name, are only produced by a fusion of races. If Americans had less prejudice, they could read history more clearly. Whence the Romans! The Magyars! The English! The Americans! The latter, at least, notwithstanding they roll up their eyes, and go into pretended fits, at the mere mention of amalgamation, are, of all the races, the most amalgamated under the sun; and, as a matter of course—the most energetic and powerful. Indeed, fusion of races seems to be a trait, distinctive of Americans. The shades of night scarce gather around them, ere they (the Americans) seek amalgation [sic] with even the very race which they affect most to despise. Talk of the "instincts of nature"—the hypocrites![42]

In describing the national benefits of amalgamation, Allen uses the language of romantic racialism common to nineteenth-century thought, insisting that each race has a particular character, the strengths of which it brings to the nation:

The African race is superior to other races, also, in kindness and religious tendencies; but what sort of a *nation* would a race of mere kind, religious folks, however kind and pious, be? The Anglo-Saxon race is superior to other races in calculating intellect and physical force; but what sort of a *nation* would a race of mere calculating intellects and physical men, however superior, be? . . . The civilization of the African, unmingled with the civilization of any other race, while it would develop more largely than any other race, the good, the beautiful, the artistic, the religious, would develop too little of physical force, calculating intellect, daring enterprise, and love of gain, to make a nation great, energetic and powerful. The civilization of the Anglo-Saxon, unmingled with the civilization of any other race, would develop too much of the fierce, active, and warlike, and too little of the kind, gentle, charitable, and merciful, to make a nation stable, grand, and truly great. The greatness of the American *nation* is, unquestionably, owing no less to the various elements of which it is composed, than to its climate and favorable circumstances. Harmony of character, which is the soul of true greatness, is only produced by a bringing together of qualities of mind and heart which are dissimilar, not antagonistic.[43]

Through the mixture of the aggressive Anglo-Saxon race and the kind African race, Allen argues, a balanced national character develops. This consequence accords with God's plan: "The plain truth, is, God has made us of one blood, and thereby to intermingle. We progress by adhering to this rule, we go backward by its violation."[44]

Yet Allen acknowledged the difficulty of dividing people into categories of race and nation. One correspondent, "Communipaw," wondered that if all people were "of one blood," then would all people be members of the same race? Allen stumbled as he tried to answer this question: "'Of *one* blood are *all* the nations of the earth created.' Here is a plain statement of the *oneness* of race of all mankind; and yet no one better knows than Communipaw, that, on entering the field of ethnography, we are compelled, for scientific purposes, to speak of 'this race,' and 'that race,' of 'mixed races,' and so on."[45]

As these letters make clear, while Allen's marriage the following year may indeed have been a matter of love, it was also in keeping with his racial and political beliefs and with a lifetime of claiming the rights of humanity and citizenship. In addition, it can be seen that the events of Allen's life—his college education, his legal training, his professorship, his vote, and, finally, his marriage—were all part of a trajectory of self-assertion as a citizen and as a man, refuting any argument about his supposed inferiority.

The Mob, the "Mary Rescue," and the Escape

In April 1851, Allen gave a series of lectures in Fulton, New York, where he visited the home of the Reverend Lyndon King, a minister in the Wesleyan Methodist "comeouter" church and "one of the ablest advocates of the social, political, and religious rights of the colored man." Allen took a special interest in Mary E. King, the minister's daughter, and, during her attendance at New York Central College, they struck up a romantic relationship.[46] After discussing marriage in December 1852, they decided to wait and think over "the whole field of difficulties, embarrassments, trials, insults, and persecutions" they would encounter as a married couple. Allen reports that they were engaged a month later, in January 1853, Mary King having the "moral heroism" to challenge the system of "American Caste,—the most cruel under the sun."[47]

Allen, himself the child of a mixed-race marriage, had no illusions about the cruelty of the caste system, both South and North. He writes of the legal and extralegal pressures surrounding interracial liaisons:

> The laws of the Southern States, on the one hand, . . . have deliberately, and in cold blood, withheld their protection from every woman within their borders, in whose veins may flow but half a drop of African blood; while the prejudice against color of the Northern States, on the other hand, is so cruel and contemptuous of the rights and feelings of colored people, that no white man would lose his caste in debauching the best educated, most accomplished, virtuous and wealthy colored woman in the community, but would be mobbed from Maine to Delaware, should he with that same woman attempt honorable marriage.[48]

Allen and Mary King were soon to experience the power of the caste system in their own lives.

As in the case of Harriet Gold, King's family was divided over her engagement. Her father, Lyndon, and sister Julia approved of the match, while her brothers and stepmother angrily opposed it. Recounting his experiences, Allen insists that he bore no ill will toward the family but felt "only pity for those who nurture a prejudice, which, while it convicts them of the most ridiculous vanity, at the same time shrivels their own hearts and narrows their own souls." In contrast, he quotes a portion of a letter from Mary King that demonstrates her "noble soul": "Friends may forsake me, and the world prove false, but the sweet assurance that I have your most devoted love, . . . is the only return I ask."[49]

As in the Cornwall scandal, the news of the engagement soon became public, and among some of Allen's neighbors it provoked the "better off dead" response that occurs in almost every discussion of interracial marriage. Others who did not declare they would rather see their children dead than married to a person of African descent nonetheless condemned the marriage as "dreadful," "vulgar," and "sinful." Allen and King did have the support of John C. and Sarah Dunn Porter, their friends and Central College students.[50] The Porters truly embraced the college's doctrine of the "unity, equality, and brotherhood of the human race," which, as Allen notes, was rare even among self-proclaimed abolitionists and Christians. Events surrounding the engagement reached a crisis point for Allen and King when her brother the Reverend John B. King came to visit and talked his father into opposing the marriage. Allen notes ironically that the younger Reverend King had been raising funds in Washington, D.C., for a "comeouter" church: this man who rejected fellowship with slaveholders also rejected a brother-in-law of color.[51]

Community opposition in Fulton had been building; on January 30 it exploded into mob violence. A crowd of four hundred to five hundred men approached the Porter house, where King and Allen were visiting. They planned to escort King home, torture Allen ("mutilations too shocking to be named"), kill him in a spiked barrel, and tar and feather Porter. A "Committee" of "respectable" men, however, while opposing the relationship, wanted to spare the village from violence. After all, the marriage had not yet taken place. These men approached Allen and told him they could save his life if King went with them and Allen left the village. Under tight security Allen was barricaded in the village hotel and then secreted away by sleigh to Syracuse, while King was taken home. The leaders of the mob boasted of having "rescued" Mary, and when the story was covered in the *Syracuse Star*, it became known as the proslavery counterpart to the abolitionist rescue of Jerry McHenry: the "Jerry Rescue" had now been matched by the "Mary Rescue."[52] The *Star* report clinched the connections between abolitionism and amalgamation in the public mind by identifying Mary's father as "Rev. Mr. King, Pastor of a regular Wesleyan Methodist, Abolition, Amalgamation church."[53]

King suffered extreme persecution and virtual imprisonment during the weeks after the mob scene. Held as if under house arrest, she was not permitted to meet Allen in Syracuse or communicate with people who approved of her engagement. Abolitionists rose to her defense. L. D. Tanner excoriated Lyndon King in the abolitionist press for his opposition to his daughter's marriage and for his treatment of her, charging that "God by his providence" was testing King's commitment to abolitionism and racial equality "and is asking you and your associates, before this State and this nation, whether you meant it." He urged King to reconsider his disapproval and linked the father's restraint of his daughter to the support of slavery: "It becomes not you, sir, to be the manacle-maker of humanity, not to be the devil's turnkey, in the great Bastile of slavery."[54]

Allen received reports of Mary's plight from his friend Porter, who had put himself in danger because of his hospitality to Allen: "*It is impossible for you to conceive what a convulsion this village of Fulton has been thrown into,*" Porter wrote him. King's family tried all kinds of maneuvers to make sure the marriage never took place: they tried to lure Allen to an isolated house (which he assumed was a trap), and they sent him a letter—not in Mary's handwriting—breaking off the engagement.[55]

In response to all the publicity surrounding the controversy, Allen published his own side of the story in the *Syracuse Standard* on February 8, 1853. This article was reprinted in many other newspapers.[56] After correcting several false rumors, Allen closes with a statement of pride and dignity:

> To the Committee who so kindly lent me their protection on that memorable night, I offer my thanks and lasting gratitude.
>
> To the poor wretches who sought to take my life, I extend my pity and forgiveness.
>
> As to myself—having in my veins, though but in a slight degree, the blood of a despised, crushed, and persecuted people, I ask no favors of the people of this country, and get none save from those whose Christianity is not hypocrisy, and who are willing to "do unto others as they would that others should do unto them"—and who regard *all* human beings who are equal in character as equal to one another.[57]

At their February 1853 convention, Liberty Party members also linked the "Jerry Rescue" and the "Mary Rescue" and the issues of abolition and amalgamation. After several resolutions praising the Jerry rescuers, supporting them in their legal trials and denouncing the Fugitive Slave Law, the convention offered this observation on the "Mary Rescue": "Resolved, That the recent outrage upon that accomplished and worthy man, Professor William G. Allen, and the general acquiescence, not to say general rejoicing, in this outrage, are among the fearful evidences that, on the subject of slavery, the deeply-corrupted heart of the American people is but too probably past cure."[58]

In the battle for control of the public perception of the controversy, Mary King's brother William S. King published an article in the *Syracuse Daily Journal* insisting that Mary and Allen were never actually engaged.

In fact, he contends that Mary had rejected Allen three times, always expressing "her abhorrence of the idea of 'amalgamation.'"[59] Events soon proved this version to be untrue. King pretended to have accepted a teaching job in Pennsylvania, and from there she traveled to New York City to meet Allen. They were married on March 30, 1853, by the Reverend Thomas Henson, a black Baptist minister and abolitionist activist.[60] After hiding in Boston for ten days, they then sailed for England on April 9 aboard the *Daniel Webster,* a ship whose name provides an ironic comment on the lack of safety for free blacks in the North and the senator's role in the Jerry and Mary rescues.[61]

The proslavery press registered its strong disapproval of the ultimate failure of the "Mary Rescue." The *Syracuse Weekly Star* condemned this "unholy amalgamation" and insisted that European wage slavery was worse than the American kind: "If the victims of English and Continental tyranny do not turn their backs, disgusted with the foul connection, their degradation must be infinitely greater than we had supposed."[62] The *Utica Gazette* called it no surprise that Allen went through with the marriage: "Allen is said to be unworthy of and ashamed of his color, and has always said that when he married he would have a white girl. . . . His marriage, it seems, is now a fixed fact, *in black and white.*"[63]

Despite the overwhelming antagonism Allen and King faced, they did receive some letters of support, most notably from Harriet Beecher Stowe. The Reverend Timothy Stowe (who, according to Allen, was not related to the famous author) also offered King words of encouragement and placed the controversy in a larger context:

> I am aware, you are aware, that the world will severely condemn you; so it did Luther, when he married a nun; it was then thought to be as great an outrage on decency, for a minister to marry a nun, as it now is for a white young lady to marry a colored gentleman. You have this consolation, that God does not look upon the countenance—the color of men; that in his eye, black and white are the same. . . . It is probably the design of Providence in this case, to call the attention of the public to the fresh consideration of what is implied in the great doctrine of human brotherhood. Is it true or not, that a colored man has all the rights of a white man? Is this a question still mooted among Abolitionists? If so, then we may as well settle it now as at any other time, and though the controversy may be, and must be a very painful one to your feelings, yet, the result will be a better understanding of the great principles of our common nature and brotherhood.[64]

Like Harriet Gold's sister, Stowe suggests that some good was to come from this event.

The coverage of the incident in the abolitionist press shows that perceptions of race were at the very heart of the controversy. One columnist notes that the selective outrage of the "skin-scanning aristocracy" over interracial marriage was highly gendered and linked to the slave power: "Had Mr. Allen been about to marry a woman a few shades darker than himself, or one perfectly black, . . . or, further, had Mr. Allen been a white *slaveholder*, fully exercising the rights which the slave code gives every master over his female slaves, those abominable rowdies would not have been at the expence of getting up a mob to mob him."[65] H. N. Gilbert exposes the illogic of the concern with blood quantum. He notes that Allen is "one-fourth African and three-fourths Anglo-Saxon," and that "if it be a sin for him to marry a white girl, it is, on their own reasoning, a three-fold greater sin to marry a black girl."[66] The people who opposed the marriage, Gilbert charged, were misled by their misunderstanding of the equality of all people: "How few of these believe in the great doctrine of *equal rights* and a *universal brotherhood*. How few practically admit that God is the Common father of us all, and that ALL are his brethren, black or white, bond or free."[67]

Despite this public support from some abolitionists, Allen was rather bitter about the lack of support he received from Central College:

> Though the trustees were willing, at heart, to face the storm of prejudice, worldly wisdom, they considered, dictated that they should not incur the odium which they could not avoid bringing upon the college, if they persisted in retaining me longer as one of their professors. The trustees thought it would be better to be cautious, and save the college for the good it might do in the future. Such a union as ours was, in fact, but one of the logical results of the very principles on which the college was founded. . . . They were now evidently anxious that I should resign, though, of course, they did not express so much to me in words.[68]

Allen considered it only natural that a school dedicated to the equality and brotherhood of the races should accept an interracial marriage. In hoping for Allen's resignation, the college fell short of its radical principles. School official Asa Caldwell reported a slightly different version of events, claiming that Allen left "with the best of feelings on both sides" and "accepted an agency for this College in Europe." The college spokesman expressed regret at losing Allen and asked, "Oh! when will this bitter cup be taken from the hand of our colored people?"[69] Allen's bitterness, however, suggests that the anguish expressed at his departure may have been less than genuine. L. D. Tanner agrees that the school officials could not live up to their principles because they did not yet feel equality in their hearts. He hoped for their conversion: "That, I think, is the error at Central College—the outside is put on, but like Miss Ophelia [the Yankee in *Uncle Tom's Cabin* who at first despises both slavery and Africans], many of the departments, after all, don't feel so in their hearts."[70] In defense of the college, with Allen in hiding, King under virtual house arrest, and a hostile mob keen to harm Allen, it would have been nearly impossible for Allen simply to resume teaching.

One element of the controversy has been overlooked. Apparently Mary King was not Allen's first choice of a wife. Evidence suggests that in the fall of 1852 he wished to marry a Miss Hawes, who was also white, but he met with objections from school officials. One account suggests that Gerrit Smith "was aware he [Allen] meant to have a white wife and he feels he should be sorry to have him marry there that it would injure us so much."[71] This episode verifies Allen's claim that the school was opposed to his marrying any white woman. After his marriage, school officials certainly worried over the influence the scandal would have on the college's future. As one official wrote to Smith: "I am afraid that Prof Allen's marriage will have a tendency to injure the institution and the colored people. Not that as a question of national right I am opposed to it, but as among the things, that, being lawful, is not expedient."[72]

The Allens in England: Realities of the Promised Land

Allen's first impression of his new home was that prejudice against people of color did not exist in England and that whites and people of color married even in the best social circles.[73] Allen kept in touch with abolitionist leaders back in the United States, corresponding with William Lloyd Garrison, Charles Sumner, and Gerrit Smith. He was pleased to report in a letter to Garrison that "here the colored man feels himself among friends, and not among enemies; among a people who, when they treat him well, do it not in the patronizing (and, of course, insulting) spirit, even of hundreds of the American abolitionists, but in a spirit rightly appreciative of the doctrine of human equality." He also notes that he and his wife had not heard the "cry of 'amalgamation,'" and had concluded that prejudice against color was an American problem caused by slavery.[74]

Allen, of course, was not the first black abolitionist to leave the United States for Britain; the years 1848–1854 were a high point for visits from black abolitionists and fugitive slaves, including Frederick Douglass,

Henry Highland Garnet (Allen's former editorial associate), William Wells Brown, William and Ellen Craft, and Henry "Box" Brown. After the passage of the Fugitive Slave Law in 1850, there was a rush of fugitive slaves fleeing the United States. The next year, Brown reported from England that fugitive slaves there were having trouble finding employment and that they had become a "burden to the benevolent."[75] Newly arrived blacks needed to connect with a British patron or abolitionist group to provide introductions and to help arrange lecture tours or other employment.[76]

The Allens arrived in England nearly penniless, but their "romance of real life" had received sympathetic treatment in the British abolitionist press, and Eliza Lee Follen, the New England abolitionist, and Lady Byron offered some assistance.[77] The Allens were presented to Harriet Beecher Stowe, who was making her triumphant British tour, and appeared along with other American abolitionists at public meetings.[78] Black abolitionists in England were not free from the schisms in the movement back home, but "Allen seemed to have moved easily" among the various factions, corresponding with Garrison, Gerrit Smith, and Douglass. Allen did write to Smith about his concerns: "I have been greatly grieved of late by the controversy between Frederick Douglass and the Garrisonians."[79]

Allen was not able to win popular acclaim in England, in part because there were many black speakers on the lecture circuit already and also because of his academic style. Nevertheless, because of the public demand for lectures on abolitionism, Allen wrote a series of lectures that he gave throughout England and Scotland during the 1853–54 season: "American Slavery and the Prejudice Against Color," "The Social and Political Condition of the Free Colored People of the Northern States of America," and "The Probable Destiny of the Colored Race." In his speech on Northern free blacks, Allen attacked state laws that denied civil rights to people of color.[80] He was praised for his intellect but earned barely any money. In mid-1855 he visited Ireland and urged his listeners there to create a climate of public opinion against slavery and prejudice. The warm reception he received encouraged him to move his family to Dublin. He continued to have financial difficulties, however, eking out a living by tutoring and lecturing.[81] His enthusiasm for race relations in Britain waned; the people were not prejudiced, he observed, but they had no experience with educated people of color.[82]

After returning to London in 1860, Allen continued his involvement in the abolitionist movement and developed a new interest in education for juvenile criminals. British abolitionist friends raised money to purchase the Caledonia Training School at Islington and hired Allen as the principal in 1863, "the first instance in this country of an educational establishment being under the direction of a man of colour."[83] The Allens struggled for five years to keep the school open, but it failed after concerted efforts by competing schools put the black man's school out of business. After this experience, writes R.J.M. Blackett, "no longer was Allen exuberant about the lack of racism in England." Mary King Allen later opened a small school for girls, but it also failed. Little is known about the remainder of the Allens' lives, but it is unlikely that they ever returned to America. In 1854 Allen sounded confident of their return to the United States, but by 1858 he wrote that "all expectation of my return to America has passed away."[84]

New York Central College met a similar fate as did the Allens' London school. While the Allen-King marriage had given ammunition to the college's opponents, the more immediate cause of its decline was financial. Lacking an endowment, the college always operated on a shoestring budget. The Panic of 1857 led to drastically reduced student enrollment and donations. Gerrit Smith tried to save the college by buying the building and surrounding land in mid-1858, but it was still forced to close in January 1859. The college reopened for a brief time in 1860–61 but soon closed again. In 1863 Cyrus Grosvenor went to England to raise money to reopen the school after the war for the education of freed slaves; if this plan was ever put into effect, it was short-lived. In 1867 the building was taken over by the McGraw Union School District and served as a public school until it was demolished in 1885.[85]

A Slave Narrative by a Free Man of Color

In my chapter on the Cornwall incident, the extensive series of available letters provided a collective reaction to the Boudinot-Gold and Ridge-Northrup marriages. Noticeably absent, however, were the reactions of Elias Boudinot and John Ridge to the controversy. In this instance, the evidence is quite different. The major sources of information about William Allen's life and marriage to Mary King are two books written by Allen himself. *The American Prejudice Against Color. An Authentic Narrative, Showing How Easily the Nation Got into an Uproar* (1853), published in London the same year as their marriage, focuses on the controversy and their subsequent flight to London. Seven years later Allen published *A Short Personal Narrative*, which again recounts the story of his marriage and adds autobiographical details of his earlier life.[86] With remarkable innovation, Allen writes in the generic conventions of the slave narrative. His adaptation of this genre to tell the story of a "free man" makes a forceful connection between Northern racism and Southern slavery.

Allen's books were part of a larger publishing trend: about twenty African Americans published their "writings on slavery, racial prejudice, and black history and fiction" in Britain in the 1840s and 1850s.[87] Slave narratives were best-sellers, especially after the passage of the Fugitive Slave Law: "They were the precursors of *Uncle Tom's Cabin*, which in eight short months sold over one million copies in England. In turn, Stowe's novel increased interest in the narratives."[88] In a lucky coincidence for the Allens, Stowe also arrived in England in April 1853. The excitement generated by her visit, as well as Allen's use of a popular generic form, certainly must have helped Allen's sales: Benjamin Quarles reports that *American Prejudice* "moved quickly from the stalls."[89]

Like the authors of slave narratives, Allen includes many "authenticating documents" in order to establish his credibility, including letters from white abolitionists and excerpts from newspaper articles that testify to the truth of his story.[90] Allen's *Personal Narrative* adapts the conventions of the slave narrative in a manner that gives his story structure and undercuts his readers' assumptions about the "free" North. In slave narratives, the story generally ends when the slave reaches the North and achieves freedom; but when Allen moves north from Virginia, his trials are just beginning. Allen also dares to challenge white prejudice, an issue dodged by other slave narratives. As Frances Smith Foster observes, many Northern readers shared some of the same racial attitudes as slaveholders. Thus, authors of slave narratives had the tricky rhetorical task of persuading white audiences to work against slavery "without raising suspicions that they were advocating social equality or seriously challenging theories of racial superiority."[91] While most slave narratives avoided questions of racial prejudice and social equality, Allen's escape from the "American despotism" of prejudice tackles these issues directly. As Allen asserts, his story exemplifies "the terrible power with which slavery has spread its influences into the Northern States of the Union—penetrating even the inmost recesses of social life."[92]

Allen's use of the slave narrative genre to expose Northern racism parallels to some degree Harriet E. Adams Wilson's *Our Nig; or Sketches from the Life of a Free Black, in a Two-Story White House, North. Showing That Slavery's Shadows Fall Even There*. Wilson's autobiographical novel is an "allegory of a slave narrative, a 'slave' narrative set in the 'free' North," and, I would argue, so is Allen's *Personal Narrative*.[93] As Eric Gardner remarks, "In all slave narratives . . . , the North is portrayed as a magical land where the protagonist will eventually realize the promise of freedom."[94] Both *Our Nig* and Allen's narrative reveal the hollowness of that promise.

Allen's *Personal Narrative* begins like most slave narratives, with an account of his birth and childhood. William Wells Brown opens his narrative: "I was born at Lexington, Kentucky. My father, as I was informed, was a member of the Wickliffe family; my mother was of mixed blood; her father, it was said, was the noted Daniel Boone, and her mother a negress."[95] Frederick Douglass also notes the same uncertainty about his parentage: "I was born in Tuckahoe, near Hillsborough, and about twelve miles from Easton, in Talbot county, Maryland. . . . The opinion was also whispered that my master was my father; but of the correctness of this opinion, I know nothing."[96] The fact that Allen is adapting and transforming the slave narrative genre is evident in the first sentence: "I was born in Virginia, but not in slavery." Unlike slaves, Allen is knowledgeable about his personal history. He can say definitively who he is and where he came from.

Like many slaves, he struggled to gain literacy. With much less poignancy than Frederick Douglass learning to read from boys on the Baltimore streets, Allen used the "magic charm" of his parents' money to buy himself the instruction he desired.[97]

When Allen is invited to attend the Oneida Institute, this unexpected opportunity establishes the "South-to-North axis" common to slave narratives in which "the North became the location of enlightened Christianity, harmony, and brotherhood."[98] His salvation by Northern patrons lives up to this image of a Northern paradise, but Allen's later experience ironically and bitterly undercuts this convention.

The narrative takes an unexpected twist when the slave system also hampers Allen's departure from Virginia as a free man. In order to leave Norfolk for Baltimore, he needs not only "Free Papers" but also a "Pass" signed by a steamboat agent and a judge. Allen comments dryly: "Really, there is something preposterous about these slaveholders. They make all sorts of attempts to drive the free colored people out of their borders; but when a man of this class wishes to go of his own accord, he must then be *permitted*!"[99] Once in Baltimore, Allen discovers that his pass and free papers are of no use: he must find a white man to testify to his free status or be detained in jail. Like the fugitive slaves so dependent on the kindness of strangers, Allen finally finds a stranger to give the required testimony. Once he is on the train to Philadelphia, he has no further difficulties, and he seems indeed to have reached the promised land.

Most slave narratives usually end with freedom. "To continue the adventures of a black in the so-called free states or countries would be to expose the overwhelming prejudice and discrimination which existed therein . . . it would necessarily indict those from whom their narratives sought sympathy and aid," writes Frances Smith Foster.[100] But it is at this point that Allen's story picks up; his earlier book, *The American Prejudice Against Color*, also takes up the story here, "to illustrate fully the bitterness, malignity, and cruelty, of American prejudice against color, and to show its terrible power in grinding into the dust of social and political bondage, the hundreds of thousands of so-called free men and women of color of the North."[101]

It is this prejudice against color that requires Allen to make a second flight, continuing the South-to-North axis of the slave narrative across the Atlantic. Many fugitive slaves also made this second flight to Canada or Britain after the Fugitive Slave Law of 1850 made life in the "free North" even more perilous.[102] Here Allen's *American Prejudice* also takes on the form of a slave narrative as he recounts his second escape—not from slavery but from prejudice. As John Porter writes to Mary, "Your flight is a flight for freedom, and I can almost call you *Eliza*," referring, of course, to the fugitive slave in *Uncle Tom's Cabin*.[103] At last, their story ends with the freedom the Allens find in England, where they have received "generous and friendly consideration."[104] All is not perfect in England and Ireland, Allen's second promised land, however, as he writes that his narrative is meant to raise money for his family.[105]

Finally, with a rhetorical gesture typical of slave narratives, Allen then tries to make his unique experience representative of the experience of all black people. At the end of the 1860 book, he digresses back to a trip he made home to Virginia while a student at Oneida to illustrate "the direct influences of slavery as they affect the free man of color."[106] His point is that neither the slave nor the free person of color is truly free in the South; his personal story of marriage and mob rule shows that no free man of color is free *anywhere* in the United States: such is the "character of prejudice against color,—bitter, cruel, relentless."[107]

Allen makes sense of his experience by telling his story as a slave's quest for freedom: his choice of genre makes a devastating commentary about the unfree lives of "free" blacks. His narrative insight into the link between the taboo against miscegenation and slavery is repeated by abolitionists in their fiction and in their campaign to repeal miscegenation laws. But despite all the connections between the life of a slave and the life of a free man of color, it is important to note that Allen was *never* a slave. There are moments in the text when he is rather self-conscious about this fact, perhaps as he hesitates to overstate the parallels between his life and the life of a slave. In a famous scene from his own narrative, Douglass recalls looking out at the ships on the Chesapeake, tracing "with saddened heart and tearful eye, the countless number of sails moving off to the mighty ocean." These ships represent the freedom he desires: "You are loosed from your moorings, and are free; I am fast in my chains, and am a slave! You move merrily before the gentle gale, and I sadly before the bloody whip!" This carefully crafted passage shifts into an almost spontaneous expression of his "soul's complaint": "O God, save me! God, deliver me! Let me be free! Is there any God? Why am I a slave?"[108] Allen tries to evoke this scene with his own memories of Chesapeake Bay: "Could I forget that I have again and again stood upon the shores of the Chesapeake, and, while looking out upon that splendid bay, beheld ships and brigs carrying into unutterable misery and woe men, women and children, victims of the most cruel slavery that ever saw the sun."[109] Allen bears witness to the horrors of slavery, but Douglass has experienced them firsthand; Allen simply cannot match Douglass's moral authority and rhetorical power. His adaptation of the slave narrative, while remarkably innovative and insightful, also has its limitations.

The "Jerry Rescue" and the "Mary Rescue" put white abolitionists to the test. Both Daniel Webster and local black abolitionists, though on different sides of the Fugitive Slave Law question, used the arrest of Jerry McHenry to test the commitment of white vigilance committees to their cause. Webster dared abolitionists to commit "treason" by protecting a fugitive slave; black abolitionists like the Reverend J. W. Loguen saw Jerry McHenry's arrest as a test for their white allies: "Now is the time to try the spunk of white men. I want to see whether they have courage only to make speeches and resolutions when there is no danger."[110] The Allen-King marriage similarly tested the white abolitionist commitment to racial equality: sadly, few came to the couple's aid either during or after the "Mary Rescue."

The central question of the scandal at New York Central College is why this radical institution drew the line at interracial marriage. Like the incident at Cornwall, this controversy took place at a reformist educational institution and challenged reformers to live out their ideals of racial equality. Both incidents demonstrate the gendered nature of the intermarriage taboo, as opponents struggled to prevent white women from crossing the color line. Most notably, in both scandals the taboo against interracial marriage had the virtual power of law—even in New York and Connecticut, where there were no laws against miscegenation—and provoked extralegal mob action.

Supporters of New York Central College dedicated themselves to its philosophy of abolitionism, equality of the sexes, and the unity of the human race. Only a few, however, took these ideas to their logical conclusion by supporting intermarriage. Opponents of the college charged that integration and coeducation would lead to amalgamation, and the Allen-King engagement only proved their point.[111] The horror of interracial marriages was generally assumed: there was an implicit assertion of black inferiority. Central to the scandal, and to any debate over slavery, was the link between abolitionism and amalgamation, a diversionary tactic meant to discredit the abolitionists. This strategy was highly successful: at the end of the day, New York Central College was glad to see Allen go, and the narrative of black inferiority triumphed over the disruptive narrative of intermarriage.

These competing narratives of intermarriage were dramatized in fiction and codified in legal statutes. Allen's own rendition of his experience both anticipates and draws on these fictional and legal narratives. His decision to tell his story within the genre of the slave narrative creates a powerful link between the amalgamation taboo and the slave power. The historical evolution of slave law and miscegenation law reveals Allen's keen historical insight and social analysis.

5

"For the Better Government of Servants and Slaves": The Development of the Law of Slavery and Miscegenation

> A perpetual and impassable barrier was intended to be erected between the white race and the one which they had reduced to slavery.
>
> CHIEF JUSTICE ROGER TANEY, *Dred Scott* decision (1857)

In *The American Prejudice Against Color* (1853), William G. Allen explains that he wrote his account to serve "the Anti-slavery Cause," even though he had never been a slave and his experience of prejudice took place in the "free" North. Allen contends that the story of his controversial interracial marriage is an attack on "American Caste and skin-deep Democracy," and he emphasizes the connections between the taboo against intermarriage (even after the slaves were "freed" in the North) and Southern bondage.[1]

In this chapter I explore the historical basis of Allen's claims. Using Virginia and Massachusetts as regional models, I argue that the development of slavery and the development of miscegenation law were concurrent and closely intertwined. Tracing the process of gradual emancipation in the North after the Revolutionary War and emancipation in the South after the Civil War, I posit that the particular historical conditions of slavery and emancipation transformed the concept of "race" and perpetuated the taboo against interracial marriage well past the demise of slavery. My discussion builds on Joanne Pope Melish's analysis of gradual emancipation in New England. As she notes: "By the 1820s the discourse of slavery had been transformed into the discourse of 'race.' The process of gradual emancipation had mapped the old assumptions about slaves onto a new class of person, 'free negro'; the old assumptions about the mutability of servile characteristics had been transformed into a new conviction of their innateness and immutability."[2] These changing ideas about race also kept the taboo against interracial marriage alive and well, even after emancipation. In the face of these transformed discourses, however, black-white marriages formed a potentially powerful narrative of disruption, challenging notions of the inherent servility and inferiority of people of color. As Rachel F. Moran observes: "Black-white marriages threatened the presumption that blacks were subhuman slaves incapable of exercising authority, demonstrating moral responsibility, and capitalizing on economic opportunity. If whites could share their emotional lives and economic fortunes with blacks, how could blacks be anything less than full persons?"[3]

Virginia: From Jamestown to the *Loving* Decision

As A. Leon Higginbotham Jr. and Barbara K. Kopytoff contend, "There is probably no better place than Virginia to examine the origins of the American doctrine of racial purity and the related prohibitions on interracial sex and interracial marriage." Colonial Virginia was "the 'mother' of American slavery" and "one of the first colonies to formulate a legal definition of race and to enact prohibitions against interracial marriage and interracial sex."[4]

By the mid-seventeenth century, a generation after the introduction of Africans to Virginia, legislation on master-servant relationships drew distinctions among servants based on racial and ethnic grounds. For example, in 1643 the colony passed a tax on the labor of African women, defining them as economically productive and white women as dependent. This statute—perhaps the earliest example of the distinctive and unfavorable treatment of African people in Virginia law—also gave free black men an incentive to marry white women, because they would not have to pay taxes on their labor.[5] In 1654 the legislature ruled that Irish servants were to serve longer indentures than English servants. In 1657 a new law freed all Indian servants at the age of twenty-five and prohibited the further purchase of Indian servants. African servants were not so fortunate, however. Laws in 1659 and 1661, which decreased import duties on African slaves and punished white servants who ran away with slaves for the loss incurred by the slave owner, marked the "first official recognition of slavery in Virginia."[6]

It is no coincidence that the first regulation of interracial sex followed shortly after this legal recognition of slavery. It was in 1662, as Kathleen Brown notes, that "the colonial government first treated interracial sexual intimacy, race relations, and regulation of the labor force as related concerns."[7] Virginia's first miscegenation law fined white men and women for fornication with a "negro" at twice the rate of fornication with whites. The law was mostly concerned about where "mulatto" children fit into society: it decreed that "all children borne in this country shalbe held bond or free only according to the condition of the mother." This statute encouraged white men to have illicit sex with slave women, since any resulting children increased their wealth.[8] Meanwhile, the dehumanization of Africans under slavery continued: in 1667 baptism was declared no longer grounds for freedom; in 1669 Africans were reduced to property by an act that protected slave owners from prosecution for the "casuall killings of slaves." The law assumed that a man would not destroy "his owne estate" with "prepensed malice," the criterion for felony murder.[9] The 1670 law legalizing slavery was almost anticlimactic after these measures.[10]

The piecemeal nature of Virginia's laws regulating sex, race, and slavery is clear in the wording of many of the acts, which show the laws evolving in response to troubling social dilemmas. The "condition of the mother" law was passed because "some doubts have arrisen whether children got by any Englishman upon a negro woman should be slave or ffree [*sic*]." The law denying freedom to baptized slaves was passed because "some doubts have risen whether children that are slaves by birth, and by the charity and piety of their owners made pertakers of the blessed sacrament of baptisme, should by vertue of their baptisme be made ffree."[11] The legal code thus developed in response to questions about the status of two sets of anomalous people in the Virginia system: the biracial offspring of interracial relationships, and Christian slaves. Both categories challenged the theoretical opposition of "English, Christian, and free" and "African, heathen, and slave" that underpinned Virginia society. People simply were not supposed to be both English and African or both Christian and enslaved. But since these dual identities did exist, "Virginia's racially based system of slavery was created in the context of continuous racial mixing, legal anomalies, and recurrent attempts to patch holes in the fabric of the system."[12]

In the two decades after Bacon's Rebellion in 1676, prejudice against Africans and Indians increased. Officials effectively prevented class solidarity between white servants and black slaves by drawing legal distinctions between them. The "screen of racial contempt" served "to separate dangerous free whites from dangerous free blacks,"[13] and "the ever present fear of slave insurrection" led to the planter policy of racial separation.[14] As a result, slaves were stripped of the trappings of white masculinity during these years: property, guns, and access to white women.[15] Virginia passed its first major slave code in 1680, which would serve as "the model of repression throughout the South for the next 180 years." Under this code, slaves could not leave the plantation without a certificate, could not carry arms, could be whipped for raising their hand against a Christian, and could be killed for running away.[16] Also after Bacon's Rebellion, "sexual regulations became an increasingly important means of consolidating white patriarchal authority and defining racial difference."[17] The concern over liaisons between white women and nonwhite men is clear in the 1691 statute prohibiting interracial marriages: "And for prevention of that abominable mixture and spurious issue which hereafter may encrease in this dominion, as well by negroes, mulattoes, and Indians intermarrying with English, or other white women, as by their unlawfull accompanying with one another . . . whatsoever English or other white man or woman being free shall intermarry with a negroe, mulatto, or Indian man or woman bond or free shall within three months after such marriage be banished and removed from this dominion forever."[18]

While the law forbade both men and women from marrying outside their race, it is the "spurious issue" that might result from a relationship between a white woman and a black man that gets special mention. The law also punished, with a large fine or indentured servitude, white women who had a child out of wedlock with a "Negro" father; the child would be indentured until age thirty. Note that the statute did not punish white men for having sexual relations with slaves or make it a crime for a black woman to have an illegitimate child by a white man.[19] The miscegenation law was part of a larger statute, "An act for suppressing outlying Slaves," which was concerned with the growing number of free blacks in Virginia and possible alliances between free and enslaved blacks. In addition to regulating interracial sexuality, the law provided for the apprehension of slaves absent from service and required that any slaveholder who wanted to free his slaves would have to pay to transport them from the colony within six months.[20]

The new racial and sexual regulations did raise some dissent. An intriguing entry in the legislative journals of Virginia notes on May 11, 1699 "the Peticon of *George Ivie* & others, for the Repeale of the Act of Assembly, Against *English* people's Marrying with Negroes Indians or Mullattoes, read, & referred to the Consideracon of the House of Burgesses." According to Kathleen Brown, Ivie was the "descendant of a prominent Norfolk family"; she speculates that "for some white people, the law might have represented a loss of social contacts and an inexplicable separation of men and women."[21]

Legislation passed in 1705 demonstrates the connections among sexual regulation, racial definition, and social control as the colony made the transition from a servant to a slave society. The extensive "act concerning Servants and Slaves" codified the legal rights of servants and the non-rights of slaves. The law defined the duties of masters and servants and provided legal recourse for servants in the event of maltreatment. The act makes it clear that racial status was a distinction growing in importance in Virginia. No nonwhite person—"negro, mulatto, or Indian, Jew, Moor, Mahometan, or other infidel"—could own a "christian white servant," and if a white owner should marry a nonwhite person, all of their Christian white servants would be freed. Additional provisions punished free and servant white women for having "a bastard child by a negro, or mulatto." The ban on intermarriage between "English, and other white men and women" and "negros or mulattos" was extended, although this law revised the 1691 version by replacing banishment with six months in prison for whites and fining ministers for performing intermarriages. This legislation went on to protect the economic investment of slave owners and denied the human rights of the slave. If a master killed his slave during "correction," it would not be a felony, whereas any Negro, mulatto, or Indian who struck a white person would get thirty lashes. Slaves could not travel, own cattle, or bear arms. In order to make an example of them, runaways could be dismembered.[22]

The year 1705 marked two other important developments in Virginia's racial codes. Slaves were officially excluded from human legal status and designated "real estate," to be distributed among heirs according to the customs of land inheritance.[23] Also in 1705, Virginia first attempted racial definitions. Its definition of "mulatto" is found in "An act declaring who shall not bear office in this country," a law excluding blacks, mulattoes, and Indians from holding office and giving testimony in General Court. The rather bizarre definition held that "the child of an Indian and the child, grand child, or great grand child, of a negro shall be deemed, accounted, held and taken to be a mulatto." This attempt at clarification was likely to have confused matters. As Thomas D. Morris explains, according to this law, a mulatto was "the offspring of any racially mixed couple," but Higginbotham and Kopytoff note that the descendants of Indians were treated very differently from descendants of Africans. According to the formula, a person with one Indian grandparent and three white grandparents was legally white, while a person with one black great-grandparent was legally mulatto.[24]

In 1723 Virginia again passed stricter laws governing interracial liaisons in the context of toughening its laws regulating free blacks and slaves. In a comprehensive statute "for the better government of Negros, Mulattos, and Indians, bond or free," the lawmakers warned that current laws "are found insufficient to restrain their tumultuous and unlawful meetings, or to punish the secret plots and conspiracies carried on amongst them." Fearing the "dangerous combinations" brewing in Virginia—especially across racial lines—the law made conspiracy for rebellion a felony punishable by death; banned meetings of slaves and between slaves and free people, black or white; punished free people for harboring slaves; and limited manumission to those slaves who had performed "meritorious services" to the colony. The 1705 statute had made all mulatto children servants until age thirty-one; the 1723 revision clarified that children born to female mulatto or Indian servants were also required to serve until they turned thirty-one.[25] This revision virtually ensured the perpetuation of multiple generations of servants along maternal lines. In an additional regulation of interracial relationships, the law specified that the wife of any free black or Indian man would be tithable, regardless of her race. In other words, the financial incentive for free blacks to marry white women was taken away, since white women were now tithable, and women who crossed the color line became black in terms of their legal status. The Assembly also excluded free black, mulatto, and Indian men from voting in elections and from joining the militia, since only householders and frontier dwellers could keep a gun.[26]

This brief survey of seventeenth- and early-eighteenth-century law demonstrates how slavery and miscegenation law developed simultaneously. The fact that so many miscegenation bans are included in acts "for the better government of servants and slaves" shows how lawmakers developed and used the miscegenation taboo to control the labor force of colonial Virginia. Lawmakers were particularly concerned about interracial alliances between white servants and black slaves—and the "in-between" status of the children of interracial liaisons. They regulated interracial sexuality in order to drive a wedge between potential allies. In addition, they attached legal value to white skin, granting even the white servant class the privileges of whiteness.[27]

After the Revolution, the consequences of interracial liaisons varied as racial definitions changed. In 1785 Virginia altered its legal definition of mulatto to one with "one fourth part or more of Negro blood." By this definition a person who was "one-eighth black," that is, having one black great-grandparent, was now legally white. As Higginbotham reports, "This was the only time Virginia law was changed to allow persons with a greater proportion of black ancestry to be deemed white. All subsequent changes were in the opposite direction—making a smaller proportion of black blood bar one from being considered white."[28] The following year, in a bill drafted by Thomas Jefferson, the legislature revised the colonial marriage law, "omitting reference to ecclesiastical authority but reenacting the following: 'A marriage between a person of free condition and a slave, or between a white person and a negro, or between a white person and a mulatto, shall be null.'"[29] This "legislation making marriage between blacks and whites void was the most significant antebellum development in antimiscegenation law," writes Peter Bardaglio. These laws had two important consequences. First, they placed married interracial couples at the risk of prosecution for illicit sexual relations. Second, they meant that outside parties could challenge the marriage in estate proceedings or other legal matters.[30]

In 1792 Virginia passed a new miscegenation law, which banned marriages between "mulattos/negroes" and whites and punished the celebrant of such marriages. At the same time, the law permitted the castration of any slave convicted of trying to rape a white woman.[31] The early national period also marked a landmark decision about the presumptions of slavery, race, and evidence in freedom suits. In the 1806 case of *Hudgins v. Wright*, the Supreme Court of Virginia "declared that racial appearance was to determine who bore the burden of proof in freedom suits." In other words, people who appeared white or Indian were presumed to be free, and people who appeared to be black were presumed to be slaves.[32] As even one of the judges in the *Hudgins* case conceded, however, "When . . . these races become intermingled, it is difficult, if not impossible, to say from inspection only, which race predominates in the offspring."[33] The only remaining substantive change in Virginia's nineteenth-century miscegenation law came in 1849, when the state reaffirmed that marriages between whites and Negroes were absolutely null and void, and in 1866, when the state made a person who was one-fourth Indian a "mulatto," if not otherwise "colored."[34]

In the twentieth century, Virginia intensified its regulation of intermarriage, strictly narrowing its definitions of whiteness and legal marriage. In 1910 the definition of mulatto as a person with one-fourth or more black blood, in effect since 1785, was expanded to include people with one-sixteenth or more black blood (that is, one great-great-grandparent). Under this change many people classified as white became "colored" in the eyes of the law. In the 1924 statute "Preservation of Racial Integrity," legislators defined "white" as someone with no trace of any blood but "Caucasian" or no more than one-sixteenth American Indian blood. This "Pocahontas exception" allowed the descendants of Pocahontas and John Rolfe to be classified as white. A 1930 statute upheld the "one-drop" rule as the standard for whiteness.[35] Interracial marriage was a felony in Virginia until 1967, when the U.S. Supreme Court ruled in *Loving v. Virginia* that the law was unconstitutional. The decision quotes the rationale of the trial judge who banished the Lovings from Virginia for twenty-five years: "Almighty God created the races white, black, yellow, malay and red, and he placed them on separate continents. And but for the interference with his arrangement there would be no cause for such marriages. The fact that he separated the races shows that he did not intend for the races to mix." In its decision the Court offered an alternative historical view, noting that "penalties for miscegenation arose as an incident to slavery" and contending that "the fact that Virginia prohibits only interracial marriages involving white persons demonstrates that the racial classifications must stand on their own justification, as measures designed to maintain White Supremacy."[36]

"To the Disgrace of Our Nation": Other Southern Legislative Trends

In many ways, the Virginia example of miscegenation law embedded in slave codes served as a model for the region. Even though Maryland never had as large a slave population as Virginia, the colony also tried to regulate interracial sexuality by the middle of the seventeenth century through a confusing and constantly changing legislative process. In 1664, just two years after the first Virginia statute, the colonial assembly passed an act denying freedom to slaves who were christened. As a part of this act, the legislators took up the problem of the status of free white women married to slaves ("to the disgrace of our Nation") and the offspring of these marriages. In order to discourage such unions, the act asserted that white women married to slaves would serve their husband's master during the husband's lifetime and that their children "shall be Slaves as their fathers were." Maryland traced status through the paternal line, in contrast with Virginia's "condition of the mother." The law did not have the intended effect, however, as lawmakers were soon horrified to find that slave owners were encouraging marriages between slaves and white women because of the economic benefit of gaining additional servants. In 1681 "An Act concerning Negroes & Slaves" tried to discourage this practice by punishing the celebrant of the marriage and setting the woman and her children free if the marriage took place with the encouragement or permission of the master. The act of 1664 also created a legally separate class of people, "mulattoes born of white women." According to the "condition of the father" rule in effect, the child of a slave father and a white mother would be a slave, but the legislature hesitated to enslave the child of a white mother. Instead, mulatto children of white mothers were indentured until age thirty-one. Finally, in 1692 Maryland added a ban on marriages between white men and black women to its previous ban on marriages between white women and black men and also legislated against interracial bastardy. The confusion caused by the "condition of the father" practice was eliminated by enslaving the children of all slave parents. After several changes in the law, by 1728 the status of the "mulattoes born of white women" was resolved, and they were grouped with Negroes in the eyes of the law. The Maryland law would not be revised again until 1859.[37]

Colonial North Carolina was mostly settled by former indentured servants and otherwise poor white men. In 1715 (the year all laws were published, although the date of passage is not certain), the laws included an act governing servants and slaves, likely adopted from the laws of Virginia and Maryland. According to this statute, whites were fined fifty pounds for marrying a negro, mulatto, or Indian, and white women found guilty of interracial bastardy were to serve an extra four years or pay an extra six pounds' fine. Interracial children were indentured until age thirty-one. North Carolina made continuous changes to the laws into the nineteenth century, but the general principle of preventing intermarriage remained the same. One notable innovation was the racial definitions in the laws of 1723 and 1741 that banned marriage between "whites" and "Indians, Negroes, mustees, mulattoes, or any person of mixed blood to the third generation, bond or free." In other words, a white person could marry someone with one-sixteenth Indian or black ancestry (one great-great grandparent), but not someone with one-eighth Indian or black ancestry (one great-grandparent). The influence of Virginia on the 1741 law was also evident in the description of biracial children as an "abominable Mixture and spurious issue."[38]

By the early eighteenth century, slaves were the majority in South Carolina, the only colony where blacks dominated the population. As in Virginia, one of the most troubling crimes to the white ruling class was any alliance between black slaves and white servants. The 1717 "Act for the Better Governing and Regulating [of] White Servants" punished illicit sex, with the strongest penalties for interracial bastardy. According to the law, white men and women and free black men guilty of interracial bastardy were bound as indentured servants for seven years, and the child, even when the mother was free, was to serve until adulthood. As in the early Maryland laws, this statute did not follow the doctrine of "the condition of the mother," although South Carolina would adopt such a provision in the code of 1740. The state would not take legal action against interracial sexuality again until after the Civil War.[39]

Antebellum Northern writers were most interested in the unique situations in Georgia and Louisiana. Georgia was originally envisioned as a free labor haven for the English poor, but the ban on slavery lasted only fifteen years. In 1750 a new law permitted slavery and defined the rights of the master over the slave.[40] This statute establishing slavery in Georgia included a ban on marriage and sexual relations between "whites" and "Negroes or blacks," and made such marriages "unlawful and absolutely null and void." This was the first colonial law to declare interracial marriages null and void. After this definitive statement, Georgia did not need to address the matter again for one hundred years: an act of 1852 renewed the ban on interracial adultery and fornication, while an act of 1861 renewed the ban on interracial marriage.[41] Fiction by Lydia Maria Child ("The Quadroons") and Frank Webb (*The Garies and Their Friends*) illustrates the tragic consequences of the Georgia law that withheld recognition from interracial families. In Child's story, the octoroon daughter of a white man is sold after her father's death; in Webb's novel, the mulatto children of a white man are disinherited since they are illegitimate according to the laws of Georgia.

The greater acceptance of interracial liaisons in Louisiana, owing to Spanish and French influences, also fascinated Northern novelists. Despite the fact that the 1724 Code Noir banned intermarriage between whites and blacks and concubinage between whites and slaves, interracial liaisons were common and more socially acceptable than in English colonies.[42] By the mid-eighteenth century, New Orleans had a reputation as a sexually open city, as Ira Berlin describes, "where relationships between white men and black women were not only tolerated but also accepted and occasionally celebrated." These alliances were not recognized by the law, but they were institutionalized under the system of *plaçage*. As Berlin observes, "The white suitor and the *placee's* mother . . . carefully negotiated the arrangement that assured free colored women a lifetime commitment, legitimate before all but church and state."[43] It was the fate of these beautiful, almost-white "quadroons" and "octoroons," and their vulnerability to exploitation and abandonment, that captured the imagination of Northern abolitionist writers. Child traces the story of two octoroon sisters in her novel *A Romance of the Republic*. Despite the imposition of Anglo-American law, which in 1808 banned and nullified marriages between "free persons" and "slaves" and "free whites" and "free persons of color," the tradition of *plaçage* continued.[44] The tradition was complicated by new laws limiting the ability of fathers to emancipate their biracial children and leave property to them, and there was much conflict between Anglo-American law and the traditions of French and Spanish Louisiana as fathers sought to evade the restrictions.[45] In Frances E. W. Harper's novel *Minnie's Sacrifice*, two Louisiana planters try to ease the lives of their biracial children (and their own consciences) by "passing" them off as white. It was the reality of interracial family connections, so threatening to the system of racial slavery, that miscegenation law attempted to control.

Massachusetts and the North:
The Clash of Slavery and Abolitionism

As in Virginia, in Massachusetts the development of miscegenation law was directly related to the growth of slavery. Unlike in Virginia, however, the law in Massachusetts was designed to manage a small African population with a significant proportion of free people. In Massachusetts the law of miscegenation and slavery was more about codifying racial bias than ensuring ownership and inheritance. Why slavery developed in New England at all is a question that has puzzled historians: without a staple crop, the region had no need for a large agricultural labor force, and the black population was never more than 3 percent of the total. At first slavery was a punishment for criminal behavior and not a permanent condition, but by 1700 "slavery had evolved into a racially identifiable institution" and Africans were brought to the colony "as perpetual chattel slaves."[46]

The first recorded slaves in Massachusetts arrived in 1638 as part of the plunder from the Pequot War. In 1637 several hundred captured Pequot men had been shipped to the West Indies and traded for African slaves, while the captured Pequot women and children were kept as servants.[47] Massachusetts was also the first colony explicitly to authorize slavery by law. As Higginbotham observes, "unlike Virginia, for example, which developed a legal framework for slavery in response to societal custom, the Massachusetts Bay and Plymouth colonies statutorily sanctioned slavery as part of the 1641 Body of Liberties a mere three years after the first blacks arrived." The Body of Liberties set parameters for slavery in Massachusetts: "There shall never be any bond slaverie, villinage or Captivitie amongst us unles it be lawfull Captives taken in just warres, and such strangers as willingly selle themselves or are sold to us." Although this provision began by prohibiting slavery, it left ambiguous loopholes that would be used by colonists. For example, "When did a war become just? And which people were strangers?"[48] While Massachusetts never developed the comprehensive slave codes that Virginia did, in the seventeenth century it did follow Virginia's lead in two matters. In 1670 it was decided that biracial children would follow "the condition of the mother." And in 1694 the legislature decided that baptism did not release slaves from their servitude. This last statute was part of a "shift in the justification offered for black slavery from the grounds of religion to those of race."[49]

At the beginning of the eighteenth century, Massachusetts began strict regulation of the nonwhite population. Higginbotham questions whether this was to protect slavery as an economic institution—"by the 1700s New England was the most active slave-trading area in America"—or whether it was a reaction to the growing black population in Massachusetts, which doubled in the first half of the eighteenth century, making up 2 percent of the colony's population but 8 percent of Boston's.[50] In this context, Massachusetts passed the first miscegenation law in New England in 1705. David Fowler suggests that this ban may have been a response to the antislavery agitation in the colony at around this time, since abolitionist activity commonly brought out fears about the control of freed slaves.[51] In "An Act for the Better Preventing of A Spurious and Mixt Issue, Etc." (echoing the language of the Virginia law of 1691), legislators banned fornication and marriage between "negroes or molattos" and "English" or people "of any other Christian nation." Perhaps in an attempt to encourage black slaves and servants to take black spouses, the law also held that "no master shall unreasonably deny marriage to his negro with one of the same nation, any law, usage or custom notwithstanding." Other provisions imposed a tax on imported blacks, defining nonwhites as chattel in the eyes of the law, and ordered the severe whipping of any Negro or mulatto who struck "any person of the English or other Christian nation."[52]

Other laws reflected a fear of collusion among servants, slaves, and free blacks. In 1703 some limits were placed on manumission, requiring owners to post bonds for the support of freed slaves. In addition, Indian, black, and mulatto servants and slaves were given a 9 P.M. curfew.[53] A 1707 law forbade free blacks from harboring slaves without their master's consent.[54] Despite these attempts to regulate the nonwhite population, scholars generally concur that slavery in Massachusetts did not involve the loss of all legal rights. Black servants and slaves could petition the court with grievances against their master, while bizarre property protections accorded to slaves in Massachusetts protected the right of "human property" to hold property themselves. In addition, slaves could testify in court, and the murder of a slave was a capital crime. More frankly than Southern law, New England slave law tended to recognize the contradiction of "human agency in chattel."[55]

As in many Northern states, the post-Revolutionary fervor for liberty led to the abolition of slavery in Massachusetts. Exactly how emancipation was effected is a matter of some controversy, but a common argument holds that the Massachusetts Declaration of Rights of 1780 (which many read as abolishing slavery)—as interpreted in the *Quock Walker* cases ending in 1783—undermined the legal basis for slavery.[56] In what cannot be mere coincidence, just after the popular and judicial support for slavery had been undermined, in 1786 the new state of Massachusetts passed an "Act for the orderly Solemnization of Marriages" providing that "no person . . . authorized to marry shall join in marriage any white person with any Negro, Indian, or Mulatto, under penalty of fifty pounds, . . . and all such marriages shall be absolutely null and void."[57] It is not clear why Indians were added to the ban on intermarriages at this point, but it may have been because of the extensive intermixture between the black and Indian population. The rarity of the "full-blood" Indian meant that Indians were now lumped into an underclass of people of color who were kept separate from whites.[58] This reinforced ban on racial intermarriage likely reflected white fears about the recently freed black population and its uncertain place in the new republic. The radical abolitionists who emerged on the scene in the 1830s, including William Lloyd Garrison and Lydia Maria Child, recognized the connections among slavery, miscegenation laws, and racial prejudice and agitated for the repeal of the intermarriage ban. Their campaign achieved success in 1843.[59]

Other Northern states followed the Massachusetts lead and passed their own miscegenation laws, which were closely connected to slavery and the process of gradual emancipation following the Revolution.

In 1798 Rhode Island added the 1786 Massachusetts law almost verbatim to its existing law, "An Act to prevent clandestine Marriages." This law held that "no person . . . shall join in marriage any white person with any Negro, Indian, or mulatto, . . . and all such marriages shall be absolutely null and void."[60] Previously, in 1784, Rhode Island had adopted a gradual emancipation act freeing children born after that date at age twenty-one for males and eighteen for females. It can be argued that the miscegenation law reflected white fears of a growing black population and attempted to maintain racial castes even after slavery ended.

The only other New England state to pass a miscegenation law was Maine. As discussed earlier in chapter 2, when Maine, previously a part of Massachusetts, became a separate state in 1820 as a provision of the Missouri Compromise, it kept all Massachusetts law that did not conflict with its own state constitution. The following year Maine revised the 1786 Massachusetts law with "An Act for regulating Marriage, and for the orderly solemnization thereof." This new law simply said that "all marriages between any white person and any Negro, Indian or Mulatto . . . shall be absolutely void." Maine had few free blacks at the time but had numerous Indians, especially on the frontiers, so this law was probably aimed at them.[61]

Among the mid-Atlantic states, Pennsylvania has a progressive reputation, owing to antislavery agitation by the Quakers and German liberals, but Higginbotham cautions that "the legal treatment of free blacks in colonial Pennsylvania appears to have been as restrictive and discriminatory as in any other colony."[62] Despite the opposition of the Quakers, slavery had been firmly established in the colony by 1700.[63] Because of the large number of white servants, interracial liaisons between servants and slaves were common enough to prompt a legal response. As in colonial Virginia and Massachusetts, these laws reflect a concern about interracial alliances and especially the behavior of free blacks. In 1725 "An act for the better regulating of negroes in this province" restricted manumissions, bound out all children of free Negroes or mulattoes, and severely punished interracial marriage, cohabitation, adultery, and fornication. The Assembly ordered that no minister or judge should "upon any pretense whatsoever join in marriage any negro with any white person." The law also severely punished interracial cohabitation "under pretense of being married": the white partner could be sold as a servant and the black partner sold as a slave for life.[64] Pennsylvania, however, would lead the way in Northern emancipation, approving a gradual emancipation plan in 1780. Anticipating the language of Garrison fifty years later, the preamble to the law affirmed that people of all complexions "are the work of an Almighty hand" and that God "hath extended equally his care and protection to all."[65] While in some other Northern states, such as Massachusetts, Maine, and Rhode Island, emancipation laws were followed by miscegenation laws, in Pennsylvania, the emancipation law included a clause for the repeal of the old slave code, including the miscegenation law of 1725.[66] This is one of the reasons why the interracial Garie family in Frank Webb's novel *The Garies and Their Friends* moves to Philadelphia. But as the fictional Garies would find, even the Quaker state was determined to keep free blacks in an inferior position.

Before the English took over and renamed it New York, the Dutch government of New Netherlands had established a system that allowed black slaves rights usually restricted to white indentured servants; some slaves even achieved the unique status of "half-freedom."[67] The Dutch position on interracial sex and marriage is not clear. In 1638 the Dutch government prohibited adulterous intercourse between whites and "Heathens, Blacks, or other persons." Fowler reads this as a special punishment for interracial adultery, while Higginbotham interprets the inclusion of "other persons" to mean that interracial adultery was no worse than any other kind. Higginbotham also reports that interracial marriages were recognized under Dutch rule, which makes his reading more persuasive. After the English takeover in 1664, the Duke of York Laws made slavery a de jure institution.[68]

New York, the largest Northern slave state, passed a gradual emancipation bill in 1799. During a debate over an earlier (failed) emancipation bill in 1784, the Assembly at one point insisted on banning black suffrage and interracial marriages as a condition of emancipation. Fowler reports that it was the matter of black suffrage that prevented an emancipation bill from passing for fourteen years. In addition, it is clear that emancipation had strong opposition in New York: in the midst of the debate, the legislature passed a strengthened slave code in 1788. New York's last slaves were not freed until 1827.[69] Although upstate New York was a hotbed of abolitionist activity, especially in later decades, the slow demise of slavery in the state reveals the level of hostility toward abolitionism and free blacks.

Civil War and Reconstruction:
The Transformation of Miscegenation Law

The Civil War marked a turning point for miscegenation law. In fact, the word "miscegenation" itself was coined during the election of 1864 in order to discredit the Republican Party. Democratic journalists posing as

Republicans wrote a satirical pamphlet claiming that interracial sex and marriage were part of the Republican platform and predicting that the war would bring about widespread racial mixing: "It is a war . . . of amalgamation, so called—a war looking, as its final fruit, to the blending of the white and black."[70] The hoax was a spectacular success, embarrassing abolitionists fooled into endorsing the pamphlet and making miscegenation a major campaign issue.

In the two decades following the war, the North would virtually eliminate miscegenation laws. By 1887 Illinois, Rhode Island, Maine, Michigan, and Ohio had repealed their bans, and Indiana was the only Northern state east of the Mississippi to keep its statute.[71] Radical Republicans like Charles Sumner argued in 1872 that these laws originated in "the prejudice of color which was the very basis of slavery." For emancipation to be complete, Sumner contended that they must be repealed: "Therefore in abolishing slavery Congress must, would it complete its work, abolish all the off-shoots of slavery, all that grows out of slavery."[72] Although miscegenation law was repealed in the North, the social taboo has lingered into the present day.

The trend in the South was quite the opposite: after the failure of radical Reconstruction and the return to "home rule," legislatures passed new and stricter miscegenation laws, rejecting claims of political equality and, most emphatically, social equality. Mississippi, Alabama, South Carolina, and West Virginia passed their first intermarriage laws, while Georgia, Missouri, Kentucky, Florida, Arkansas, Tennessee, North Carolina, Delaware, Texas, and Maryland amended their existing laws, several states even adding miscegenation bans to their constitutions.[73] These laws were a sign of the white fear of black freedom and citizenship; whites felt a need for the law to define relationships no longer trusted to custom. As Martha Hodes puts it: "With the demise of slavery, the maintenance of . . . [the racial] hierarchy through other means became essential to white Southerners. Thus did the 'mixture' of European and African ancestry come to be a much more serious taboo than ever before." Most telling was the link between political rights and fears of black sexuality: "White Southerners explicitly conflated black men's alleged sexual misconduct toward white women with the exercise of their newly won political rights."[74]

"Race" and the Taboo against Interracial Marriage

A century after emancipation and the end of the Civil War, the trial judge in the *Loving v. Virginia* case declared that the Lovings' marriage was against the will of God: "The fact that he separated the races shows that he did not intend for the races to mix."[75] If the taboo against interracial marriage originated in slavery, how was it possible for this statement to be a matter of debate one hundred years after emancipation? Building on Joanne Melish's historical analysis, I would argue that the particular historical conditions of slavery and emancipation transformed the concept of "race" and perpetuated the taboo against interracial marriage into the present day. As Ira Berlin reminds us, race is more than just a social construction; it is a historical construction as well, and one that is "continually redefined."[76]

One common European justification for African slavery was that the heathen could be civilized and converted; according to custom, the slave would then be set free. Freeing slaves upon their conversion, however, was a threat to the system. This situation led to a change in the ideology of slavery: "Once the Africans began to accept the Christian God, it became impossible to insist on their inferiority based on the idea that they did not know God. Instead it became necessary to reinvent their inferiority based on the idea that God did not know *them*."[77] As described earlier, many colonies passed laws clarifying that baptism did not mean freedom for enslaved Africans.

Because religion was no longer a sign of privilege, by the early eighteenth century there was a shift toward "race" or "blood" as the category determining eligibility for freedom, citizenship, property ownership, and marriage. The development of an ideology of black inferiority centered on sex and religion. At first, black inferiority was marked by appearance and culture, but soon the children of black-white parentage started to "look less black" and thus "less inferior." Many blacks also converted to Christianity and were therefore "less savage." This problem was solved by attaching "negative connotations to certain aspects of interracial sex" and by "eliminating any beneficial consequences flowing from Christian conversion."[78]

But despite this early emphasis on race in the eighteenth century, it is important to realize that it was not "race" in the fixed, biological sense, as it would be understood in the antebellum period. Many people believed in the Enlightenment view of race: that racial differences resulted from the effects of physical and social environment. In other words, the physical difference of Africans was caused by climate, and their degraded social status was the result of the deplorable conditions of slavery.

The nineteenth century marked a radical departure from these environmental beliefs about racial differences. Scholars of racial thought agree that the American Revolution was a catalyst for these changes. Historians have often noted that the revolutionary rhetoric of freedom and equality exposed the hypocrisy of a slave society and that, consequently, the Northern states ended slavery during the early national period. While revolutionary ideas led to freedom for some slaves, it also put Southern slaveholders on the defensive. Unable to defend their practices in the language of human equality, they needed a new justification for enslaving Africans. The answer was racial inferiority, explained with a mixture of science and religion: enslaved Africans were a separate and inferior race, making slavery their natural and rightful place.[79]

In a mid-nineteenth-century debate that divided the scientific community, scientists such as Samuel G. Morton, Josiah Nott, and Louis Agassiz advocated the theory of polygenesis. According to this belief in multiple creations, racial differences existed because the races were actually separate species of humans, created at different times. Polygenesis conveniently meant that there was a hierarchy of races, in which the "caucasoid" was superior and the "Negro" was ranked last. Other scientists, such as Samuel Stanhope Smith, the Reverend John Bachman, and the British scholars James Cowles Prichard and Sir William Lawrence, maintained the traditional belief in monogenesis, or a single creation of the human species. The support of polygenesis versus monogenesis was not merely a scientific question but one fraught with political implications about the place of people of color in American society.[80] Detractors of polygenesis pointed to the Genesis account of creation, and abolitionists embraced the New Testament reminder that God "hath made of one blood, all nations of men for to dwell on all the face of the earth." But despite the controversy over theories of creation, Americans could generally agree about the inferiority of the African race.

The reactions of white Americans to Northern emancipation and the growing number of free blacks also tended to push blacks into an inferior racial category. As Melish observes, in New England there was never agreement that the negative traits attributed to enslaved Africans would still exist after slavery. Gradual emancipation, however, led to a "new conception of 'racial' difference on the part of whites in which the characteristics . . . associated with slave status were redefined as uniquely innate and permanent biological traits in persons of color, irrespective of their status." In other words, if in the eighteenth century whites attributed the servility of slaves to their condition of servitude, by the nineteenth century they believed "that all people of color were inherently servile."[81] The exclusion of free blacks from all but unskilled and domestic labor upheld this view of blacks as servile. As Ira Berlin notes, in freedom most blacks remained in the same service and unskilled work they performed as slaves, "maintaining racial perceptions of servitude that had been formed in slavery."[82]

While most free blacks were kept in a state of second-class citizenship in the North following gradual emancipation, the complete denial of citizenship to blacks on the basis of their separate and inferior racial identity was made federal policy by the infamous *Dred Scott* decision of 1857. The exclusion of black people "from the ranks of humanity and the rights of citizenship, . . . merely implied in the law at the outset of the national period," would become formalized by the decision.[83] Dred Scott was a Missouri slave who sued for his freedom on the basis of residence in free territory in the 1830s. When *Dred Scott v. Sanford* reached the Supreme Court in 1856, the Court had to consider whether residing in free territory did indeed make Scott free and whether a slave had the right to sue in a federal court. In the course of his decision, Chief Justice Roger Taney ruled that no black person could ever become a citizen of the United States. As part of his argument, he incorporated a review of the miscegenation laws of Maryland, Massachusetts, and Rhode Island, which, according to Taney,

> show that a perpetual and impassable barrier was intended to be erected between the white race and the one which they had reduced to slavery, and governed as subjects with absolute and despotic power, and which they then looked upon as so far below them in the scale of created beings, that intermarriages between white persons and negroes or mulattoes were regarded as unnatural and immoral, and punished as crimes, not only in the parties, but in the person who joined them in marriage. And no distinction in this respect was made between the free negro or mulatto and the slave, but this stigma, of the deepest degradation, was fixed upon the whole race.[84]

These laws, according to Taney, demonstrated that the original intent of the Founding Fathers was not to include black people as citizens. He also notes that states that had emancipated their slaves, such as Massachusetts in the 1780s, still had miscegenation bans or other anti-black laws.[85]

Radical abolitionists angrily denounced the *Dred Scott* decision, and black abolitionists in Boston organized an annual "Crispus Attucks Day" in protest of the Court's ruling. While many white abolitionists also criticized the ruling's effect on free blacks, their complaints exposed them to counterattack on one of their "most vulnerable points—namely, the degree to which an enemy of slavery was a friend of the Negro."[86]

The *Dred Scott* decision "codified into law, at the highest level of the American legal process, the precept of black inferiority."[87] It took a civil war and several constitutional amendments to overturn the decision, and it was not until the 1967 *Loving* case that the Fourteenth Amendment's due process and equal protection clauses were determined to apply to miscegenation laws. The issue of the legal status of blacks had outlasted the slavery system that had constructed that status from the early days of Virginia and Massachusetts. The persistence of miscegenation laws in the South and the de facto prohibition of interracial marriage in the North indicated the intractability of the problem. It is this intractable problem, the disruptive narrative of interracial marriage, that the novelists Lydia Maria Child, Frank Webb, and Frances E. W. Harper address in their fiction.

6

Abolitionists and Intermarriage:
The Interracial Marriage Question in Child,
Webb, and Harper

> I wanted to do something to undermine *prejudice*; and
> there is such a universal passion for novels, that more can
> be done in that way, than by the ablest arguments, and
> the most serious exhortations.
>
> LYDIA MARIA CHILD (1867)

The scandal over the Allen-King marriage and the development of miscegenation bans within an evolving slave code highlight the connections
among Northern prejudice, Southern slavery, and the taboo against interracial marriage. These factors meant that no person of color was truly free
in the United States. The scandals and statutes featuring interracial marriage told a similar tale: narratives of control—stories of difference, inferiority, and danger—competed with narratives of disruption—stories of
equality, democracy, and romantic love. Both factions claimed to have God
and science on their side; both claimed to protect women; both claimed
to have the best interests of the national family at heart. Whether the taboo
against intermarriage was enforced by statute or by social custom, the
stakes were equally high: control over African labor and the preservation
of white supremacy.

In the genre of fiction, narratives of interracial marriage could be a
vehicle for astute social analysis and for presenting imagined alternatives
to a racist society. As audiences would know from their prior reading
experience, stories of marriage are never just about a couple in love: they
are about social standing and inheritance as well. Jane Austen got it right:
on some level marriage is always about property, even in the Americanized
novel of manners. Our most courageous novelists explore how interracial
connections complicate the traditional marriage plot and how systems of
descent, slavery, and inheritance all combine to ban black-white marriages

in the United States. These authors—black and white, male and female—
saw fiction as a way to shape legal and social change.

In their fiction, Lydia Maria Child, Frank J. Webb, and Frances E. W.
Harper uncover existing interracial family ties, dramatize the consequences
of miscegenation laws, and explore the likely outcome of their repeal.
These writers agreed that the repeal of such laws would be a step toward
racial justice and that they must be revoked as a matter of principle. In the
1830s and 1840s, Child analyzed miscegenation law as part of a system of
prejudice that upheld the "slave power." By the time she published her
1867 novel *A Romance of the Republic*, she advocated intermarriage as the
solution to prejudice. Webb, in *The Garies and Their Friends* (1857), and
Harper, in *Minnie's Sacrifice* (1869), believed that intermarriage should be
a matter of personal choice, concurring with Child that miscegenation
laws insult the human dignity of people of color. These African American
novelists, however, did not embrace intermarriage with Child's enthusiasm. In Webb's novel—set in a Northern state that had repealed its miscegenation laws and passed a gradual emancipation law back in 1780—
interracial marriages are met with violence and social rejection. Harper
exposes the sexual exploitation of women in slavery, but then insists that,
in the face of the dangers confronted by people of color after the Civil
War, intermarriage is but a minor issue.[1] Despite their differing views
about the role of intermarriage as a healing force in American culture, all
three writers include an explicit analysis of the law and how it affects the
lives of their characters—and, by extension, the lives of the real people
these characters represent.

"This Legalized Contempt of Color": Child and the Massachusetts Intermarriage Ban

Continuing the theme of intermarriage she began in *Hobomok*, Lydia Maria Child integrated her activism, political writing, and fiction throughout
her long career. She believed that intermarriage would eliminate prejudice
and bridge the differences between the various American peoples. Hers
was a particularly daring stance, not only because of the social taboo
against intermarriage, but also because such marriages were against the law
not just in the South but in many Northern states as well. In the 1830s and
1840s, Child challenged these laws through political writing; she also used
her fiction to interrogate and reject the race-based definitions of family
and marriage imposed by the law and to demonstrate the high costs of
these laws for women of color.

When Massachusetts passed New England's first miscegenation law in 1705, it banned fornication and marriage between "negroes or molattos" and "English" or people "of any other Christian nation."[2] When the state revised the law in 1786, it added Indians to the group forbidden to marry whites.[3] The intermarriage law was mostly a symbolic defense of white privilege. Although there were a few cases in which the intermarriage ban was a factor, the law was generally not enforced.[4]

In 1831 William Lloyd Garrison launched his campaign to repeal this law; the struggle against prejudice was part of his program to eliminate slavery.[5] His call for repeal appeared in one of the first issues of the *Liberator*: "If there be a pious, just or republican member in our Legislature—one who values his own liberty of choice, or privilege of action—we call upon him to move for the obliteration of the act of June 22, 1786."[6] Garrison took this step largely in response to the influence of David Walker, the North Carolina–born African American abolitionist who had died the previous year under suspicious circumstances. Although Garrison and Walker had disagreed over using violence to end slavery, after Walker's death, Garrison, conscious of the importance of Boston's black abolitionist community, appropriated many of Walker's positions, including his "strong anticolonization stand" and "his demand that the Massachusetts racial intermarriage law be repealed" in order to "win black support for his cause."[7] In his famous *Appeal*, Walker had cited the intermarriage law as an example of how Africans were treated as brutes in America, noting that the Old Testament Jews had been allowed to intermarry while in Egypt, then added: "I would not give a *pinch of snuff* to be married to any white person I ever saw in all the days of my life. . . . I only made this extract to show how much lower we are held, and how much more cruel we are treated by the Americans, than were the children of Jacob, by the Egyptians."[8] Taking a more favorable view of intermarriage than Walker, Garrison used the earliest issues of the *Liberator* to thunder against "the marriage law" in Massachusetts and promote the potential benefits of intermarriage: "If He has 'made of one blood all nations of men for to dwell on all the face of the earth,' then they are one species, and stand on a perfect equality; their intermarriage is neither unnatural nor repugnant to nature, but obviously proper and salutary; it being designed to unite people of different tribes and nations."[9] Garrison also illustrates the absurdity of defining racial identity as required by the law: "Come, thou sagacious discriminator of skins, define thy boundary line! Let us know the exact shade and the particular curl of the hair which justly deprive a man of his right of choice! We have all shades in the nation—match them, and dispel our doubts! If marriage, as thou sayest, is the creature of color and not of affection, ought we not also to consult the bulk and height of the body? Shall fat and lean persons be kept apart by penalties? or shall we graduate love by feet and inches? And why not? Do not people differ as much in size as in color?"[10]

Garrison's arguments for repeal were primarily religious and political. Again and again he contended that the marriage law conflicted with Christianity and democracy. He condemned the law for assaulting the marriage covenant, for making children illegitimate, and for insulting God, who, after all, had created people of all complexions. In fact, he called prejudice against color the ultimate sin, for through it people dared to criticize God's handiwork: "I would as soon deny the existence of my Creator, as quarrel with the workmanship of his hands," he writes. "He has made the whole family of man to differ in personal appearance, habits and pursuits."[11] If the ban against intermarriage challenged the will of God, Garrison also contended that the law itself violated the Declaration of Rights of Massachusetts and the provisions of the Declaration of Independence, which do not give legislatures the right to regulate the race of marriage partners.[12] Wielding these political and religious arguments, Garrison and other abolitionists struggled to repeal the ban on intermarriage.

In the legislative session for 1831–32, state representative John P. Bigelow proposed an amendment to repeal the intermarriage ban, but without success. The press ridiculed the amendment and suggested that Bigelow had personal motivations for introducing it. As the Pennsylvania *Inquirer* insinuated, "We should not be surprised if Mr. Bigelow has been paying his devotions to some 'elegant creole,' and has adopted this method of exonerating himself from a portion of the obloquy in consequence."[13] Having failed in 1831–32, the movement for repeal would not be revived until 1838. Nevertheless, as Donald Jacobs notes, the campaign got the attention of the black abolitionist community: "Boston's blacks had heard Garrison, and . . . his ideas began to strike a more responsive chord among Boston's black leadership." Black support was essential to the *Liberator*'s survival: in 1834, three-quarters of the subscribers were black.[14] In the meantime, abolitionist societies were springing up all over Massachusetts, organizing around the issues of slavery and educating members about the evils of racial prejudice. In 1836 abolitionist societies throughout the North began a petition campaign for a variety of causes, most notably to protest slavery in Washington, D.C. The campaign against the Massachusetts intermarriage ban during the 1830s took place in this context of abolitionist activism at the local and national level.[15]

In 1839, antislavery women from Lynn, Brookfield, Dorchester, and Plymouth presented the Massachusetts state legislature with a petition signed by more than 1,300 women urging repeal of all laws drawing distinctions between people on the basis of color. The target of the petition drive was the intermarriage ban.[16] For example, the Lynn Female Anti-Slavery Society adopted the following resolution: "That all laws making a distinction on account of color, are unnecessary and unchristian, having a tendency to degrade a class of people entitled to the common and equal rights of citizens, who have been long and cruelly oppressed."[17] The female antislavery societies used the same dual religious and political argument initiated by Garrison at the beginning of the decade. In addition, they insisted that "it was as outraged wives and mothers that they fought slavery, an institution that openly disregarded and often defiled domestic arrangements."[18] Despite these arguments that the defense of slave women was their duty, the protesters received a storm of negative publicity; their adversaries suggested that the repeal drive masked a desire for interracial sexual experiences. As the *Boston Morning Post* sneered, the petition from Lynn "is rather a cut at the white Lynn beaux—or, perhaps some of these ladies despair of having a *white* offer, and so are willing to try *de colored race*."[19] The House of Representatives issued a report on the matter, declaring that "it is inconsistent with the modesty of a virtuous woman to solicit the repeal of laws restraining the union of the white and black races in marriage," arguing that the law did not make distinctions on the basis of race because it affected all races equally (that is, blacks could not marry whites and whites could not marry blacks), and dismissing the "bitter words" of the petitioners as "insulting to the memories of our ancestors."[20] Here the suggestion of female sexual impropriety was mobilized to prevent racial equality—the same strategy that was used to attack Mary King for her involvement with Professor William Allen.

At this point Child entered the controversy and offered public support to the abolitionist women. This was not the first time she had publicly denounced the intermarriage ban. Six years earlier, in the final chapter of her landmark abolitionist textbook, *An Appeal in Favor of That Class of Americans Called Africans* (1833), she had called for an end to prejudices against people of color, from miscegenation laws to segregated schools and public transportation. In her *Appeal*, her rhetorical strategy is first to reassure readers about the consequences of repealing intermarriage bans and then to appeal to their sense of justice and patriotism. She assures nervous white readers that repeal will not lead to a wave of intermarriages and that someday intermarriage will not even be an issue: "I believe the feeling in opposition to such unions is quite as strong among the colored class, as it is among white people. . . . While the prejudice exists, such unions cannot take place; and when the prejudice is melted away, they will cease to be a degradation, and of course cease to be an evil." Social concerns aside, Child argues that the intermarriage law is unjust and that the affections should not be a matter for government interference. Freedom to choose a spouse, she declares, is as fundamental a right as freedom of religion. In addition, she points out, the law is a "*useless* disgrace" to Massachusetts, affecting only a small number of the lower classes, who are guilty only of a difference in "taste." The law makes the biracial children of "*honest*" families illegitimate, while the law and customs of the Southern states do nothing about "*immoral* connexions."[21]

As editor of the *National Anti-Slavery Standard,* Child took a similar approach to her advocacy of the repeal, simultaneously reassuring readers about the effects of repeal and appealing to their sense of justice with cross-cultural and historical examples. She emphasizes that abolitionists do not *advocate* amalgamation and that the fear of amalgamation is a "bugbear" raised by enemies of the cause. Abolitionists believe that if there truly is a "natural antipathy between the races, the antipathy will protect itself," and thus laws banning marriages are simply unnecessary. In reference to the South, addressing the argument that emancipation will lead to widespread amalgamation, she counters that amalgamation is an integral part of the slavery system through the sexual exploitation of enslaved women. It is this abuse that emancipation would prevent: "By universal emancipation, / We want to *stop* amalgamation." Fears of amalgamation, Child explains, are used simply to distract the public from the serious sin of slavery. Being a Christian and an American requires a person to work for equal justice and equal opportunity for all; integral to that equality is the repeal of the intermarriage law.[22] In order to get her readers to view the issue differently, Child places the intermarriage ban in historical perspective. Responding to legislators who argue that a change in the law would insult their Massachusetts ancestors, she reminds them of the witchcraft trials, a chapter of colonial history they would all like to forget. Like the judges at these infamous trials, the current legislators "are as little aware what a comedy they are preparing for posterity."[23]

After witnessing the harsh treatment of the abolitionist petitioners by the press and the legislature, Child offered her support with an individual petition on March 20, 1839. In this document she does not try to persuade nervous potential converts to the abolitionist cause; rather, she makes an argument for political justice, using her authority as "a free-born woman, sharing moral and intellectual advantages with all the sons and daughters of this intelligent Commonwealth." Her reasoning falls into three main categories: the law does not work, the law interferes with private life, and the law harms the image of the Commonwealth. She begins with a commonsense argument: repeal the law because it does not restrain vice or have any other useful effect. While the law is useless, however, its "unjustifiable interference with domestic institutions" still has many harmful results: it infringes on private choice, bastardizes children, and violates freedom, just as a law banning Catholic-Protestant marriages would. Finally, she argues, the ban has an impact beyond its destruction of individual lives: "Strongly tinged with the vile system of slavery, in which it originated . . . this legalized contempt of color in Massachusetts has a direct tendency to sustain slavery at the South." In all, the law is "a disgrace to the statute book of a free and intelligent Commonwealth." Child does not intertwine religious and political arguments in the manner of Garrison or the women of Lynn. She is not trying to convert the legislature to the Christian principles of anti-prejudice embraced by the abolitionists; with a specific political goal in sight, she speaks in a language of freedom and patriotism that her audience can understand. At the end of her petition, Child also adds her protest against "the contemptuous treatment offered to her sisters in Lynn" and insists that all petitioners deserve respect from their representatives.[24]

While Child directly and publicly challenged Massachusetts' intermarriage ban in her political writing, she displaced her fictional critique of the law to a Southern setting in her 1842 story "The Quadroons."[25] Previously, in her *Appeal*, she had described respectable interracial families in Massachusetts who were harmed by the intermarriage ban: "I know two or three instances where women of the laboring class have been united to reputable, industrious colored men. These husbands regularly bring home their wages, and are kind to their families. If by some of the odd chances . . . their wives should become heirs to any property, the children may be wronged out of it, because the law produces them illegitimate."[26] Despite Child's firsthand knowledge of these "honest" Northern families, she chose not to write about their trials in her fiction, perhaps making a strategic rhetorical decision after a decade of race riots in Northern cities which were often sparked by resistance to "amalgamationists" and "abolitionists."

Instead she turned to the infamous "quadroons" to show the interconnection between miscegenation laws and the "slave power."

"The Quadroons" first appeared in Maria Weston Chapman's antislavery gift annual, the *Liberty Bell*.[27] Chapman, a leader in abolitionist circles, ran the Massachusetts Anti-Slavery Fair and edited the *Liberty Bell*, which was sold at the fair. The *Liberty Bell*, published between 1839 and 1857, featured essays, letters, poems, and stories by leading intellectuals and abolitionists, including Ralph Waldo Emerson, Harriet Beecher Stowe, Margaret Fuller, Henry Wadsworth Longfellow, William Lloyd Garrison, and Lydia Maria Child. The gift annual, a "yearly testimonial to the validity of abolitionist principles," reached out to tentative antislavery supporters. As Anne Warren Weston (Chapman's sister) noted, the annual was "an instrumentality by which the truth can be conveyed to classes among whom our periodical Anti-Slavery literature finds a very imperfect circulation."[28] In the 1842 *Liberty Bell*, in which Child's story appeared, Eliza Lee Follen reassures female readers that abolitionism is indeed "Women's Work": "Is it not natural and right that women should feel most for the sufferings and degradation of their own sex? And are not women the greatest sufferers from slavery?" She urges her readers to continue to sign petitions "for the liberation of women from the vilest bondage."[29]

In her story, Child carries out Follen's appeal for an abolitionist, interracial sisterhood. She tries to address the controversial topic of interracial marriage and the sexual exploitation of enslaved women without alienating her white female audience; given the social context in which women were branded "not virtuous" for their political activism around this issue, hers was no easy task. Her strategy is to write a sentimental tragedy showing how the intermarriage ban and slavery affected one family. Her "quadroon" heroines fall into the "tragic mulatta" category, a type Child is often credited with inventing. Beautiful, educated, and "almost" white, they are heroines Child's readers could relate to and feel sympathy for. In her fiction, Child illustrates the domestic consequences of intermarriage bans by appealing to her readers' emotions—a stark contrast to the appeal for political justice in her petition.

In "The Quadroons," Rosalie, who is "one-quarter" African (one African grandparent), lives in a cottage in the Georgia countryside with her white "husband," Edward, and their daughter Xarifa. As in Massachusetts, marriages between blacks and whites in Georgia were "unlawful" and "absolutely null and void."[30] Rosalie and Edward were "married" in a church ceremony that had no legal standing: "The tenderness of Rosalie's conscience required an outward form of marriage; though she well knew that a union with her proscribed race was unrecognised by law." Rosalie nevertheless claims that she is satisfied "without the protection of the state," and the narrator tells us that their "marriage" was "sanctioned by Heaven, though unrecognised on earth" (89). Because of political ambition, Edward, after ten years of happiness with Rosalie, decides to marry the blond Charlotte. Rosalie angrily refuses to be "the other woman" and soon dies of a broken heart. Charlotte is also devastated when she hears the whispers about her husband's previous connection.

Several years later the dissipated Edward dies in a drunken fall from his horse. It is then discovered that Xarifa's grandmother had been a slave and that her manumission papers were never recorded. Technically, therefore, Xarifa is also a slave; she is sold at auction to a wealthy planter who wants her as his mistress. Xarifa's British music teacher, George, is her only friend in the world; in fact, her father had hired him hoping that the "English freedom from prejudice should lead him to offer legal protection to his graceful and winning child" (96). Ideally, George would marry her and take her to England. But when he tries to help her escape from slavery, he is shot and killed, leaving her without any protectors. Xarifa's "pure temple" is "desecrated" by her licentious master, and like any white victim of seduction tales, she dies of grief and madness (98).

In "The Quadroons," Child illustrates how intermarriage bans do not prevent interracial relationships but merely leave women of color vulnerable and without legal protections. Even in his loving relationship with Rosalie, Edward is free to abandon her for Charlotte, "unfettered by the laws of the land" (91). Child blames Edward for his moral weakness, and he suffers for it, but she also blames society for not recognizing interracial marriages and for making it so easy for Edward to discard Rosalie. With the fate of Xarifa, Child indicts society for forbidding consensual marriages while looking the other way when the "amalgamation" takes place within the coercion of slavery.

Some current critics condemn Child's "tragic mulattas" for reinforcing the prejudice of her readers; they do not like the heroines' preference for white men and their lack of self-reliance. Modern readers prefer Child's militant stories, like "Slavery's Pleasant Homes" (which appeared in the *Liberty Bell* in 1843), in which the heroine is darker-skinned, takes a lover from among her fellow slaves, and dies resisting her master; her lover then kills their master in revenge.[31] Child herself realized that "The Quadroons" was "embarrassingly cloying." As she wrote to her editor Maria Weston

Chapman: "You . . . will laugh at it heartily, but the young and romantic will like it. It sounds, in sooth, more like a girl of sixteen, than a woman of forty." This letter, according to Child's biographer Carolyn Karcher, demonstrates Child's "awareness of the conflicting demands her fiction had to meet from sophisticated antislavery activists and unconverted general readers."[32]

But despite Child's self-deprecating comments, only the most deliberate misreading could dismiss "The Quadroons" as just another Southern plantation romance. The story can be best understood in the context of the fierce political efforts to change a law embedded in the history and mythology of Massachusetts and the equally fierce efforts to maintain it, an issue as important in its local significance as was the equally entrenched institution of slavery in the South. In other words, "The Quadroons" is a Northern story masked as a Southern tale, an allegory for the very situation the New England abolitionists were agitating against. It has a political edge that rebukes not only an unjust law but also, by obvious implication, a foolishly romanticized version of the New England past that denies the local experience of slavery and prejudice.[33] It is only in the context of the campaign for repeal of the Massachusetts intermarriage law that we can read the story accurately.

Child's gift was an extraordinary ability to tailor her message to specific audiences. Her political publications appeal to her readers' beliefs in American freedom and place the intermarriage law in the broader context of slavery and Massachusetts history. Her fiction demonstrates that the personal is indeed political and illustrates the impact of intermarriage bans on women of color. Along with other abolitionist women, Child challenged the definition of family outlined by Massachusetts law. After several years of agitation, they were successful: the repeal passed on February 24, 1843, signaling a major victory for the abolitionist campaign against slavery and prejudice.[34] The repeal energized the abolitionist movement, inspiring continued efforts against slavery and segregation in schools and public places. After this legal victory, Child, in her effort to challenge American prejudice, continued to portray interracial marriages in her fiction.

The Garies and Their Friends:
Intermarriage in the "Free" North

Whereas Child and other white abolitionists believed that racial prejudice would disappear following the demise of slavery and its legal framework,

Frank Johnson Webb, as a Northern free man of color, knew better. As Joanne Melish explains, " 'Black' and 'white' were not vestigial legal categories sustained by the persistence of slavery; rather, they were independent social identities—only arbitrarily related to physical characteristics—which had become institutionalized as successors to the legal categories of 'slave class' and 'slave-owning class' and performed the same function: to organize labor and social relations."[35] In other words, race kept even free people of color in an inferior position. One of the few novels by black authors published before the Civil War, *The Garies and Their Friends* (1857) tells the story of the violence and prejudice free blacks encountered in the North, echoing in many ways the experience of William Allen in his life and marriage.[36]

Born a free black in Philadelphia in 1828, Webb was raised in turbulent times.[37] Philadelphia, a city with strong Southern ties, was perhaps the Northern city most hostile to blacks and abolitionists. "Although the 15,000 blacks who lived in Philadelphia in 1830 comprised less than ten percent of the city's total population," writes Elise Lemire, "there had been a thirty percent increase in the black population since 1820 which gave whites the impression that the city was ever darkening in color."[38] In addition, "Philadelphia was becoming a center of abolitionist activity" by both blacks and whites. Between 1829 and 1849 there were six major riots against blacks and abolitionists, interspersed with fighting between Irish Catholic immigrant and native Protestant gangs. Fear of amalgamation as a consequence of abolitionism was commonly cited as a reason for mob violence. In the midst of this violence, black men lost any political recourse, for their right to vote was taken away in 1838. Webb grew up during this tumultuous time, and his novel reflects his city in turmoil.[39]

In June 1856, Frank Webb and his wife, Mary, left Philadelphia for England, joining the many black abolitionists who left the United States to escape the risk of kidnapping under the Fugitive Slave Law and the increasingly hostile atmosphere for people of color. Like the Allens three years earlier, the Webbs were assisted by the circle of British abolitionists, including Lady Byron, the earl of Shaftesbury, the duchess of Sutherland, and Lord Brougham. Most important, the Webbs had a letter of introduction from Harriet Beecher Stowe, which opened many doors for them in aristocratic circles. Mary had started giving dramatic readings in the United States, and she began presenting readings in England soon after their arrival.[40] Stowe supported Mary's dramatic talent, even writing a dramatization of *Uncle Tom's Cabin* for her. While Stowe publicly relished

her role as patron of the arts and friend of the African race, she privately
admitted how difficult it was to guide the Webbs through English society:
"How soon one grows weary of doing what one *writes* about."[41]

It is not known whether Webb began working on *The Garies and Their
Friends* in England or in the United States, but, like Allen, he published
his book in London.[42] The novel includes introductions by two of his
abolitionist patrons, Stowe and Lord Brougham, and a dedication to Lady
Byron. Stowe seems to misunderstand the purpose of the novel, writing
that it addresses the question of whether the African race is "capable of
freedom, self-government, and progress" (xix). For Webb, this is not a
matter of dispute: Northern blacks are hampered not by a lack of ability
but by the disastrous effects of racial prejudice on the black community.
The novel was published in England by Routledge in its "Cheap Series,"
which appealed to readers outside the upper classes. Routledge was "widely
recognized as the chief promoter of American authors to the British public," and its best-sellers included *Uncle Tom's Cabin*.[43] It is not known,
however, whether Webb's novel was available in the United States prior to
the 1969 Arno Press–*New York Times* reprint.

The plot features two families in Philadelphia, the black Ellises and the
interracial Garies. The novel uses both "the rhetoric and motifs of senti-
mentalism" in its valorization of domestic life over the political reality of
the antebellum North, complete with race riots and segregation.[44] The
novel opens, like Child's story "The Quadroons," with an interracial family unrecognized by the laws of Georgia. Clarence Garie's "wife," Emily,
and his two children are in fact his slaves, since the law will not permit
him to marry Emily or manumit his family. A common motif in abolitionist literature is the careless Southern man who dies without freeing his
black family; this plot device is found in Child's work, Stowe's *Uncle Tom's
Cabin*, and Dion Boucicault's play *The Octoroon*. Webb's novel counters
this standard plot with the question, What would happen if one of those
men did the right thing? In other words, what if a Southern planter
brought his family to the free North, where he could manumit them and
legally marry his wife? Because of Emily's fears about their precarious
status, the Garies move to Philadelphia, and—because Pennsylvania had
repealed its amalgamation laws in 1780—she and Clarence are legally married.[45] Northern life, however, does not offer them the freedom they had
anticipated. As William and Mary Allen found, many Northerners, regardless of the liberality of the law, were violently opposed to intermarriage and
black economic progress. In the novel, a mob attacks the home of the

wealthy Mr. Walters and maims another family friend, Mr. Ellis, as he tries to warn the Garies about the danger. In the midst of this horrific race riot, Clarence and Emily Garie are killed by a mob shouting, "Down with the Abolitionist—down with the Amalgamationist!" (221). Noel Ignatiev claims that the riot is based on an actual 1849 event in which a mob led by a violent gang, the Killers, attacked a tavern, called the California House, owned by a black man who had recently married a white woman.[46]

Following the riot, the Garies' two light-skinned children, also named Emily and Clarence, are left without relatives, so the family lawyer decides that they should "pass" into white society. Clarence is sent off to boarding school with strict orders not to reveal the secret of his maternity, but Emily remains with the black Ellises. Webb leaves no doubt as to the relative wisdom of these decisions: Emily grows into a well-adjusted, happy young woman, while Clarence becomes a nervous wreck. He asks Emily to leave her black fiancé and join him in the white world, but she refuses: "I, thank God, am with the oppressed" (335). Clarence is sick, body and soul, from his isolation and the pressure of keeping his secret. He cannot tell his beloved, "Birdie," about his background after she remarks that an interracial engagement is "strange and unnatural" (331). His engagement to Birdie is finally broken when his lineage is revealed to her enraged father. As Ariela Gross observes, "The greatest blow to a white man's honor would be to be deceived into bestowing the honors of whiteness on a 'negro.'"[47] Both Birdie and Clarence die of broken hearts. Clarence is often held up as an example of the "tragic mulatto," but Webb's portrayal makes it clear that the biracial character is tragic only when he tries to pass. Despite the different race-gender configuration in the marriage of the elder Garies and their son's engagement—in the former the man is white while in the latter the woman is white—both relationships are equally offensive to the white families and the white community.

As in most fiction featuring black-white marriages, the law plays a central role. It is the law that sets the plot in motion by forcing the Garie family to leave Georgia and move north. As Garie explains to his uncle, "I'm going north, because I wish to emancipate and educate my children— you know I can't do it here" (100). In addition, he and Emily wish their marriage to be recognized by the state: "It is not my fault that we are not legally married; it is the fault of the laws" (101). Once they get to Philadelphia, however, they still have difficulty legalizing their marriage. The first minister they approach refuses to marry them, denying "the propriety of amalgamation" and declaring that "the negro race" is "marked out by the hand of God for servitude." Garie is completely surprised by this attitude in the "free" North: "I did not for a moment have an idea that he would hesitate to marry us. There is no law here that forbids it" (137). Fortunately they find another minister to marry them; he counsels them to face the "prejudices of society" with courage and patience (138).

Just as the law forces the Garies to leave the South, the neglect of Northern law enforcement leads to their tragic deaths. When Mr. Walters, a prosperous businessman and leader in the black community, learns the details of the mob's plans for attacking black neighborhoods, he goes to the mayor to ask for protection. With "apathy and indifference," the mayor claims there is nothing he can do to prevent the rioting (202). To add insult to injury, the murders of the elder Garies are then covered up by "a very unsatisfactory and untruthful verdict" at the inquest (226).

In an additional travesty of justice, the law strips the Garie orphans of their rightful inheritance. Most of their father's fortune remained in Georgia, and according to Georgia law, because they are "the offspring of a slave-woman," they cannot automatically inherit property from a white father. Without "a will in their favour"—Garie's will has mysteriously disappeared—the inheritance goes to Garie's nearest living white relative, his cousin Mr. Stevens, a shady Philadelphia lawyer (252–53). As the novel reveals, Mr. Stevens knew about this legal situation and murdered his own cousin during the riots in order to inherit the fortune, inciting the local fears of abolitionism and amalgamation for his personal economic gain.

Webb's answer to his question—What would happen to an interracial family who moved north in search of freedom and legal recognition?—is not an optimistic one. Clarence Garie Sr., for all his good intentions, is not a heroic figure. For one thing, he is no abolitionist despite what the angry mob calls him. When the Garies go north, he hires an overseer to run his plantation, leaving the vast majority of his slaves in bondage. Although Garie realizes that his family will face some prejudice in the North (57), his naïveté about race relations leaves them exposed to danger. As the rioters approach his house, he observes in wonder: "It's a mob—and that word Amalgamationist—can it be pointed at me? It hardly seems possible; and yet I have a fear that there is something wrong" (221). Garie bravely defends his home, but his actions come too late to save himself and his wife.

The fate of the Garies complicates the question of interracial marriage. Although his wife and children were protected from slavery, the hostility of Philadelphians to abolitionists and amalgamationists (lumped together as one and the same) destroys the happy family. The Garies' marriage is a loving one, and Webb endorses their right to be legally married. This endorsement is not enthusiastic, however, for in this dangerous environment, interracial marriage is no cure for the problem of prejudice.

After the deaths of their parents, the best thing for the Garie children—and, by implication, for all biracial individuals—is to seek refuge in the black community, where they are wanted and needed. The real hero of the novel is not Garie but Mr. Walters, who organizes the black community to defend itself against the riot. Walters also takes in young Emily and Clarence after their parents' death; the one failure of his leadership, which feels inconsistent with his philosophy of black uplift and pride, occurs when he allows himself to be persuaded to send Clarence away to "pass" (274–76).

Webb's novel demonstrates Joanne Melish's contention that, despite the absence of a law dividing black and white, "by 1850 in the North 'race' had come to perform the same function in social relations that the law performed in legal ones."[48] Webb exposes the violent prejudice of the urban North, often overlooked in abolitionist condemnations of Southern slavery. That this tragedy is set in Pennsylvania, a state that had eliminated both slavery and miscegenation laws seventy years earlier, refutes the abolitionist belief that the repeal of miscegenation laws and the abolition of slavery would gradually eliminate racial prejudice. Whereas Child criticizes the law for preventing the formation of legitimate interracial families, Webb observes that even the protection of the law cannot guarantee the safety and social status of such families.

Reconstructing the "American Family": Child's "Romance" and Harper's "Sacrifice"

The Civil War and its aftermath transformed the narratives of interracial marriage as they became part of the discussion over the fate of the former slaves. As Lyde Cullen Sizer notes in her work on Northern women writers, "The emphasis on whiteness and blackness in the years just after the war reflected the intense anxiety both conservative and progressive Northern white women had about the consequences of the war."[49] Stories of North-South romances were used to explore national reunification after the war, and interracial marriage added another layer of complexity to these stories.[50] And so, as Sizer observes, "the intertwined lives of black and white people become political messages about the failures and possibilities of national reunion and repair."[51]

At the end of the Civil War, abolitionists such as Child and Frances

E. W. Harper turned their energies toward the work of Reconstruction. They joined Frederick Douglass's call for the "full and complete adoption" of blacks "into the great national family of America."[52] Their postwar novels create a dynamic interracial conversation about the fate of the 3.5 million newly emancipated slaves and present their visions for postbellum America. Child, in *A Romance of the Republic* (1867), portrays interracial marriage as the means of bringing blacks into the "American family." Harper's work, like Webb's, is more skeptical about the possibilities of intermarriage and offers an alternative model of political engagement rooted in domestic and community life. In her novel *Minnie's Sacrifice* (1869), she suggests that the color line would not be easily erased and that "national healing" would also undermine Northern protection of the former slaves. Harper showed remarkable prescience here: as the historian David Blight notes, the desire for sectional reunion seriously undercut the commitment to the emancipated slaves: "The tragedy of Reconstruction is rooted in this American paradox: the imperative of healing and the imperative of justice could not, ultimately, cohabit the same house."[53]

The term "miscegenation," having been coined in the 1864 election to discredit the Republican Party, signified a key issue in Reconstruction politics, used by pro-Southern Republicans and Democrats alike. According to Eric Foner, President Andrew Johnson welcomed emancipation, but "in condemning slavery he dwelled almost obsessively on racial miscegenation as the institution's main evil."[54] When he vetoed the Civil Rights Bill in 1866, he argued that full citizenship for blacks discriminated against whites and that the bill would lead to racial intermarriage.[55] Miscegenation fears were also central to anti-Republican politics. In the 1868 election, "one of the most explicitly racist presidential campaigns in American history," the Democratic vice presidential candidate, Francis P. Blair Jr., asserted that Republican rule would lead to miscegenation and that this "racial intermixing would reverse evolution, produce a less advanced species incapable of reproducing itself."[56]

Child and Harper were both dismayed by Johnson's approach to Reconstruction. Johnson hated the slaveholding aristocracy, but he believed that white men should rule the South. In May 1865 he offered amnesty and pardon to all former Confederates who pledged allegiance to the Union and supported emancipation. The wealthiest plantation owners were excluded from this process, but Johnson proved willing to pardon them individually. The seized plantations that abolitionists had hoped would be distributed among freedmen and poor whites went back to their previous owners. Emboldened by the president's leniency, the states of the former Confederacy went on to pass repressive "Black Codes," which controlled and limited the economic options of the black labor force. Radical Republicans in Congress passed extensive legislation, including three constitutional amendments, to protect the former slaves, but congressional Reconstruction would be short-lived.[57] Black political power was suppressed by the vigilante violence of the Ku Klux Klan and other groups; by 1876, Southern "redemption" (a return to "home rule" by white Democrats) would be almost complete. After the return to "home rule," legislatures passed new and stricter miscegenation laws, even while the North virtually eliminated such statutes. Child and Harper were writing at a pivotal moment in the early days of Reconstruction; both foresaw the betrayal of their abolitionist dreams.

The two authors had different reactions to President Johnson's obstruction of rights for the former slaves and the use of miscegenation in national politics. Child felt great anxiety about the effects of the Johnson administration on Reconstruction: "I wish I *could* feel confidence in President Johnson, but I *cannot*. He seems to be to be destitute of sympathy for the colored race."[58] What Carolyn Karcher describes as the "tragic derailment of Reconstruction under Andrew Johnson" caused Child to lose confidence in political activity, ironically at the moment when her political authority was at its highest. After publishing a series of letters critical of the president, this leading abolitionist figure withdrew from the political arena and decided that her role lay in what the literary critic Jane Tompkins would call the "cultural work" of Reconstruction. While politicians argued over black suffrage and land redistribution, Child worked on two long-range projects: the elimination of prejudice and the empowerment of the freedpeople. She turned her attention to compiling a reader for ex-slaves, *The Freedmen's Book*, published in December 1865. A combination "primer, anthology, history text, and self-help manual" written for the benefit of the former slaves, it was also designed to challenge white prejudice with its examples of black literary achievement, including several of Harper's poems. In addition, the book encouraged former slaves to assert their rights through legal and political channels; unfortunately, for dealing with life in the Reconstruction South this advice was already inadequate.[59]

Harper reacted to the weakening Northern commitment to the ex-slaves with continued political activism. An experienced lecturer on the abolitionist circuit, she undertook a demanding schedule of lectures for the African Methodist Episcopal Church, visiting every Southern state except

Arkansas and Texas between 1866 and 1869.[60] The theme of her lectures was "Literacy, Land, and Liberation." To this end she "promoted literacy, self-determination, women's rights, and human dignity for all Americans, while she lambasted Klan terrorism, chastised domestic violence, condemned intemperance, and reprimanded the federal government for its indifference to the black citizenry."[61] In her volume of poetry, *Sketches of Southern Life* (1872), Harper also provided commentary on Reconstruction through her ex-slave character Aunt Chloe. "An uneducated but decidedly informed and intelligent woman," writes Frances Smith Foster, "Chloe is a radical departure from the victimized slave woman and the tragic mulatto."[62] Child's reader and Harper's oratory and poetry were all designed to empower the former slaves and give them a voice in the cultural and political arenas; in addition, their fiction guided readers through the challenges of the Reconstruction era.

In addition to *The Freedmen's Book*, Child's cultural response to Reconstruction included *A Romance of the Republic*, in which she reconstructed the nation though interracial marriages. The subject had been brewing in her mind for a few years. As she wrote to Congressman William P. Cutler of Ohio in 1862: "The horror that many people have of future social equality, and intermarriage of the races, makes me smile. The argument is so shallow! the fear is so contradictory of itself! If there *is* an 'instinctive antipathy,' as many assert, surely that antipathy may be trusted to prevent amalgamation. If there is *no* instinctive antipathy, what reason is there for the horror? . . . *My* belief is, that when generations of colored people have had a fair chance for education and the acquisition of wealth, the prejudice against them, originating in their degraded position, will pass away."[63] Perhaps the repeal of Northern miscegenation laws gave her greater confidence in her scheme for national and racial reconciliation. As Child explained to Francis Shaw, "Having fought against *slavery* till I saw it go down in the Red Sea, I wanted to do something to undermine *prejudice*; and there is such a universal passion for novels, that more can be done in that way, than by the ablest arguments, and the most serious exhortations."[64]

A Romance of the Republic returns to the "tragic mulatta" theme Child had developed in her abolitionist fiction twenty-five years earlier. The novel features two sisters, Rosa and Flora, who live with their widowed father on the outskirts of antebellum New Orleans. Upon their father's death, the girls find out that their "Spanish mother" was actually a "quadroon" and a slave; they too are thus slaves, scheduled to be sold at auction to pay their father's debts.

The rake of the novel, Gerald Fitzgerald, seizes this opportunity to control the girls: he buys them, marries Rosa in a sham ceremony (she is unaware that marriage to a slave is illegal in Louisiana), and settles them in a secluded sea island cottage. His power as their master leaves the sisters vulnerable to abuse: he makes advances to Flora (causing her to fake her death and run away) and then marries a white bride. Here Child illustrates how the laws against intermarriage do not prevent interracial liaisons; all they do is deprive women of color of legal protections. Rosa asks Gerald to manumit her because she is pregnant and knows the "bitter significance of the law"—that the child follows the condition of the mother.[65] He never frees her, but in a moment of madness Rosa gets her revenge. The legal Mrs. Fitzgerald has also given birth to a baby boy, Gerald Jr., and Rosa switches the babies. Her son is raised as the Fitzgerald heir, while the legal heir is sold as a slave.

As the plot progresses, both sisters are helped by white friends to escape from slavery. They also both marry white men: Rosa weds the proper Bostonian Alfred King, her father's friend's son, and Flora marries the German Franz Blumenthal, her father's former clerk. The story resumes nineteen years later at the start of the Civil War: both intermarriages are happy, and the sisters are finally reunited. Rosa's rash act so many years ago, however, now produces dangerous consequences. She has a lovely fifteen-year-old daughter, Eulalia, whose beauty is owing to the combination of her parents' different features, like "mixing flowers" (302). Eulalia has fallen in love with the young Gerald Fitzgerald; her mother is tormented by the knowledge that he is actually Eulalia's half-brother. This plot complication reflects a sinister side of the secret interracial family ties that were an outgrowth of slavery: the hidden genetic identity of mixed-race children creates the threat of incest. Rosa confesses her actions and tells Mrs. Fitzgerald that the boy she has raised is not her son.

In addition to the threat of incest caused by switching the babies, there also remains the problem that the true Fitzgerald heir has spent a lifetime in slavery. Rosa's husband, Alfred King, dedicates himself to setting this situation right. In another instance of the novel's timely coincidences, the young Gerald Fitzgerald meets his half-brother and virtual twin, George Falkner (the true Fitzgerald heir), during the war as both fight for the Union Army. The Fitzgerald family refuses to recognize the all-white George as their true heir, because he has been raised as a slave, lacks education and genteel manners, and, most important, has a mulatto wife. Rosa's husband is very wealthy, however, and with his own money he restores George Falkner to his rightful inheritance. He arranges an education for George and his wife and gives him a job in his European business office. Like the Allens, the Falkners have to leave the United States for Europe, where their interracial marriage is more acceptable.

When Rosa's and Flora's families are reunited after the war, Flora is delighted by the multilingual babble of the reunion: "What a polyglot family we are!" (432). Her husband agrees: "Nations and races have been pretty thoroughly mixed up in the ancestry of our children . . . African and French, Spanish, American, and German" (432). Here Child anticipates the early-twentieth-century appropriation of the image of the "melting pot" and offers the mixing of peoples as the solution to American racial and ethnic strife.

In Child's novel the work of Reconstruction is a domestic matter. The scenes that take place prior to the Civil War, which constitute much of the book, feature the political activism of the abolitionists. After the war, however, the activists make Reconstruction a private endeavor, as the novel centers on the "reconstruction" of one family. The former slaves in the novel are treated much better by Rosa's and Flora's families than the real former slaves were treated by the U.S. government: George Falkner's inheritance is restored, and the sisters' former slave-servants are employed within the household and family business.

The image of two happy multiracial households suggests that the race problem in the United States could be solved one family at a time. While the novel "works to eliminate categories of racial difference," as Dana Nelson notes, there are some limitations to Child's vision. She does not appreciate the value of black culture: "The novel fails to imagine social cross-*cultural* relationships to complement romantic cross-*racial* ones."[66] Child's patriotic conclusion, in which "all the family, of all ages and colors" sing "The Star-Spangled Banner" (441), also feels at odds with the stark political realities of the postbellum period. But despite this flag-waving ending, Child's "romance" is harshly critical of the "republic." The "romantic" elements of her story—the things that could not possibly happen in real life—are actually true-to-life consequences of slavery. Throughout the novel, according to Nelson, "Child is uncompromising in emphasizing the irony central to her title: the poetic qualities seemingly advertised by a 'romance' of the 'republic' turn out to be among the most shameful facts of U.S. history."[67]

A Romance of the Republic received a few favorable notices from those who had worked to eliminate slavery and prejudice. *The Nation* praised Child for raising the question of "the social and domestic relations to be sustained hereafter between our innumerous freemen and our numerous freedmen" and heralded the novel's "most catholic liberality and charity" (while noting that the novel was not appropriate for the schoolroom).[68] The *National Anti-Slavery Standard*, which Child had edited from 1841 to 1843, exulted that Child had written "the second great novel based upon slavery and its painfully romantic incidents" (*Uncle Tom's Cabin*, of course, being the first). The reviewer also urged that the rebellious states not be readmitted "without additional protection to the blacks vouchsafed by the Federal government," and praised the book for its ability to inspire Northern commitment to the former slaves: "The appearance of this novel is therefore most opportune to deepen and intensify the feeling which shall demand the extinction of every remaining vestige of the odious slave system, with the amplest guarantees of future security."[69] Nevertheless, as Karcher recounts, "many of Child's closest friends responded to it with embarrassed silence, polite platitudes, or 'cold' dismissal."[70] Apparently even former abolitionists were not ready to consider Child's vision of a multiracial America, and she was devastated by the reactions of many of her abolitionist friends: "I had some expectations, quite modest, at the time I published 'The Romance of the Republic'; but I found out then what the interest of friends amounted to, and I shall never dream again, not even the merest little bit of a dream."[71]

Frances E. W. Harper's novel *Minnie's Sacrifice* demonstrates that direct political activism was a necessary complement to Child's campaign against prejudice in this time of dire emergency in the South. Frances Ellen Watkins Harper, born free in Maryland in 1825, was long recognized as a popular poet and abolitionist speaker and also became a pioneer in fiction.[72] Her commitment to abolitionism was solidified by an 1853 Maryland law providing that any person of color who entered the state by the Northern border could be sold as a slave. This law effectively exiled Maryland natives who were residing or traveling in the North.[73] At the time the law was passed, Harper was teaching at a school in Pennsylvania, and so she was unable to return home.

Rediscovered in the 1990s by Frances Smith Foster, *Minnie's Sacrifice* was first published in Philadelphia in 1869 in the *Christian Recorder*, the journal of the African Methodist Episcopal (AME) Church. Foster's work with the Afro-Protestant press requires us to rethink our assumption that black writers wrote mainly for white audiences. She finds that "African American writers were about the business of creating and reconstructing literary subjects, themes, and forms that best suited their own aesthetics and intentions and . . . they assumed and did enjoy an extensive black readership." Foster also argues that *Minnie's Sacrifice* may be most fruitfully read by emphasizing its specific context: "published in a black paper, by a black woman, for black readers—during Reconstruction."[74] Unlike Child, Harper wrote about the war and Reconstruction from a black point of view and as a firsthand witness; she derived additional literary material from her experiences as a lecturer.[75] She also had the historical advantage of having witnessed two more years of Reconstruction; by 1869 the Freedmen's Bureau had been discontinued, and the Ku Klux Klan had begun to terrorize the South. As she reported from the field, "I think the former ruling class in the South have proved that they are not fit to be trusted with the welfare of the whites nor the liberty of the blacks."[76] In contrast to Child's personal and cultural approach to Reconstruction, *Minnie's Sacrifice* was written "with a focus on the pressing political issues of the day, including suffrage, lynching, and acquisition of land and education for the ex-slaves."[77]

The plot of *Minnie's Sacrifice* is similar to that of Harper's 1893 novel *Iola Leroy*.[78] The parallel protagonists, Louis and Minnie, have both been raised as white even though they were slaves by birth. Louis's mother was seduced by her master and gave birth to a "child of shame" (3). In a retelling of the Moses story, a source of African American inspiration and a "visionary motif" in Harper's writing, the planter's daughter rescues the fair-skinned baby from slavery.[79] Ten years earlier, Harper had noted her interpretation of Moses in an American context: "I like the character of Moses. He is the first disunionist we read of in the Jewish Scriptures. The magnificence of Pharaoh's throne loomed up before his vision," but he "chose rather to suffer with the enslaved, than rejoice with the free. He would have no union with the slave power of Egypt."[80] Louis is passed off as the planter's ward (ironically, he is his biological son) and raised as white, never knowing the secret of his origins.

Minnie is the daughter of a quadroon woman and her master, St. Pierre Le Grange. The jealous mistress, Mrs. Le Grange, insists that Minnie be sold after she is mistaken for one of the Le Grange children: "I was almost ready to die with vexation; but this shall never happen again" (16). Le Grange does not have the heart to sell his own child, so he only pretends to sell Minnie and instead sends her North to be raised by a Quaker couple. Like Louis, Minnie is raised as white and does not know the secret of her "tainted blood."

After establishing Louis and Minnie's secret identities, the narrative then jumps ahead ten years, with Minnie and Louis still ignorant of their maternity. Upon hearing of a black woman's experience of prejudice, Minnie tells her adoptive parents that "it must be dreadful to be colored" (46). Soon after, Minnie's birth mother encounters her on the street and claims her with great joy; it is a happy reunion once Minnie gets over the shock of discovering her racial identity. Louis learns his secret when he enlists in the Confederate army. His black grandmother is horrified and insists that he be told: "That boy is going to lift his hand agin his own people" (57). Louis then decides to desert the Confederate side and go north; agreeing with his grandmother, he says, "I can never raise my hand against my mother's race" (60). Like Moses, who embraces his Hebrew identity once it is revealed, Louis goes on to lead his people out of the American Egypt, the system of slavery and racial prejudice.

After the war, Minnie and Louis get married. Even though they both can pass for white, they claim their black identity and return to the South to work with the newly freed slaves (like Emily Garie, they choose to remain on the side of the oppressed). As Minnie writes to Louis, the South needs an "army of civilizers; the army of the pen, and not the sword" (68). Reconstruction is dangerous work, however, and the couple receive death threats. Their hope for Northern protection against the former slaveholders fades away as the Northern states vote down black suffrage: "Every item of Northern meanness to the colored people in their midst was a message of hope to the rebel element of the South" (85). Minnie dies in this atmosphere of vigilante violence. Unfortunately, this key chapter has been lost, so we do not learn the specific circumstances of "Minnie's sacrifice," although the implication is that she has been lynched by the Klan.[81] The novel concludes with Minnie's funeral and Louis's decision to continue their work: "Sorrow and danger still surrounded his way, and he felt his soul more strongly drawn out than ever to share the fortunes of the colored race" (89–90).

For Harper, Minnie's character is a direct response to the "tragic mulatta" who plays such a central role in Child's fiction. In her concluding address to her readers, Harper explains the origins of her character: "While some of the authors of the present day have been weaving their stories about white men marrying beautiful quadroon girls, who, in so doing were lost to us socially, I conceived of one of that same class to whom I gave a higher, holier destiny; a life of lofty self-sacrifice and beautiful self-consecration, finished at the post of duty, and rounded off with the fiery crown of martyrdom, a circlet which ever changes into a diadem of glory" (91). The moral of the story is that everyone with African blood, even those who could "pass," must work for the uplifting of the race: "The lesson of Minnie's sacrifice is this, that it is braver to suffer with one's own branch of the human race . . . [than to] pass . . . for mere personal advantages . . . and at the expense of self-respect" (91).

While some current critics share Harper's disdain for mulatta characters designed to appeal to white readers, Hazel Carby offers an alternative reading for these heroines: "Historically the mulatto, as narrative figure, has two primary functions: as a vehicle for an exploration of the relationship between the races and, at the same time, an expression of the relationship between the races. The figure of the mulatto should be understood and analyzed as a narrative device of mediation."[82] I would argue that Child and Harper share this narrative strategy of mediation, even though their characters choose different affiliations. The fate of these intermediary characters is shaped by their creators' views on race and culture: Child dreamed of the day when race would be erased as a social category, while Harper viewed racial identity as a reality of American culture, one that required intermediate figures to make a choice.

It follows, then, that Harper portrays miscegenation, through Louis and Minnie's heritage, as part of the legacy of slavery; intermarriage is a possibility, but not the answer to an immediate crisis. She contends that, in an era of racist violence and political repression, there are no easy answers. When Minnie and Louis hear the news of a black-white marriage, they are happy for the loving couple, but they do not see it as a sign of hope for the future. As Louis says: "The question of the intermingling of the races in marriage is one that scarcely interests this question. The question that presses upon us with the most fearful distinctness is how can we make life secure in the South" (81). This is the question that most concerns Harper; as she wrote to a friend in Philadelphia, "how have our people been murdered in the South, and their bones scattered at the grave's mouth! Oh, when will we have a government strong enough to make human life safe?"[83] She warns her readers that the North would choose national unity over protecting the former slaves and dismisses Child's vision as woefully inadequate for the crisis ahead.[84]

According to Child, intermarriage was the solution to the race problem in America; her narratives of disruption, however, were too radical for most of her contemporaries. Just as the Boudinot-Gold marriage defined the limits of the missionary spirit in Cornwall and the Allen-King marriage left abolitionists in upstate New York running scared, so did Child's advocacy of intermarriage, in fiction and in real life, mark a limit for abolitionists. Harper and Webb recognized this reality and suggested that intermarriage should be permitted in principle, but it was not for them a priority or a solution to racial prejudice. This is not to portray Child as a naïve optimist and Harper and Webb as shrewd realists. Their disagreement perhaps lies more in their rhetorical strategies than in their sentiments: Child worked for the elimination of prejudice by offering a positive model, while Harper and Webb combated prejudice by revealing its ongoing horrors and offering inspirational examples of black leadership. The trends in lawmaking suggest that a majority of the Northern population agreed with Harper's and Webb's position, as the last miscegenation laws in the North were repealed during Reconstruction.

The fiction discussed in this chapter illustrates the unjust consequences of the miscegenation laws and predicts the likely outcome of their repeal. In Child's fiction, "quadroons" in Georgia and Louisiana are left vulnerable by relationships not legitimized by law. The repeal of miscegenation laws, according to Child, would create protection for women and promote racial and national reconciliation through newly legal intermarriages. Webb's "quadroon" character Emily Garie is similarly vulnerable because she cannot be legally married to her white husband in Georgia. Unlike the nefarious rakes and careless fathers of other abolitionist fiction, Clarence Garie tries to do the right thing by moving his family to Philadelphia. Even though he and Emily are legally married there, the family still meets a tragic end, demonstrating that emancipation and the repeal of intermarriage bans will not lead to the racial utopia Child envisions. Harper agrees that miscegenation laws and slavery caused the exploitation of enslaved women, but, law or no law, she insists that the right to intermarry is a hollow victory in the violence of the Reconstruction era South. Harper refuses to be distracted by the issue of intermarriage; she knows that the fuss over intermarriage is really "about" political rights, equality, and safety for African Americans. Rather than being the source of national healing that Child had imagined, miscegenation was used as a threat into the twentieth century to promote white supremacy and to deny civil rights to people of color.

EPILOGUE

*Into the Post-*Loving *Era*

> There can be no doubt that restricting the freedom to
> marry solely because of racial classifications violates the
> central meaning of the Equal Protection Clause.
>
> LOVING V. VIRGINIA (1967)

In November 2000, Alabama voters repealed the section of their state constitution that banned "any marriage between a white person and a Negro, or a descendant of a Negro." Alabama was the last state to have a miscegenation law on its books. The law was unenforceable and unconstitutional, according to the 1967 *Loving v. Virginia* decision by the U.S. Supreme Court, and proponents of the repeal initiative called the provision "embarrassing and insulting" and a "shameful relic" of Alabama's racist past. The referendum did not create much public debate beyond a fringe opposition, but the real story may lie with the 40 percent of voters who elected to keep the law.[1] The taboo against interracial marriages remains a flash point for American race relations; it is part of the "hidden history" of American culture that has been over three centuries in the making.[2]

Miscegenation laws have always had implications beyond their regulation of interracial marriage, playing a significant role in landmark cases involving race and civil rights. The infamous *Dred Scott* decision of 1857, for example, offered this legislation as evidence that the founders did not intend African Americans to become citizens. After the Civil War, the Supreme Court in *Pace v. Alabama* (1883) upheld miscegenation laws by accepting the "equal application" theory that these laws did not violate the equal protection clause of the Fourteenth Amendment because they punished black and white transgressors equally.[3] As Eva Saks writes, "*Pace* was

171

both a rehearsal and an important symbolic antecedent for the 'separate but equal' rhetoric of the United States Supreme Court's decision upholding the constitutionality of segregated passenger trains, *Plessy v. Ferguson* (1896)."[4]

The *Pace* decision would not be challenged until the milestone case *Perez v. Lippold* (1948), in which the California Supreme Court struck down the state's miscegenation law, the first time a state court had done so since Reconstruction.[5] Soon after the *Perez* case, intermarriage bans played a role in the cases collectively known as *Brown v. Board of Education of Topeka* (1954). In the Virginia portion of the case, lawyers for the state repeatedly raised the question whether desegregation also would lead to the repeal of laws against intermarriage. The Supreme Court rejected the narrative of race lurking beneath "separate but equal"—the pernicious notion that in fact the races were not equal—and ruled that "separate educational facilities are inherently unequal" and in violation of the equal protection clause.[6] As Richard Kluger notes, despite the limited language of *Brown*, the case "had in effect wiped out all forms of state-sanctioned segregation" as the Court broadened the premise of *Brown* to apply to a wide range of situations.[7] In the wave of civil rights decisions handed down by the Warren Court in the 1950s and 1960s, the Court ruled in *Loving v. Virginia* (1967) that miscegenation laws were unconstitutional, striking down the "last major category of legally enforced discrimination based solely on race."[8]

Ironically, at the same time that the black civil rights movement succeeded in removing discriminatory laws based on race, new federal programs aimed at assisting Indians made blood quantum an increasingly important issue. "Once the 1960s began to see federal programs and policies directed at rectifying some of the wrongs," Patricia Penn Hilden explains, "blood quantum reemerged as an essential factor in most federal guideline definitions of Indianness."[9] Dating back to the passage of the General Allotment Act, or Dawes Act (1887), "blood quantum" is meant to measure an individual's "degree of Indian blood." Unlike African Americans, who have been assigned their racial identity through a "one-drop rule," Indians are said to lose their "authentic Indianness" as their Indian blood quantum decreases.[10] This alleged "genetic distance" from their "full-blood" ancestors continues to increase, according to demographic figures. As Fergus M. Bordewich reports, "In 1970, more than 33 percent of all Indians were married to non-Indians; a decade later, the number had grown to 50 percent, and it has continued to climb." In light of these statistics, Bordewich insists that "the principle, or the pretense, that blood should be a central defining fact of being Indian will soon become untenable."[11]

Many Indian activists and writers challenge the federal blood quantum criteria as an attack on Indian sovereignty. In response to a calculus of blood that promises the "vanishing" of Indians with each generation, N. Scott Momaday offers the trope of memory in the blood, or blood memory, which blurs "distinctions between racial identity and narrative." Through blood memory, as Chadwick Allen explains, Indian authenticity is measured not by blood quantum but by a process of cultural memory and storytelling. Contemporary writers such as Leslie Marmon Silko, James Welch, Joy Harjo, Linda Hogan, and Gerald Vizenor explore this trope as well. For Indian writers, intermarriage need not lead to cultural erasure as measured by government formulas; the power of blood memory asserts true Indian identity.[12]

The disruptive narrative of interracial marriage continues into the present day. As in the nineteenth century, the taboo against intermarriage and the obsession with racial identity are linked to the struggle for resources and power. These questions are reenacted in current controversies over affirmative action, interracial adoption, census categories, voting districts, and Indian sovereignty. What has changed, as we saw in the 2000 Alabama ballot question, is that resistance to interracial marriage has been internalized; it remains strong even though such opposition is no longer as acceptable in public discourse.

The changes in legal codes have not led to substantial changes in private codes: nationwide, intermarriage in the post-*Loving* era remains relatively rare, even as the last racial barriers continue to fall. Even interracial dating remains somewhat controversial. In 2002, Taylor County High School in Georgia made headlines when students organized its first integrated prom. Since desegregation thirty-one years earlier, the high school, like many Southern schools, had stopped sponsoring dances. In their place, parents and students had organized separate proms for black and white students. But despite the students' enthusiasm for the new unified prom, there were no interracial couples, and students quoted in the media coverage emphasized that the issue was school unity rather than interracial dating. The following year, some students elected to return to the "whites only" prom format.[13]

The taboo against interracial marriage has denied the family ties that have been part of the American experience from the very beginning. As the face of America continues to change, the question remains whether historical knowledge and cultural critique can help to reverse centuries of fear and prejudice so that we may see ourselves as one nation made "of one blood."

NOTES

Introduction

1. See chapter 4 of this text for a full treatment of the Allen-King marriage. William G. Allen, *The American Prejudice Against Color. An Authentic Narrative, Showing How Easily the Nation Got into an Uproar. By William G. Allen, A Refugee from American Despotism* (1853; reprint, New York: Arno Press and New York Times, 1969), 1, 86, 89.

2. Cheryl I. Harris, "Whiteness as Property," in *Critical Race Theory: The Key Writings That Formed the Movement*, ed. Kimberlé Crenshaw et al. (New York: New Press, 1995), 277.

3. My work has benefited from the insights of critical race theory, a development in legal studies that, as Cornel West explains, confronts "the historical centrality and complicity of law in upholding white supremacy." Cornel West, foreword to Crenshaw et al., *Critical Race Theory*, xi.

4. Several literary histories provide a valuable introduction to the body of "miscegenation fiction," tracing the tradition from its late-eighteenth-century roots into the twentieth century. James Kinney, in *Amalgamation! Race, Sex, and Rhetoric in the Nineteenth-Century American Novel* (Westport, Conn.: Greenwood Press, 1985), assembles a catalog of sixty miscegenation novels, and Werner Sollors, in *Neither Black nor White yet Both: Thematic Explorations of Interracial Literature* (New York: Oxford University Press, 1997), discusses themes in black-white miscegenation fiction in a sweep of world literature. Other scholars, such as Judith R. Berzon (*Neither White nor Black: The Mulatto Character in American Fiction* [New York: New York University Press, 1978]); William J. Scheick (*The Half-Blood: A Cultural Symbol in Nineteenth-Century American Fiction* [Lexington: University Press of Kentucky, 1979]); and Juda Bennett (*The Passing Figure: Racial Confusion in Modern American Literature* [New York: Peter Lang, 1997]), have been concerned with "mixed-blood" characters and their marginal place in American society. Although these studies form an important foundation for my work, they tend to focus on the subgenre as a whole, and the texts of the early national and antebellum periods are treated as precursors for later innovations.

Martha Hodes's *White Women, Black Men: Illicit Sex in the Nineteenth-Century South*

(New Haven: Yale University Press, 1997) provides an important model for writing about the lives of real people; this study adds a Northern perspective to the field. More recently, the collection edited by Werner Sollors, *Interracialism: Black-White Intermarriage in American History, Literature, and Law* (New York: Oxford University Press, 2000), brings together some of the most important scholarship on the topic of black-white marriages, while Monika Kaup and Debra Rosenthal's collection *Mixing Race, Mixing Culture: Inter-American Literary Dialogues* (Austin: University of Texas Press, 2002) challenges us to think beyond national borders about the theme of miscegenation in New World literature. Randall Kennedy's *Interracial Intimacies: Sex, Marriage, Identity, and Adoption* (New York: Pantheon Books, 2003) is a useful introduction to this topic. My emphasis on reformers also complements and extends the scope of previous scholarship. For example, Elise Lemire, in *"Miscegenation": Making Race in America* (Philadelphia: University of Pennsylvania Press, 2002), explores antebellum literary works that demonize sex between blacks and whites; in contrast, I am interested in texts that counter this dominant discourse and seek to imagine alternatives.

5. David Carr, *Time, Narrative, and History* (Bloomington: Indiana University Press, 1986), 61.

6. Tzvetan Todorov, *Genres in Discourse* (New York: Cambridge University Press, 1990), 29.

7. Barry R. Schaller, *A Vision of American Law: Judging Law, Literature, and the Stories We Tell* (Westport, Conn.: Praeger, 1997), 31.

8. My work builds on the insights of Law and Literature studies. One common position among legal scholars is that literature can provide the emotional content, the "story" behind the dry logic of the law, making empathy and justice more possible. See, for example, Martha Nussbaum, *Poetic Justice: The Literary Imagination and Public Life* (Boston: Beacon Press, 1995); Schaller, *Vision of American Law*; and Marisa Anne Pagnattaro, *In Defiance of the Law: From Anne Hutchinson to Toni Morrison* (New York: Peter Lang, 2001). While I agree with this position to some extent, I do not agree with the sharp lines these scholars draw between genres. Narrative is not a literary "extra" that can help us understand the law better. It is rooted in our very experience; the law itself is a story of what we as a society fear and what we hope for. These scholars argue that we can understand the law better by adding thoughtful consideration of literary genres and that these disparate genres can give us valuable perspectives. I would counter that the genres of law and literature are not so different after all and that the best interpretive strategy is to recognize these important commonalities, these shared narrative traits. Laura Hanft Korobkin's approach seems more useful here: "How do culturally powerful stories and strategies circulate from literary to litigative sites and back again?" See her *Criminal Conversations: Sentimentality and Nineteenth-Century Legal Stories of Adultery* (New York: Columbia University Press, 1998), 14.

9. Nussbaum, *Poetic Justice*, xviii.

10. Sollors, *Neither Black nor White*, 3.

11. Peggy Pascoe, "Miscegenation Law, Court Cases, and Ideologies of 'Race' in Twentieth-Century America," *Journal of American History* 83, no. 1 (June 1996): 48 n. 11. See Hodes, *White Women, Black Men*, 9, and Elise Lemire, "Making Miscegenation: Discourses of Interracial Sex and Marriage in the United States, 1790–1865" (Ph.D. diss., Rutgers University, 1996), 241, for arguments against using the term.

Chapter One

1. Theda Perdue, intro. to *Cherokee Editor: The Writings of Elias Boudinot* (Knoxville: University of Tennessee Press, 1983), 24. See also Charlotte Hyams Peltier, "The Evolution

of the Criminal Justice System of the Eastern Cherokees, 1580–1838" (Ph.D. diss., Rice University, 1982), 189.

2. *Arkansas Gazette*, October 2, 1839, quoted in Rennard Strickland, *Fire and the Spirits: Cherokee Law from Clan to Court* (Norman: University of Oklahoma Press, 1975), 77 n. 35.

3. Theda Perdue makes a strong case for this argument (*Cherokee Editor*, 10–11). Bernd C. Peyer agrees that Perdue's argument is "very plausible"; see Peyer's chapter on Boudinot in *The Tutor'd Mind: Indian Missionary-Writers in Antebellum America* (Amherst: University of Massachusetts Press, 1997), 182. See also Mary Young, "The Cherokee Nation: Mirror of the Republic," *American Quarterly* 33, no. 5 (Winter 1981): 502–24.

4. Donald Philip Corr, "'The Field Is the World': Proclaiming, Translating, and Serving by the American Board of Commissioners for Foreign Missions, 1810–40" (Ph.D. diss., Fuller Theological Seminary, 1993), 3.

5. William G. McLoughlin, *Cherokees and Missionaries, 1789–1839* (New Haven: Yale University Press, 1984), 102–5. Despite the financial benefits of this close relationship with the federal government, it quickly created a difficult dilemma for the ABCFM missionaries in the field. Their experiences with the Indians often led them to oppose government policy, which they did at the risk of losing government support.

6. Robert F. Berkhofer Jr., *The White Man's Indian: Images of the American Indian from Columbus to the Present* (New York: Knopf, 1978), 150.

7. Joseph Tracy, *History of the American Board of Commissioners for Foreign Missions*, 2d ed. (New York: M. W. Dodd, 1842), 58, 65.

8. Theodore S. Gold, *Historical Records of the Town of Cornwall, Litchfield County, Connecticut* (Hartford: Case, Lockwood, and Brainard, 1877), 29.

9. James W. Parins, *John Rollin Ridge: His Life and Works* (Lincoln: University of Nebraska Press, 1991), 1–9; Thurman Wilkins, *Cherokee Tragedy: The Ridge Family and the Decimation of a People*, rev. 2d ed. (Norman: University of Oklahoma Press, 1986), 97–118.

10. Mary Brinsmade Church, "Elias Boudinot: An Account of His Life Written by His Granddaughter," Town History Papers of the Woman's Club of Washington, Connecticut, October 1, 1913, Cornwall Historical Society no. 346, Cornwall, Conn.

11. Perdue, *Cherokee Editor*, 6.

12. Parins, *John Rollin Ridge*, 9.

13. Susannah Watie to Elias Boudinot, January 1821, quoted in Jedidiah Morse, *A Report to the Secretary of War of the United States on Indian Affairs, Comprising a Narrative of a Tour Performed in the Summer of 1820* (New Haven: S. Converse, 1822), 272.

14. Wilkins, *Cherokee Tragedy*, 122.

15. Parins, *John Rollin Ridge*, 10–11.

16. Ellen K. Rothman, *Hands and Hearts: A History of Courtship in America* (New York: Basic Books, 1984), 22–23; Cathy Davidson, *Revolution and the Word: The Rise of the Novel in America* (New York: Oxford University Press, 1986), 113.

17. Wilkins, *Cherokee Tragedy*, 131–33.

18. Ibid., 146.

19. Edward C. Starr, *A History of Cornwall, Connecticut: A Typical New England Town* (New Haven: Tuttle, Morehouse, Taylor, 1926), 143.

20. Wilkins, *Cherokee Tragedy*, 146–47.

21. *American Eagle* (Litchfield, Conn.), March 22, 1824, quoted in Ralph Henry Gabriel, *Elias Boudinot, Cherokee, and His America* (Norman: University of Oklahoma Press, 1941), 62–63.

22. *Quarterly Report of the Foreign Mission School in Cornwall, Conn.*, March 1, 1824, no. 16, 2–3.

23. "Marriage at Cornwall," *Religious Intelligencer*, April 10, 1824, 714–15.

24. "Marriage of John Ridge," *Boston Recorder*, March 27, 1824, 55.

25. "The Foreign Mission School," *Religious Intelligencer*, January 22, 1825, 539.

26. Starr, *History of Cornwall*, 148.

27. Gabriel, *Elias Boudinot*, 64–65.

28. Peyer, *The Tutor'd Mind*, 180.

29. Church, "Elias Boudinot," 3, 10.

30. Mary Gold Brinsmade to Rev. Herman Vaill, July 14, 1825, Herman Landon Vaill Collection, Manuscripts and Archives, Yale University Library.

31. Gabriel, *Elias Boudinot*, 66–72.

32. Stephen Gold to Rev. Vaill, June 11, 1825, Vaill Collection.

33. Gabriel, *Elias Boudinot*, 76–77.

34. Harriet Gold to Rev. and Flora Vaill, June 25, 1825, Vaill Collection.

35. *Niles' Weekly Register*, July 9, 1825, 298; Frank Luther Mott, *American Journalism, a History: 1690–1960*, 3d ed. (New York: Macmillan, 1962), 188.

36. "Miscellany," *Boston Recorder*, August 19, 1825, 140.

37. "Indian Improvement," *Religious Intelligencer*, August 20, 1825, 188.

38. Morse, *Report to the Secretary of War*, 73–75.

39. Harriet Gold to Rev. and Flora Vaill, June 25, 1825, Vaill Collection.

40. Ibid.

41. Starr, *History of Cornwall*, 139–40.

42. General Daniel Bourbon Brinsmade to Rev. Vaill, July 14, 1825, Vaill Collection.

43. Stephen Gold to Rev. Vaill, June 11, 1825, Vaill Collection.

44. Gen. Brinsmade to Rev. Vaill, June 29, 1825, Vaill Collection.

45. Gen. Brinsmade to Rev. Vaill, July 14, 1825, Vaill Collection.

46. Rev. Cornelius B. Everest to Stephen Gold, July 2, 1825, Cornwall Historical Society, Cornwall, Conn. Publication of material on the Foreign Mission School is by permission of the Cornwall Historical Society.

47. Rev. Vaill to Harriet Gold, June 29, 1825, Vaill Collection.

48. Mary Gold Brinsmade to Rev. Vaill, July 14, 1825, Vaill Collection.

49. Catherine Gold to Rev. and Flora Vaill, July 30, 1825, Vaill Collection.

50. Undated letter quoted in Gabriel, *Elias Boudinot*, 86–87; Rev. Everest to Rev. Vaill, August 10, 1825, Vaill Collection.

51. Rev. Everest to Stephen Gold, July 2, 1825, Cornwall Historical Society.

52. Rev. Vaill to Harriet Gold, June 29, 1825, Vaill Collection.

53. Catherine Gold to Rev. and Flora Vaill, July [?] 1825, Vaill Collection.

54. Rev. Vaill to Mary Gold Brinsmade, August 2, 1825, Vaill Collection.

55. Lucia McMahon, " 'While Our Souls Together Blend': Narrating a Romantic Readership in the Early Republic," in *An Emotional History of the United States*, ed. Peter N. Stearns and Jan Lewis (New York: New York University Press, 1998), 67.

56. Mary Gold Brinsmade to Rev. Vaill, July 14, 1825, Vaill Collection.

57. Gen. Brinsmade to Rev. Vaill, July 14, 1825, Vaill Collection.

58. Catherine Gold to Rev. and Flora Vaill, July [?] 1825, Vaill Collection.

59. Catherine Gold to Rev. and Flora Vaill, July 30, 1825, Vaill Collection.

60. Flora Gold Vaill to Rev. Vaill, September 19, 1825, Vaill Collection.

61. Abby Gold Everest to Rev. and Flora Vaill, September 5, 1825, Vaill Collection.

62. Rev. Everest to Rev. Vaill, September 14, 1825, Vaill Collection.

63. Marginal note from Harriet Gold in Flora Gold Vaill to Rev. Vaill, September 19, 1825, Vaill Collection.

64. Mary Gold Brinsmade to Rev. Vaill, July 14, 1825, Vaill Collection.

65. Gabriel, *Elias Boudinot*, 77–85.

66. Col. Benjamin Gold to Rev. Vaill, September 1, 1825, Vaill Collection.

67. Catherine Gold to Rev. and Flora Vaill, July 30, 1825, Vaill Collection.

68. Rev. Vaill to Col. Gold, September 5, 1825, Cornwall Historical Society.

69. Gen. Brinsmade to Rev. Vaill, July 14, 1825, Vaill Collection.

70. Church, "Elias Boudinot," 12; Gabriel, *Elias Boudinot*, 89–90.

71. Rev. Vaill to Harriet Gold, March 5, 1826, Vaill Collection.

72. Harriet Gold to Rev. and Flora Vaill, January 2, 1826, Vaill Collection.

73. Rev. Samuel Worcester to Jeremiah Evarts, October 24, 1825, in Papers of the American Board of Commissioners for Foreign Missions (hereafter ABCFM), 18.3.1, 5:227, Houghton Library, Harvard University (microfilm). Publication of material from the Papers of the ABCFM is by permission of the Houghton Library, Harvard University. Worcester later worked on Cherokee translations with Elias Boudinot and went to jail for his resistance to Cherokee removal. See McLoughlin, *Cherokees and Missionaries*, 239–65.

74. McLoughlin, *Cherokees and Missionaries*, 136–37.

75. Rev. Daniel S. Butrick to Jeremiah Evarts, October 12, 1824, ABCFM, 18.3.1, 4:2.

76. Butrick to Evarts, November 21, 1824, ABCFM, 18.3.1, 4:5.

77. Butrick to ?, September 29, 1825, ABCFM, 18.3.1, 4:18.

78. William Chamberlain to Evarts, journal, May–November 1825, ABCFM, 18.3.1, 4:43.

79. David Brown to Evarts, September 29, 1825, ABCFM, 18.3.1, 5:289.

80. McLoughlin, *Cherokees and Missionaries*, 188.

81. John Ridge, letter to editor, *Christian Herald*, December 20, 1823; quoted in Peyer, *The Tutor'd Mind*, 182.

82. Ridge to Elizur Butler, July 7, 1826, ABCFM, 18.3.1, 4:69.

83. Elias Boudinot, "An Address to the Whites, Delivered in the First Presbyterian Church, on the 26th of May, 1826, by Elias Boudinott, A Cherokee Indian" (Philadelphia: William F. Geddes, 1826); reprinted in Perdue, *Cherokee Editor*, 69; Elias Boudinot to Rev. Vaill, November 21, 1827, Vaill Collection.

84. Boudinot to Rev. Vaill, January 23, 1829, Vaill Collection.

85. Perdue, *Cherokee Editor*, 10. Wilkins and Peyer also support Perdue's argument.

86. Wilkins, *Cherokee Tragedy*, 147.

87. Perdue, *Cherokee Editor*, 10.

88. Parins, *John Rollin Ridge*, 12.

89. Chamberlain to Evarts, July 30, 1824, ABCFM, 18.3.1, 4:37.

90. "Speech of John Ridge, A Cherokee Chief," *Liberator*, March 17, 1832, 44.

91. Peyer, *The Tutor'd Mind*, 183; Worcester to R. Anderson, December 22, 1825, ABCFM, 18.3.1, 5:229.

92. There is some discrepancy among the various sources about the exact wedding date. Wilkins and Gabriel say the wedding took place on March 28, but I agree with John Andrew, who dates the wedding May 1. On April 29 Flora Gold Vaill wrote to her husband that Boudinot was expected to arrive in Cornwall the next day, with the ceremony planned for May 1. Flora Gold Vaill to Rev. Vaill, April 29, 1826, Vaill Collection.

93. Church, "Elias Boudinot," 12.

94. Wilkins, *Cherokee Tragedy*, 193–95. The exact chronology of Boudinot's tour is not clear. We do know that he also spoke in Salem, Boston, and Philadelphia. For coverage of his appearances in Charleston and New York, see *New York Observer*, February 25, 1826, 31; March 4, 1826, 35; March 25, 1826, 46.

95. An intriguing footnote to the Boudinot scandal: by 1831 Boudinot's sister Nancy Watie was married to John Wheeler, the white printer of the *Cherokee Phoenix*. Wheeler joined Samuel Worcester and Elizur Butler in testing the Georgia requirement that whites in the Cherokee Nation sign an oath of allegiance to the state or leave. He was arrested and sentenced to four years' hard labor; Wheeler then took the oath and was released. He emigrated to the Cherokee Nation West (Arkansas) in 1834. See Daniel F. Littlefield Jr. and

James W. Parins, *American Indian and Alaska Native Newspapers and Periodicals, 1826–1924* (Westport, Conn.: Greenwood Press, 1984), 89.

96. Evarts to Rev. Timothy Stone, August 26, 1825, ABCFM, 1.01, 5:359–61; quoted in John Andrew, "Educating the Heathen: The Foreign Mission School Controversy and American Ideals," *Journal of American Studies* 12, no. 3 (1978): 338.

97. Andrew, "Educating the Heathen," 340.

98. Tracy, *History of the American Board*, 125.

99. *Report of the American Board of Commissioners for Foreign Missions* (Boston: Crocker and Brewster, 1825), 95.

100. Ibid. (1826), 103.

101. Ibid. 104.

102. Ibid. 106.

103. Andrew, "Educating the Heathen," 341.

104. Genevieve McCoy, "Sanctifying the Self and Saving the Savage: The Failure of the ABCFM Oregon Mission and the Conflicted Language of Calvinism" (Ph.D. diss., University of Washington, 1991), 5. McCoy also notes that the ABCFM believed that an Oregon mission would escape the pressures of competition for land being felt by the southeastern tribes. The mission came to a violent end during a measles epidemic; fearing that they were being deliberately infected in order to make room for the whites, the Indians killed the missionaries Marcus and Narcissa Whitman.

105. Gold, *Historical Records*, 29.

106. Ibid., 85.

107. Starr, *History of Cornwall*, 137.

108. Edwin W. Small and Miriam R. Small, "Prudence Crandall: Champion of Negro Education," *New England Quarterly* 17 (December 1944): 513–17.

109. Andrew, "Educating the Heathen," 337.

110. Starr, *History of Cornwall*, 147.

111. Wilkins, *Cherokee Tragedy*, 99.

Chapter Two

An earlier version of this chapter was published in *Legal Studies Forum* 23, no. 1–2 (1999): 37–70. Reprinted by permission of the publisher.

1. Elise Virginia Lemire posits this relationship as well as a connection between notions of race and the miscegenation taboo in "Making Miscegenation: Discourses of Interracial Sex and Marriage in the United States, 1790–1865" (Ph.D. diss., Rutgers University, 1996). Unlike Lemire, I am most interested in *pro*-intermarriage discourses.

2. Rachel F. Moran, *Interracial Intimacy: The Regulation of Race and Romance* (Chicago: University of Chicago Press, 2001), 5.

3. David Brion Davis, "Constructing Race: A Reflection," *William and Mary Quarterly* 54, no. 1 (January 1997): 7. See also Audrey Smedley, *Race in North America: Origin and Evolution of a Worldview* (Boulder: Westview Press, 1993), 15–16. For a discussion of the contrast between early modern and modern usages of race, see Karen Ordahl Kupperman, "Presentment of Civility: English Reading of American Self-Presentation in the Early Years of Colonization," and Joyce E. Chaplin, "Natural Philosophy and an Early Racial Idiom in North America: Comparing English and Indian Bodies," *William and Mary Quarterly* 54, no. 1 (January 1997): 193–95 and 229–31.

4. See Henry Kamen, *The Spanish Inquisition: An Historical Revision* (London: Weidenfield and Nicolson, 1997), esp. chap. 11, "Racialism and Its Critics." See also Smedley, *Race in North America*, 66–69.

5. David Sanders, *Lost Tribes and Promised Lands: The Origins of American Racism* (New York: HarperPerennial, 1992), 65–73.

6. Kamen, *The Spanish Inquisition*, 231.

7. Smedley, *Race in North America*, 62–63.

8. Charles M. Segal and David C. Stineback, *Puritans, Indians, and Manifest Destiny* (New York: G. P. Putnam's Sons, 1977), 33.

9. Ann Taves, "Sexuality in American Religious History," in *Retelling U.S. Religious History*, ed. Thomas A. Tweed (Berkeley: University of California Press, 1997), 36, quoting Roger Williams, *A Key into the Language*.

10. Hannah Franziska Augstein, intro. to *Race: The Origins of an Idea, 1760–1850* (Bristol: Thoemmes Press, 1996), xi.

11. Reginald Horsman, *Race and Manifest Destiny: The Origins of American Anglo-Saxonism* (Cambridge: Harvard University Press, 1981), 98–99. See also Augstein, *Race*, xi–xviii; Bernard W. Sheehan, *Seeds of Extinction: Jeffersonian Philanthropy and the American Indian* (Chapel Hill: University of North Carolina Press, 1973), 15–44; Winthrop D. Jordan, *White Over Black: American Attitudes toward the Negro, 1550–1812* (Chapel Hill: University of North Carolina Press, 1968), 287–94.

12. Horsman, *Race and Manifest Destiny*, 115.

13. Lemire, "Making Miscegenation," 15.

14. Augstein, *Race*, x.

15. Horsman, *Race and Manifest Destiny*, 2, 62–65.

16. Robert J. C. Young, *Colonial Desire: Hybridity in Theory, Culture, and Race* (New York: Routledge, 1995), 16–17.

17. Horsman, *Race and Manifest Destiny*, 2. Crèvecoeur, in his famous *Letters from an American Farmer*, writes that the American is a mixture of nations, but he makes it clear that this mixture is European: "What then is the American, this new man? He is either a European or the descendant of a European, hence that strange mixture of blood, which you will find in no other country. . . . Here individuals of all nations are melted into a new race whose labors and posterity will one day cause great changes in the world" (Letter III, "What is an American?").

18. Lemire, "Making Miscegenation," 15.

19. R. F. Foster, *Modern Ireland, 1600–1972* (London: Penguin, 1989), 32. Nicholas P. Canny, *The Elizabethan Conquest of Ireland: A Pattern Established, 1565–76* (New York: Barnes and Noble Books, 1976), 161. See also Smedley, *Race*, 52–62, 85–88.

20. Foster, *Modern Ireland*, 25.

21. Nicholas P. Canny, *Kingdom and Colony: Ireland in the Atlantic World, 1560–1800* (Baltimore: Johns Hopkins University Press, 1988), 41; Edmund Curtis and R. B. McDowell, intro. to *Irish Historical Documents, 1172–1922* (London: Methuen, 1943), 10–12; Foster, *Modern Ireland*, 12.

22. *Irish Historical Documents*, 53. "Gossipred," according to the *OED*, means "the relationship of gossips" and "spiritual affinity," with particular reference to Irish customs.

23. Smedley, *Race*, 53.

24. Canny, *Kingdom and Colony*, 41.

25. David D. Smits, "'We are not to grow wild': Seventeenth-Century New England's Repudiation of Anglo-Indian Intermarriage," *American Indian Culture and Research Journal* 11, no. 4 (1987): 6–7. Canny reminds us of the limits of the Irish-Indian analogy, however, noting "that whatever the analogies drawn between the Irish and the American Indians, the reality was that English and Scots settlers of the seventeenth century encountered little difficulty in living in close proximity to the Irish" (*Kingdom and Colony*, 66).

26. Foster, *Modern Ireland*, 32–34; Canny, *The Elizabethan Conquest*, 125, 160.

27. See Sydney E. Ahlstrom, *A Religious History of the American People* (New Haven: Yale University Press, 1972), 129: "[Puritans] found much specific guidance in the Scriptures, very often in the Old Testament, for the ordering of personal life, the regulation of society, and the structuring of the Church." Sacvan Bercovitch, *Typology and Early American Liter-*

ature (Amherst: University of Massachusetts Press, 1972), is an important source. See also Werner Sollors, *Beyond Ethnicity: Consent and Descent in American Culture* (New York: Oxford University Press, 1986), 40–65.

28. Lloyd E. Berry, intro. to *The Geneva Bible: A Facsimile of the 1560 Edition* (Madison: University of Wisconsin Press, 1969), 22; P. Marion Simms, *The Bible in America* (New York: Wilson-Erickson, 1936), 90.

29. Thomas M. Davis, "The Traditions of Puritan Typology," in Bercovitch, *Typology and Early American Literature*, 44–45.

30. Jill Lepore, *The Name of War: King Philip's War and the Origins of American Identity* (New York: Alfred A. Knopf, 1998), 5–6.

31. Raymond E. Brown et al., eds., *The Jerome Biblical Commentary* (Englewood Cliffs, N.J.: Prentice-Hall, 1968), 65 (hereafter *JBC*).

32. G. E. Thomas, "Puritans, Indians, and the Concept of Race," *New England Quarterly* 48 (March 1975): 7. All biblical citations in this discussion are from the Geneva Bible.

33. William Bradford, *Of Plymouth Plantation, 1620–1647*, ed. Samuel Eliot Morison (New York: Alfred A. Knopf, 1966), 25.

34. *JBC,* 554.

35. Bradford, *Of Plymouth Plantation*, 205.

36. *JBC*, 340–41.

37. *JBC*, 433.

38. John J. O'Rourke, in the *JBC*, cautions that Paul is not directly referring to inter-marriage here, but the rest of O'Rourke's analysis makes it difficult to avoid such an interpretation: "By his acceptance of the gospel, the Christian is of a different species, so to speak, from the unbeliever; the believer cannot live like the one without faith. Contact with unbelievers is necessary, but a sharing of their way of life is impossible" (*JBC*, 282).

39. This is the argument that the Reverend Daniel Butrick and other supporters of the Boudinot-Gold marriage made: they were suitable partners because they were both Christians. See Butrick to ?, September 29, 1825, ABCFM 18.3.1, 4:18.

40. See, for example, Gal. 3:28, 1 Cor. 12:13, Col. 3:11, Eph. 6:5–9.

41. Kamen, *The Spanish Inquisition*, 34.

42. Thomas, "Puritans, Indians," 27.

43. The treatment and religious status of the Indians was further complicated by the popular theory that the Indians were part of the Ten Lost Tribes of Israel. What would it mean for the new chosen people to encounter the original chosen people? If the Indians were actually long-lost descendants of the Jews, then they deserved an exalted place in society, and their conversion to Christianity would be a sign of the millennium. See Segal and Stinebeck, *Puritans, Indians, and Manifest Destiny*, 143; and Sanders, *Lost Tribes*, 14–15, 363–76. This fascination with Indians-as-Jews lasted well into the nineteenth century. Elias Boudinot, whose name the Cherokee Indian Buck Watie adopted on enrolling in the Cornwall Foreign Mission School, wrote a three hundred–page book, drawing connections between Indian and ancient Jewish language and customs. See Elias Boudinot, *A Star in the West; or, a Humble Attempt to Discover the Long Lost Ten Tribes of Israel, Preparatory to Their Return to Their Beloved City, Jerusalem* (Trenton: D. Fenton, 1816).

44. Smits, "We are not to grow wild," 24–25, 25 n. 1; Gary Nash, *Red, White, and Black: The Peoples of Early America* (Englewood Cliffs, N.J.: Prentice-Hall, 1974), 279; David Fowler, "Northern Attitudes toward Interracial Marriage: A Study of Legislation and Public Opinion in the Middle Atlantic States and the States of the Old Northwest" (Ph.D. diss., Yale University, 1963), 26–28.

45. John Rolfe to Sir Thomas Dale, quoted in Robert S. Tilton, *Pocahontas: The Evolution of an American Narrative* (New York: Cambridge University Press, 1994), 14.

46. David D. Smits, "'Abominable Mixture': Toward the Repudiation of Anglo-Indian

Intermarriage in Seventeenth-Century Virginia," *Virginia Magazine of History and Biography* 95, no. 2 (April 1987): 166–67, 173–75, 184. It is important to note that Powhatan had a change of heart regarding intermarriages; he later refused a proposal for his youngest daughter from Governor Thomas Dale.

47. Ibid., 191–92.

48. Kathleen M. Brown, *Good Wives, Nasty Wenches, and Anxious Patriarchs: Gender, Race, and Power in Colonial Virginia* (Chapel Hill: University of North Carolina Press, 1996), 2.

49. Richard S. Dunn, *Sugar and Slaves: The Rise of the Planter Class in the English West Indies, 1624–1713* (Chapel Hill: University of North Carolina Press, 1972), 228, 253.

50. Virginia Bernhard, "Beyond the Chesapeake: The Contrasting Status of Blacks in Bermuda, 1616–63," *Journal of Southern History* 54, no. 4 (November 1988): 562–63.

51. To cite two of the most notorious examples, in 1290 Edward I expelled non-converted Jews from England, two hundred years before the Spanish expulsion of the Jews. Queen Elizabeth I attempted to expel "Negroes" and "Moors" from England in 1601. See Sanders, *Lost Tribes*, 25; Douglas A. Lorimer, *Colour, Class, and the Victorians: English Attitudes to the Negro in the Mid-Nineteenth Century* (Leicester: Leicester University Press, 1978), 21–22; S.E. Ogude, "Literature and Racism: The Example of *Othello*," in *Othello: New Essays by Black Writers*, ed. Mythili Kaul (Washington, D.C.: Howard University Press, 1987), 154.

52. Fowler, "Northern Attitudes toward Interracial Marriage," 31, 45, 57, 79, A96.

53. Ibid., A96, A97.

54. Byron Curti Martyn, "Racism in the United States: A History of the Anti-Miscegenation Legislation and Litigation" (Ph.D. diss., University of Southern California, 1979), 111–12.

55. Fowler, "Northern Attitudes toward Interracial Marriage," 50–52; Martyn, "Racism in the United States," 121.

56. Smedley, *Race in North America*, 201.

57. Lemire, "Making Miscegenation," 15.

58. Chaplin, "Natural Philosophy," 252.

59. Tilton, *Pocahontas*, 24.

60. Sheehan, *Seeds of Extinction*, 4.

61. Thomas Jefferson to Colonel Benjamin Hawkins, February 18, 1803, in *The Writings of Thomas Jefferson*, ed. Andrew A. Lipscomb and Albert Ellery Berg (Washington, D.C.: Thomas Jefferson Memorial Association, 1903–4), 10:363.

62. Thomas Jefferson to Captain Hendrick, the Delawares, Mohiccons, and Munries, n.d., in *The Complete Jefferson*, ed. Saul K. Padover (New York: Tudor, 1943), 503. See also Jefferson to the Chiefs of the Wyandots, Ottawas, Chippewas, Powtewatamies, and Shawanese, January 10, 1809, in *Complete Jefferson*, 509.

63. Jordan, *White Over Black*, 477.

64. Tilton, *Pocahontas*, 24–25.

65. William Wirt, *Life and Character of Patrick Henry* (Philadelphia: Porter and Coates, 1818?), 258. Wirt was a champion of Indian rights; he represented the Cherokees in the landmark cases *Cherokee Nation v. Georgia* and (1831) and *Worcester v. Georgia* (1832).

66. Wirt, *Life and Character of Patrick Henry*, 259.

67. Fowler, "Northern Attitudes toward Interracial Marriage," A97.

68. During the controversy over the Ridge-Northrup marriage at Cornwall, the ABCFM missionaries referred to Crawford's support of Indian-white marriage several years earlier. See Rev. Daniel S. Butrick to Jeremiah Evarts, November 21, 1824, ABCFM 18.3.1, 4:5, and Rev. William Chamberlain to Jeremiah Evarts, August 24, 1825, ibid., 4:43.

69. *American State Papers: Indian Affairs*, (Washington, D.C.: Gales and Seaton, 1834), 2:26–28.

70. *Strictures Addressed to James Madison on the Celebrated Report of William H. Crawford, Recommending the Intermarriage of Americans with the Indian Tribes* (Philadelphia: Jesper Harding, 1824), 5–6.

71. Ibid., iii–iv. The election of 1824 was a four-way race among members of the Democratic-Republican Party: Crawford, John Quincy Adams, Andrew Jackson, and Henry Clay. Crawford's unlikely prospects were further diminished when he suffered a paralyzing stroke; he finished third in the race. Although Jackson won the popular and electoral vote, no candidate received a majority, and so the election was decided by the members of the House of Representatives, who elected Adams president. See Robert V. Remini, *The Life of Andrew Jackson* (New York: Harper and Row, 1988), 150–56.

72. *Niles' Weekly Register,* July 9, 1825, 298.

73. Sheehan, *Seeds of Extinction,* 7.

74. Ibid., 177–80.

75. Martyn, "Racism in the United States," 131–132.

76. *Acts and Resolves, Public and Private, of the Province of Massachusetts Bay, 1692–1780,* 21 vols. (Boston: Wright and Potter, 1869–1922), 1:578; Fowler, "Northern Attitudes toward Interracial Marriage," 50–52.

77. Samuel Sewall, *The Diary of Samuel Sewall, 1674–1729,* ed. M. Halsey Thomas, 2 vols. (New York: Farrar, Straus, and Giroux, 1973), 1:532; Martyn, "Racism in the United States," 124.

78. *Acts and Laws of the Commonwealth of Massachusetts,* chap. 3, sec. 7, 10 (1786–87); Martyn, "Racism in the United States," 223.

79. Daniel R. Mandell, "Shifting Boundaries of Race and Ethnicity: Indian-Black Intermarriage in Southern New England, 1760–1880," *Journal of American History* 85, no. 2 (September 1998): 466.

80. Fowler, "Northern Attitudes toward Interracial Marriage," 107; Carter G. Woodson, "Relations of Negroes and Indians in Massachusetts," *Journal of Negro History* 5 (1920): 45–62.

81. William Apess, *The Experiences of Five Christian Indians of the Pequot Tribe,* in *On Our Own Ground: The Complete Writings of William Apess, a Pequot,* ed. Barry O'Connell (Amherst: University of Massachusetts Press, 1992), 159.

82. See my discussion of the repeal campaign in chapter 6.

83. *The Public Laws of the States of Rhode Island and Providence Plantations, 1798* (Providence: Carter and Wilkinson, 1798), 481–86.

84. Fowler, "Northern Attitudes toward Interracial Marriage," 108.

85. Ruth Wallis Herndon and Ella Wilcox Sekatau, "The Right to a Name: The Narragansett People and Rhode Island Officials in the Revolutionary Era," in *After King Philip's War: Presence and Persistence in Indian New England,* ed. Colin G. Calloway (Hanover: University Press of New England, 1997), 125–26, 143 n. 96.

86. *Maine Laws,* chap. 70, sec. 2 (1821), quoted in Martyn, "Racism in the United States," 322; Fowler, "Northern Attitudes toward Interracial Marriage," 109.

87. Fergus M. Bordewich, *Killing the White Man's Indian: Reinventing Native Americans at the End of the Twentieth Century* (New York: Doubleday, 1996), 73.

88. Maureen Ann Konkle, "Writing the Indian Nation: U.S. Colonialism, Native Intellectuals, and the Struggle over Indian Identity" (Ph.D. diss., University of Minnesota, 1997), 86.

89. Mandell, "Shifting Boundaries," 474–78. Mandell also suggests that African American husbands' access to their Indian wives' land was a matter of controversy. See Daniel R. Mandell, "The Saga of Sarah Muckamugg: Indian and African American Intermarriage in Colonial New England," in *Sex, Love, Race: Crossing Boundaries in North American History,* ed. Martha Hodes (New York: New York University Press, 1999), 72–90.

90. Rennard Strickland, *Fire and the Spirits: Cherokee Law from Clan to Court* (Norman: University of Oklahoma Press, 1975), xiii–xiv, 49.

91. Konkle, *Writing the Indian Nation*, 35.

92. Strickland, *Fire and the Spirits*, 51–52, xi–xii, 18, 207, 65–66. See also Charlotte Hyams Peltier, "The Evolution of the Criminal Justice System of the Eastern Cherokees, 1580–1838" (Ph.D. diss., Rice University, 1982), 186–91; and Mary Young, "The Cherokee Nation: Mirror of the Republic," *American Quarterly* 33, no. 5 (Winter 1981): 502–24.

93. *Laws of the Cherokee Nation: Adopted by the Council at Various Periods* (Tahlequah: Cherokee Advocate Office, 1852), 10 (hereafter *LCN*). In my research I used the original 1852 edition of *LCN*. The reprint edition, vol. 5 of the *Constitutions and Laws of the American Indian Tribes* series (cited below), may be more accessible for researchers.

94. *Constitution and Laws of the Choctaw Nation*, vol. 11 of *Constitutions and Laws of the American Indian Tribes* (1869; reprint, Wilmington, Del.: Scholarly Resources, 1973), 76–77.

95. Letter from David Brown, *Religious Intelligencer*, October 15, 1825, 311.

96. *LCN* (1852), pt. 1, 57.

97. Ibid., pt. 1, 131–32.

98. "Intermarriages," *Cherokee Phoenix*, April 3, 1828, 4.

99. *LCN*, pt. 1, 32, 93.

100. *Constitution and Laws of the Choctaw Nation*, 106.

101. *LCN*, pt. 1, 104–5; *Constitution and Laws of the Cherokee Nation*, vol. 7 of *Constitutions and Laws of the American Indian Tribes* (1875; reprint, Wilmington, Del.: Scholarly Resources, 1973), 221–24; *Compiled Laws of the Cherokee Nation*, vol. 9 of *Constitutions and Laws of the American Indian Tribes* (1881), 274–78; *Constitution and Laws of the Cherokee Nation*, vol. 10 of *Constitutions and Laws of the American Indian Tribes* vol. 10 (1892), 329–34; *Constitution and Laws of the Choctaw Nation*, vol. 12 of *Constitutions and Laws of the American Indian Tribes* (1888), 225–27.

102. *Compiled Laws of the Cherokee Nation*, 274–78.

103. Theda Perdue, *Slavery and the Evolution of Cherokee Society, 1540–1866* (Knoxville: University of Tennessee Press, 1979), 49–50, 57.

104. *LCN*, pt. 1, 38.

105. *Constitution and Laws of the Choctaw Nation*, 12: 206.

106. *LCN*, pt. 1, 120–21.

107. Daniel F. Littlefield Jr., *The Cherokee Freedmen: From Emancipation to Citizenship* (Westport, Conn.: Greenwood Press, 1978), 9; *LCN*, pt. 2, 44, 55, 71.

108. *LCN*, pt. 2, 7, 19.

109. Jack D. Forbes, *Africans and Native Americans: The Language of Race and the Evolution of Red-Black Peoples*, 2d ed. (Urbana: University of Illinois Press, 1993), 199–200.

110. William G. McLoughlin, "Red Indians, Black Slavery, and White Racism: America's Slaveholding Indians," *American Quarterly* 26 (October 1974): 382.

111. Horsman, *Race and Manifest Destiny*, 193.

112. James H. Merrell, "The Racial Education of the Catawba Indians," *Journal of Southern History* 50 (August 1984): 379.

113. Ibid. 382.

114. Colin G. Calloway, "Introduction: Surviving the Dark Ages," in *After King Philip's War: Presence and Persistence in Indian New England*, ed. Colin G. Calloway (Hanover: University Press of New England, 1997), 7.

115. Thomas L. Doughton, "Unseen Neighbors: Native Americans of Central Massachusetts, a People Who Had 'Vanished,' " in Calloway, *After King Philip's War*, 220.

116. Herndon and Sekatau, "Right to a Name," 125–28.

117. Letter from Brown, 311.

118. Perdue, *Slavery and the Evolution of Cherokee Society*, 84–85.

119. Strickland, *Fire and the Spirits*, 99.

120. Peter Wallenstein, "Native Americans Are White, African Americans Are Not: Racial Identity, Marriage, Inheritance, and the Law in Oklahoma, 1907–1967," *Journal of the West* 39, no. 1 (January 2000): 57. See also chap. 5, "The Sexual Color-Line in Red and Black: Antimiscegenation and the Sooner State," in Charles F. Robinson II, "The Antimiscegenated Conversation: Love's Legislated Limits (1868–1967)" (Ph.D. diss., University of Houston, 1998).

121. Segal and Stinebeck, *Puritans, Indians, and Manifest Destiny*, 221.

122. Ibid. See also McLoughlin, "Red Indians," 372.

123. Ann L. Stoler, "Making Empire Respectable: The Politics of Race and Sexual Morality in Twentieth-Century Colonial Cultures," *American Ethnologist* 16, no. 4 (November 1989): 635. Although Stoler's subject is early-twentieth-century colonialism, I have found that some of her analysis also applies to the nineteenth-century American context.

124. Circe Sturm, *Blood Politics: Race, Culture, and Identity in the Cherokee Nation of Oklahoma* (Berkeley: University of California Press, 2002), 86.

125. Samuel Worcester to Jeremiah Evarts, March 9, 1829, ABCFM 18.3.1, 5:248.

126. Tessie Liu, "Teaching the Differences among Women from a Historical Perspective: Rethinking Race and Gender as Social Categories," in *Unequal Sisters: A Multicultural Reader in U.S. Women's History*, ed. Vicki L. Ruiz and Ellen Carol DuBois, 2d ed. (New York: Routledge, 1994), 571–83.

Chapter Three

1. Many critics contend that writers like Sedgwick and Child also contributed to the racial ideology of the time. As Ezra Tawil argues, "Women's and men's frontier romances not only shared a fundamentally similar racial ideology, but also worked together to produce it." See Ezra Tawil, "Domestic Frontier Romance, or, How the Sentimental Heroine Became White," *Novel* 32, no. 1 (Fall 1998): 100.

2. Portions of this chapter are drawn from my article "Reading and Writing *Hope Leslie*: Catharine Maria Sedgwick's Indian 'Connections,'" *New England Quarterly* 75, no. 3 (September 2002): 415–43, and are used here by permission.

3. Mary Kelley, intro. to Catharine Maria Sedgwick, *Hope Leslie; or, Early Times in the Massachusetts* (New Brunswick, N.J.: Rutgers University Press, 1987), xx–xxi.

4. Sedgwick, *Hope Leslie*, 93; hereafter cited in the text.

5. See also the courtroom scene in which Magawisca declares, "Take my own word, I am your enemy; the sun-beam and the shadow cannot mingle. The white man cometh—the Indian vanisheth. Can we grasp in friendship the hand raised to strike us?" (292).

6. Review of *Hope Leslie* by Catharine Maria Sedgwick, *North American Review* 26 (1828): 418.

7. "Miss Sedgwick's Novels," review, *American Ladies Magazine* 2 (1829): 237.

8. Review of *Hope Leslie* by Catharine Maria Sedgwick, reprinted in *Pittsfield (Mass.) Sun*, July 5, 1827.

9. Kelley, intro., to *Hope Leslie*, xxxviii–xxxix.

10. John Demos, *The Unredeemed Captive: A Family Story from Early America* (New York: Vintage Books, 1994).

11. Kelley, intro, xxxviii–xxxix.

12. Demos, *Unredeemed Captive*, 19–35, 189, 201, 207–13, 227, 242–43. Eunice visited her relatives in 1740, 1741, 1743, and 1761.

13. Catharine Maria Sedgwick, *Life and Letters of Catharine M. Sedgwick*, ed. Mary E. Dewey (New York: Harper and Brothers, 1871), 129–30. See *American National Biography*,

s.v. "Eleazar Williams." Sedgwick may have distanced herself from Williams after he began claiming to be the lost dauphin of France in the 1840s.

14. Laurel Hill in Stockbridge is the setting of Magawisca's sacrifice, according to local lore. Sedgwick, either in error or with creative license, does get her facts wrong here. According to the Stockbridge historian Lion G. Miles, there is almost no evidence for an Indian village at Stockbridge in the seventeenth century, despite what some accounts say. The Housatonic Valley in Berkshire Country was a traditional hunting area until early in the eighteenth century, and there is no historical or archaeological evidence for any permanent year-round village in this area.

15. Demos, *Unredeemed Captive*, 181–84; Patrick Frazier, *The Mohicans of Stockbridge* (Lincoln: University of Nebraska Press, 1992), 16–17.

16. Hilary E. Wyss, *Writing Indians: Literacy, Christianity, and Native Community in Early America* (Amherst: University of Massachusetts Press, 2000), 87–90.

17. Colin G. Calloway, *The American Revolution in Indian Country: Crisis and Diversity in Native American Communities* (New York: Cambridge University Press, 1995), 85. For the history of the mission town, see also Frazier, *Mohicans of Stockbridge*; and James Axtell, "The Rise and Fall of the Stockbridge Indian Schools," *Massachusetts Review* (Summer 1986): 367–78.

18. The Jones and Brown families were also connected to the Williams family; see Frazier, *Mohicans of Stockbridge*, 46, 54, for details.

19. After the death of Sergeant in July 1749, Stephen Williams filled in as the Indians' minister for a month that winter (ibid., 82–89).

20. Ibid., 99–100, 102–3; Axtell, "Rise and Fall of the Stockbridge Indian Schools," 371–75.

21. Lion G. Miles, "The Red Man Dispossessed: The Williams Family and the Alienation of Indian Land in Stockbridge, Massachusetts, 1736–1818," in *New England Encounters: Indians and Euroamericans, ca. 1600–1850*, ed. Alden T. Vaughan (Boston: Northeastern University Press, 1999), 276–302.

22. Indian Memorial, May 27, 1762, Lynch Collection, Stockbridge Library Historical Collections, Stockbridge, Mass. Publication is by permission of the Stockbridge Library.

23. Miles, "Red Man Dispossessed," 284, 290–91, 293.

24. Frazier, *Mohicans of Stockbridge*, 188–90.

25. Calloway, *American Revolution in Indian Country*, 85, 100–101, 107.

26. Indian Memorial, September 2, 1783, Stockbridge Indian Collection, Stockbridge Library Historical Collections. In 1870 the Stockbridge Indians, by then living in Wisconsin, petitioned the Massachusetts government for support on the grounds that "they were tripped of their birth-right by fraud, force, and other improper means." Not surprisingly, the state attorney general and the legislature rejected their claim. See Charles Allen, *Report on the Stockbridge Indians, to the Legislature. House No. 13, Commonwealth of Massachusetts* (Boston: Wright and Potter, 1870).

27. Miles, "Red Man Dispossessed," 295; Frazier, *Mohicans of Stockbridge*, 237–45. See also Rev. David D. Field, "A History of the Town of Stockbridge," in *A History of the County of Berkshire, Massachusetts* (Pittsfield, Mass.: Samuel W. Bush, 1829), 239–72.

28. On November 28, 1783, Theodore Sedgwick paid thirty pounds for 1.5 acres from the widow Elisabeth Pewamoqanquoh (Pewauwgausquoh, Puvanwyansquoh), alias Wauwanynqeunot (Wauwaumpequunaunt, Wauwaupequunot, Wauwauyugennot, Wauwauyausquoh). On April 28, 1786, he purchased 0.55 acres for ten pounds and eight pence from the widow Elisabeth Whwumen (Oneweemeene, Uhweemeen, Whwemane). On January 4, 1788, he bought 1.25 additional acres from her for ten pounds. On May 17, 1788, he bought less than an acre from "Jehoiakim Mtochksin, Gentleman" (Mtohksin) for thirty shillings. For the archival records, see (first purchase) Berkshire County Middle Registry

(BCMR), Book 21, 363, Sedgwick II Papers, 5.2, Massachusetts Historical Society (MHS), Boston; (second purchase) BCMR, Book 24, 341–42, Sedgwick II Papers, 5.5, MHS; (third purchase) BCMR, Book 37, 205–6, Sedgwick II Papers 5.7, MHS; (fourth purchase) BCMR, Book 37, 215–16. I owe an enormous debt to Lion G. Miles, who generously shared additional primary sources and explained the primary materials I already had. Publication of the Sedgwick materials is by permission of the Massachusetts Historical Society.

29. Frazier, *Mohicans of Stockbridge*, 94, 198, 225.

30. According to Lion G. Miles, records of Jehoiakim Mtohksin's Revolutionary service come from a number of sources, mostly unpublished. For an account of his heroism at the siege of Boston, see Rev. Cutting Marsh to Col. George Boyd, August 23, 1838, Cutting Marsh Papers, State Historical Society of Wisconsin, Madison. Mtohksin is mentioned as a captain in several journals of participants on General John Sullivan's 1779 expedition against the Indians in New York. See Frederick Cook, ed., *Journals of the Military Expedition of Major General John Sullivan, 1779* (Auburn, N.Y.: Knapp, Peck, and Thomson, 1887), 249, 260, 272n, 315, 349, 368.

31. Again, Sedgwick apparently assumed that the Mohicans lived on the Housatonic River in the seventeenth century, when they used it only as a hunting ground. It is also possible that she takes creative liberties here.

32. The first removal of the Stockbridge Indians to New York took place in the fall of 1784. About seventy members of the tribe then moved to the White River country of Indiana in 1818. When they lost that land, they moved to Green Bay, Wisconsin, in 1821, to be followed by the New York members of the tribe between 1822 and 1829.

33. Frazier, *Mohicans of Stockbridge*, 234.

34. Of course, Magawisca's arm is cut off by her own father (not by the English), a fact that certainly disrupts the culpability intended by my reading.

35. Frazier, *Mohicans of Stockbridge*, 234–35.

36. *The Power of Her Sympathy: The Autobiography and Journal of Catharine Maria Sedgwick*, ed. Mary Kelley (Boston: Massachusetts Historical Society, 1993), 46–47.

37. Ibid., 49–50.

38. Miles notes, however, that Sedgwick gets some of her facts mixed up when she describes the story of her mother's rescue. The incident occurred in August 1754, when a party of Schaghticoke Indians raided into Berkshire County. Sedgwick says in her autobiography that "the Indians did not come," but in fact they killed a man on the road in Lenox and penetrated to the house of a Mr. Chamberlain in Stockbridge, where they killed a servant and two children. See Sarah Cabot Sedgwick and Christina Sedgwick Marquand, *Stockbridge, 1739–1939: A Chronicle* (Great Barrington, Mass.: Berkshire Courier, 1939), 73–75.

39. Sedgwick, *The Power of Her Sympathy*, 49.

40. Catharine Maria Sedgwick (hereafter CMS) to Nathan Appleton, October 17, 1855, Appleton Family Papers, 8.4, MHS. Miles indicates that Sedgwick is incorrect about the Indian burial ground. In 1809 the Stockbridge tribe granted the cemetery to Dr. Oliver Partridge for ten dollars in services rendered, provided he did not till or break the soil. See Book 50, p. 47, of the Berkshire County Middle Registry in Pittsfield, Mass.

41. See Jill Lepore, *The Name of War: King Philip's War and the Origins of American Identity* (New York: Alfred A. Knopf, 1998).

42. Dwight was also the author of "Memoirs of Henry Obookiah" (New Haven, 1818), an account of the life and death of one of the school's most famous converts.

43. Catharine Maria Sedgwick, *A New-England Tale; or Sketches of New-England Character and Manners* (New York: E. Bliss and E. White, 1822), 14; idem, *Redwood; A Tale* (New York: E. Bliss and E. White, 1824), 2:283.

44. Hubert M. Sedgwick, *A Sedgwick Genealogy: Descendants of Deacon Benjamin Sedgwick* (New Haven: New Haven Colony Historical Society, 1961), 3–5, 11–12, 29–30.

45. See the Sedgwick Family Papers, MHS; Benjamin Sedgwick Collection, Connecticut State Library, History and Genealogy Unit, State Archives, Hartford; T. S. Gold Family Papers, Archives and Special Collections, Thomas J. Dodd Research Center, University of Connecticut.

46. CMS to Katherine Sedgwick Minot, February 5, 1831, Catharine Maria Sedgwick Papers (CMS Papers) I, 1.14, MHS; published as "Letter to Katherine Sedgwick Minot," February 5, 1831, in *Life and Letters of Catharine M. Sedgwick*, ed. Mary E. Dewey (New York: Harper and Brothers, 1871), 216.

47. CMS to Charles Sedgwick, February 5, 1831, CMS Papers I, 1.14. On this trip Sedgwick also met some western Indians: "They were arrayed in all their finery for a visit to their great Father. . . . They were extremely polite." CMS to Katherine Sedgwick Minot, February 2, 1831, CMS Papers I, 1.14.

48. CMS to Henry Sedgwick, February 15, 1831, CMS Papers III, 3.12.

49. Journal, vol. 11, June 9, 1830, CMS Papers I. Sedgwick most likely refers to Jeremiah Evarts, *Essays on the Present Crisis in the Condition of the American Indians, first published in the National Intelligencer, under the signature of William Penn* (Boston: Perkins and Marvin, 1829).

50. Emily Sedgwick Welch, *A Biographical Sketch: John Sedgwick, Major-General* (New York: De Vinne Press, 1899), 10.

51. CMS to Henry Dwight Sedgwick, August 14, 1825?, Francis J. Child Papers, MHS.

52. Little did Sedgwick know that her cousins would meet a tragic end. Harriet died in 1836, only ten years after her marriage and Elias was assassinated in 1839 for having signed the Treaty of New Echota, which led to the infamous Trail of Tears. For a discussion of the rhetoric of "civilization or extinction," see Lucy Maddox, *Removals: Nineteenth-Century American Literature and the Politics of Indian Affairs* (New York: Oxford University Press, 1991).

53. Alan Taylor, *William Cooper's Town: Power and Persuasion on the Frontier of the Early American Republic* (New York: Alfred A. Knopf, 1995), 4.

54. James Fenimore Cooper, *The Pioneers, or the Sources of the Susqueharra, A Descriptive Tale*, ed. James Franklin Beard (Albany: State University of New York Press, 1980), 94; hereafter cited in the text.

55. Cooper anticipates William Lloyd Garrison's critique of the colonization movement's futile attempt to make the United States an all-white nation: "Indeed, let us shut up our ports against our own mariners, who are returning from an India voyage, and whose cheeks and muscles could not wholly withstand the influence of the breezes and tropics to which they were exposed." William Lloyd Garrison, *Thoughts on African Colonization* (1832; reprint, New York: Arno Press, 1968), 119.

56. Fergus M. Bordewich, *Killing the White Man's Indian: Reinventing Native Americans at the End of the Twentieth Century* (New York: Doubleday, 1996), 48.

57. James Fenimore Cooper, *The Last of the Mohicans; A Narrative of 1757*, ed. James Franklin Beard (Albany: State University of New York Press, 1983), 159 hereafter cited in the text.

58. *Mohicans* is the novel most frequently discussed when critics deal with Cooper and the intermarriage question, and there is no consensus on what the novel says about Cooper's racial thought. For example, Leslie Fiedler in *Love and Death in the American Novel* (New York: Stein and Day, 1982) contends that Cooper's "horror of miscegenation led him to forbid even the not-quite white offspring of one unnatural marriage to enter into another alliance that crossed race lines. The last of the Mohicans is portrayed as the last, the Vanishing American shown to have vanished because (so at least Cooper believed) the color line is eternal and God-given" (207). In her introduction to *Hobomok and Other Writings on Indians* by Lydia Maria Child (New Brunswick, N.J.: Rutgers University Press, 1997), Carolyn Karcher agrees that the novel reveals Cooper's fears of amalgamation: "Shifting the

focus back to race war as the correct prototype of relations between whites and Indians, Cooper raised the specter of a love affair between a white woman and an Indian only to dispel it, first by revealing that the woman was not white after all, then by killing off the would-be lovers and burying them in separate graves, so that even in death, their blood would not mingle" (xxv). Jane Tompkins does not read the plot so literally, arguing in *Sensational Designs: The Cultural Work of American Fiction, 1790–1860* (New York: Oxford University Press, 1985) that the subject of the novel is "cultural miscegenation." Nonetheless, racial identity is still central to Tompkins's reading. Natty Bumppo, who is "neither red nor pale," must cling to the notion that he has been true to his "gifts" as a white man; cultural identity is rooted in faithfulness to kind (114, 118–19). In the 1983 SUNY edition, James Franklin Beard defends Cooper's attitude toward racial intermarriage as "pragmatic, but not racist" (intro. to *The Last of the Mohicans* by James Fenimore Cooper [Albany: State University of New York Press, 1983], xxxvi). As Cooper writes in *Notions of the Americans: Picked up by a Travelling Bachelor*, ed Gary Williams (Albany: State University of New York Press, 1991): "As there is little reluctance to mingle the white and red blood . . . I think an amalgamation of the two races would in time occur. Those families of America who are thought to have any of the Indian blood, are rather proud of their descent; and it is a matter of boast among many of the most considerable persons of Virginia, that they are descended from the renowned Pocahontas" (490). Barbara Mann argues in "Whipped Like a Dog: Crossed Blood in *The Last of the Mohicans*," *James Fenimore Cooper: His Country and His Art* 10 (1999): 48–61, that "the rift between colonial British and American policy on miscegenation" is central to the novel and that "Cooper may have intended Natty as a miscegenate passing for white" (49, 52). Finally, Geoffrey Rans contends in *Cooper's Leather-Stocking Novels: A Secular Reading* (Chapel Hill: University of North Carolina Press, 1991) that the novel offers more than a single meaning of amalgamation: while the plot "traces Anglo-Saxon fear of miscegenation," it "also offers Munro's defiant miscegenation . . . as well as his pious hope of racial equality before God, Heyward's embarrassed racism, and Tamenund's dignified espousal of racial intermarriage as desirable" (37). I agree with Rans that Cooper displays a range of reactions to amalgamation, but I contend that the fate of Cora and Uncas makes the strongest impression. Like Jefferson, Cooper can only envision theoretical intermarriages in the distant future.

59. Rans, *Cooper's Leather-Stocking Novels*, 121–23.

60. Review of *The Last of the Mohicans* by James Fenimore Cooper, *North American Review* 26 (1828): 373.

61. Review of *The Last of the Mohicans* by James Fenimore Cooper, *North American Review* 23 (1826): 163.

62. James Fenimore Cooper to the duchess de Broglie, March 22, 1827, letter 107 in *Letters and Journals of James Fenimore Cooper*, ed. James Franklin Beard, 6 vols. (Cambridge: Belknap Press of Harvard University Press, 1960), 1:199.

63. James Fenimore Cooper, *The Prairie: A Tale*, ed. James P. Elliott (Albany: State University of New York Press, 1985), 4; hereafter cited in the text.

64. Susan M. Ryan, "The Grammar of Good Intentions: Benevolence and Racial Identity in Antebellum American Literature" (Ph.D. diss., University of North Carolina, 1998), 220.

65. James Fenimore Cooper, *The Wept of Wish-ton-Wish* (Columbus: Charles E. Merrill, 1970); hereafter cited in the text. Lydia Maria Child gave the novel a kind review: "This novel falls far short of some of Mr. Cooper's previous volumes; but it is well sustained, and interesting" (*Massachusetts Weekly Journal*, November 21, 1829, 4).

66. Lepore, *The Name of War*, 208.

67. Cooper may also have had a family connection to his story. As John McWilliams notes of Cooper's wife: "Susan de Lancey's grandmother was the daughter of Colonel Caleb

Heathcote. . . . Cooper could not have written *The Wept of Wish-ton-Wish* without his wife's family in mind. . . . Perhaps the entire tale is based on a family legend, or portion of Heathcote history." See John P. McWilliams, *Political Justice in a Republic: James Fenimore Cooper's America* (Berkeley: University of California Press, 1972), 248 n. 11.

68. Susanne Opfermann, "Lydia Maria Child, James Fenimore Cooper, and Catharine Maria Sedgwick: A Dialogue on Race, Culture, and Gender," in *Soft Canons: American Women Writers and Masculine Tradition*, ed. Karen L. Kilcup (Iowa City: University of Iowa Press, 1999), 29; H. C. Carey and Lea to James Fenimore Cooper, April 9, 1827, James Fenimore Cooper Papers, box 2, folder 13, American Antiquarian Society, Worcester, Mass.

69. James Franklin Beard, intro. to Cooper, *The Pioneers*, xix.

70. Taylor, *William Cooper's Town*, 54–63.

71. Susan Scheckel, "'In the Land of His Fathers': Cooper, Land Rights, and the Legitimation of American National Identity," in *James Fenimore Cooper: New Historical and Literary Contexts*, ed. W. M. Verhoeven (Atlanta: Rodopi, 1993), 125–50.

72. David E. Wilkins, *American Indian Sovereignty and the U.S. Supreme Court: The Masking of Justice* (Austin: University of Texas Press, 1997), 28, 31, 32, 35.

73. *Johnson and Graham's Lessee v. McIntosh*, 21 U.S. (8 Wheaton) 543 (1823); reprinted. in Wilcomb E. Washburn, *The American Indian and the United States: A Documentary History* (New York: Random House, 1973), 4:2546; emphasis added.

74. Ibid., 2538.

75. Opfermann, "Lydia Maria Child," 36.

76. Scheckel, "In the Land of His Fathers," 134.

77. Review of *The Leather-Stocking Tales* by James Fenimore Cooper, *U.S. Magazine and Democratic Review* 28 (March 1851), 287.

78. Lydia Maria (Francis) Child to Catharine Maria Sedgwick, August 28 [before 1828], CMS Papers III.

79. Catharine Maria Sedgwick to Lydia Maria (Francis) Child, May 28, 1827, CMS Papers III.

80. Although the Abenaki and Penobscot Indians had mostly been driven away almost one hundred years earlier, several Indian families still lived nearby, and Child visited them often. See Carolyn L. Karcher, intro. to *A Lydia Maria Child Reader*, pt. 1 (Durham: Duke University Press, 1997), 25–28.

81. Sedgwick also explores French colonial history in her story "The Catholic Iroquois." See the gift annual *Atlantic Souvenir: A Christmas and New Year's Offering* (Philadelphia: Carey and Lea, 1826), 72–103.

82. Carolyn L. Karcher, *The First Woman in the Republic: A Cultural Biography of Lydia Maria Child* (Durham: Duke University Press, 1994), 114.

83. Olive Patricia Dickason, "From 'One Nation' in the Northeast to 'New Nation' in the Northwest: A Look at the Emergence of the Métis," in *The New Peoples: Being and Becoming Métis in North America*, ed. Jacqueline Peterson and Jennifer S. H. Brown (Lincoln: University of Nebraska Press, 1985), 19; see 19–28.

84. J. B. Brebner, "Subsidized Intermarriage with the Indians: An Incident in British Colonial Policy," *Canadian Historical Review* (1925): 33–36.

85. Sylvia Van Kirk, *"Many Tender Ties": Women in Fur-Trade Society in Western Canada, 1670–1870* (Winnipeg, Manitoba: Watson and Dwyer, 1980), 28.

86. Child, *Hobomok*, 133; hereafter cited in the text.

87. Lydia Maria Child, "The Indian Wife," in *The Coronal* (Boston: Carter and Hendee, 1832), 165–66; hereafter cited in the text.

88. Van Kirk, *"Many Tender Ties,"* 4.

89. Werner Sollors, *Beyond Ethnicity: Consent and Descent in American Culture* (New York: Oxford University Press, 1986), 129.

90. *Blackstone's Commentaries: with Notes of Reference to the Constitution and Laws of the Federal Government of the United States; and of the Commonwealth of Virginia*, ed. St. George Tucker (Union, N.J.: Lawbook Exchange, 1996), 437.

91. Van Kirk, *"Many Tender Ties,"* 49–50, 87–89, 95.

92. Review of *Hobomok* by Lydia Maria Child, *North American Review* 19 (1824): 262–63.

93. Karcher, intro. to *Hobomok*, xxxiv.

94. Karcher, *First Woman in the Republic*, 38–39.

95. "Recent American Novels," *North American Review* 21 (1825): 94–95.

96. Lydia Maria Child, *The First Settlers of New England: or the Conquest of the Pequods, Narragansets and Pokanokets: As Related by a Mother to Her Children and Designed for the Instruction of Youth* (Boston: Monroe and Francis, 1829); hereafter cited in the text. For an outstanding discussion of *First Settlers*, see Karcher, *First Woman in the Republic*, 86–96.

97. Karcher, *First Woman in the Republic*, 90.

98. Karcher, intro. to *Lydia Maria Child Reader*, pt. 1, 30.

99. Karcher, *First Woman in the Republic*, 93; Lepore, *The Name of War*, 205.

100. Karcher, *First Woman in the Republic*, 87, 637 n. 28.

101. Rev. Cornelius B. Everest to Stephen Gold, July 2, 1825, Cornwall Historical Society, Cornwall, Conn.

Chapter Four

1. Jayme A. Sokolow, "The Jerry McHenry Rescue and the Growth of Northern Antislavery Sentiment during the 1850s," *American Studies* 16, no. 3 (1982): 431–32.

2. Donald Yacavone, *Samuel Joseph May and the Dilemmas of the Liberal Persuasion, 1797–1871* (Philadelphia: Temple University Press, 1991), 144.

3. The "Jerry Rescue Trials" received extensive newspaper coverage. See, for example, *New York Herald*, January 30, and February 1 and 2, 1853; *Boston Transcript*, February 2, 1853; *Boston Daily Advertiser*, February 1, 1853.

4. William G. Allen, "Jerry Rescue Celebration," *Frederick Douglass' Paper*, October 29, 1852.

5. Catherine M. Hanchett, " 'Dedicated to Equality and Brotherhood': New York Central College, C. P. Grosvenor, and Gerrit Smith," paper presented at the Madison County Historical Society, Oneida, N.Y., February 16, 1989, Cortland County Historical Society, Cortland, N.Y., (photocopy), 1.

6. John R. McKivigan, "The American Baptist Free Mission Society," *Foundations* 21 (October–December 1978): 341–42. See also Edwin Scott Gaustad, *Historical Atlas of Religion in America* (New York: Harper and Row, 1976), 57–60.

7. Kenneth R. Short, "New York Central College: A Baptist Experiment in Integrated Higher Education, 1848–61," *Foundations* 5 (July 1962): 250–51.

8. McKivigan, "American Baptist Free Mission Society," 340.

9. John R. McKivigan, *The War against Proslavery Religion: Abolitionism and the Northern Churches, 1830–1865* (Ithaca: Cornell University Press, 1984), 93–94.

10. Edwin R. Warren, *The Free Missionary Principle, or Bible Missions: A Plea for Separate Missionary Action from Slaveholders!* (Boston: J. Howe, 1846), 29, 31, 46.

11. A. T. Foss and E. Mathews, *Facts for Baptist Churches* (Utica, N.Y.: American Baptist Free Mission Society, 1850), iii–iv.

12. McKivigan, "American Baptist Free Mission Society," 346.

13. Short, "New York Central College," 251.

14. Hanchett, "Dedicated to Equality," 4–5.

15. ABFMS, *Fourth Annual Report*, May 1847, 17; quoted in Short, "New York Central College," 251.

16. The name was quickly changed because of confusion over its meaning. The word "Free" was intended to advertise the college's abolitionist principles, but many people interpreted it to mean "no tuition."

17. "The Free Institution," *Christian Contributor and Free Missionary*, April 26, 1848.

18. Seymour B. Dunn, "The Early Academies of Cortland County," in *Cortland County Chronicles*, 2 vols. (Cortland, N.Y.: Cortland County Historical Society, 1957), 1:71–72. Douglass was a particularly enthusiastic supporter of the college. In *Frederick Douglass' Paper* (previously the *North Star*), published in nearby Rochester, he urged his readers to send their children to the school that "placed its heel upon the venomous viper of American prejudice against color" (April 26, 1850).

19. Walter Dyson, *Howard University, the Capstone of Negro Education: A History, 1867–1940* (Washington, D.C.: Graduate School of Howard University, 1941), 349. The college hired two other African American professors, Charles Lewis Reason and George Boyer Vashon. Reason, Allen, and Vashon succeeded one another in their professorships.

20. James Oliver Horton and Lois E. Horton, *In Hope of Liberty: Culture, Community, and Protest among Northern Free Blacks, 1700–1860* (New York: Oxford University Press, 1997), 215, 213–19. See also Paul Goodman, *Of One Blood: Abolitionism and the Origins of Racial Equality* (Berkeley: University of California Press, 1998), 45–53. Lydia Maria Child's husband, David Lee Child, was a founding member and trustee of the Noyes Academy; see Carolyn L. Karcher, *The First Woman in the Republic: A Cultural Biography of Lydia Maria Child* (Durham: Duke University Press, 1994), 202.

21. Curtis Marshall, "Eleutherian College," *Indiana History Bulletin* 25 (1948): 200–203.

22. Horton and Horton, *In Hope of Liberty*, 52. By 1852 African American students had attended the Institute at Easton, Pa.; the Normal School of Albany, N.Y.; Bowdoin College; Rutland College in Vermont; Jefferson College in Pennsylvania; Athens College in Athens, Ohio; Hanover College in Indiana; the medical school of the University of New York; Castleton Medical School in Vermont; Berkshire Medical School in Massachusetts; Rush Medical School, Chicago; Eclectic Medical School, Philadelphia; Homeopathic College, Cleveland; the medical school of Harvard University; Gettysburg Theological Seminary; Dartmouth Theological School; and the Theological Seminary of Charleston. See Carter Godwin Woodson, *The Education of the Negro prior to 1861* (Washington, D.C.: Associated Publishers, 1919), 276–77.

23. Foss and Mathews, *Facts for Baptist Churches*, 400.

24. *First and Second Report of the New York Central College Association* (Utica, 1849–50); quoted in Albert Hazen Wright, *Cornell's Three Precursors, vol. 1, New York Central College* (Ithaca: New York State College of Agriculture, 1960), 39.

25. "Original Design of the Founders of the College," in *First and Second Report*; quoted in Wright, *Cornell's Three Precursors*, 17.

26. *Catalogue of the Officers and Students of New York Central College: For the Year 1853–54* (Homer, N.Y.: Dixon and Gould, 1854), 23–24.

27. William G. Allen, *A Short Personal Narrative, by William G. Allen, (Colored American,) Formerly Professor of the Greek Language and Literature in New York Central College, Resident for the Last Four Years in Dublin* (Dublin: William Curry and J. Robertson, 1860), 5–7. For a biographical sketch, see C. Peter Ripley et al., eds., *The Black Abolitionist Papers*, vol. 1, *The British Isles, 1830–1865* (Chapel Hill: University of North Carolina Press, 1985), 358–59.

28. Allen, *Short Personal Narrative*, 8–11, 13. Oneida's president, the Reverend Beriah Green, was a controversial figure because of his support for integrated schools and intermarriage. On one occasion in 1834, as the *National Intelligencer* reported, "a procession marched through the city, blowing horns, rattling tin pans, &c.; and, among other acts offensive to good order, they hung the Rev. Dr. Beriah Green, of the Oneida Institute, or Manual Labor College, in effigy. The immediate cause of these outrageous proceedings,

was the fact, that Dr. Green solemnized a marriage between a negro man and a white girl" ("Riot in Utica," February 5, 1834).

29. William G. Allen, *Wheatley, Banneker, and Horton* (Boston: Laing, 1849).

30. William G. Allen, *The American Prejudice Against Color. An Authentic Narrative, Showing How Easily the Nation Got into an Uproar. By William G. Allen, A Refugee from American Despotism* (London: W. and F. G. Cash, 1853; reprint, New York: Arno Press and The New York Times, 1969), 3–4.

31. Allen, *Short Personal Narrative*, 14–15.

32. "A Blow to Colorphobia," *Frederick Douglass' Paper*, July 24, 1851.

33. Quoted in "McGrawville College," *Frederick Douglass' Paper*, May 20, 1852.

34. *Black Abolitionist Papers, 1830–1865* (Sanford, N.C.: Microfilming Corporation of America, 1981), microfilm, 6:0131, 6:0953, 7:0067, 7:0221, 7:0312, 7:0484 (hereafter BAP, microfilm).

35. Frederick Douglass, "A Letter from the Editor," *Frederick Douglass' Paper*, July 30, 1852.

36. "Address on 'Orators and Oratory,'" *Liberator*, October 29, 1852.

37. Phyllis F. Field, "Republicans and Black Suffrage in New York State: The Grassroots Response," *Civil War History* 21, no. 2 (1975): 136–39; John L. Stanley, "Majority Tyranny in Tocqueville's America: The Failure of Negro Suffrage in 1846," *Political Science Quarterly* 84, no. 3 (September 1969): 413–15.

38. "Letter from Wm. G. Allen," *Frederick Douglass' Paper*, November 12, 1852, BAP, microfilm, 7:0826.

39. "British and Foreign Anti-Slavery Society," *Frederick Douglass' Paper*, June 23, 1854, BAP, microfilm, 8:0888.

40. See Field, "Republicans and Black Suffrage," and Stanley, "Majority Tyranny in Tocqueville's America," for a discussion of the referenda on black suffrage.

41. Nathaniel H. Carter et al., *Reports of the Proceedings and Debates of the Convention of 1821* (Albany: E. and E. Hosford, 1821), 190, 386.

42. "Letter from Wm. G. Allen," *Frederick Douglass' Paper*, May 20, 1852. See also "Letter from Wm. G. Allen," *Frederick Douglass' Paper*, July 30, 1852.

43. "Letter from William G. Allen," *Frederick Douglass' Paper*, June 10, 1852.

44. "Letter from Wm. G. Allen," *Frederick Douglass' Paper*, May 20, 1852.

45. "Letter from William G. Allen," *Frederick Douglass' Paper*, August 13, 1852.

46. Allen, *American Prejudice*, 4; *Fulton, New York* (Fulton: Morrill Press, 1901), 52; Leon N. Brown, "Pioneer Oswego County Preachers and Their Churches" in *Publication of the Oswego County Historical Society*, vol. 4 (Oswego, 1940), 15–27. In one of the few separate mentions of Mary King in the records, Timothy Stow, after attending the New York Central College commencement exercises, noted that she gave an oration titled "Our Country and Its Destiny." See Timothy Stow, "McGrawville College," *Frederick Douglass' Paper*, July 30, 1852.

47. Allen, *American Prejudice*, 4–8.

48. Ibid., 12–13.

49. Ibid., 13–14, 17.

50. The local historian Catherine Hanchett has found listings for both Porters in college records. See "New York Central College Students: A List Compiled by C. M. Hanchett," May 1997, Cortland County Historical Society.

51. Allen, *American Prejudice*, 20–26.

52. Ibid., 30–47.

53. Ibid., 53.

54. "Letter from L. D. Tanner to Lyndon King," *Frederick Douglass' Paper*, March 4, 1853. King responded to this public upbraiding in a later issue, calling the charges "*un-*

founded, abusive and *slanderous!*" but without making any specific rebuttals. Douglass noted King's evasiveness: "Whether the above letter is such a contradiction as will cover the ground of the allegations made by Mr. Tanner, the good sense of our readers will decide." Lyndon King, "L. D. Tanner's Letter," *Frederick Douglass' Paper*, April 1, 1853.

55. Allen, *American Prejudice*, 65, 59–68.

56. See, for example, "To the Public," *Frederick Douglass' Paper*, March 4, 1853.

57. Allen, *American Prejudice*, 74.

58. "Liberty Party Convention," *Frederick Douglass' Paper*, March 4, 1853. The government indicted fourteen whites and twelve blacks for their role in the "Jerry Rescue," but only one black man was convicted. The anniversary of the event was celebrated for the rest of the decade. See Horton and Horton, *In Hope of Liberty*, 255. For a contemporary report of the 1857 celebration, see "The Jerry Rescue Celebration," *National Anti-Slavery Standard*, October 24, 1857.

59. "The Fulton Rescue Case," *Syracuse Daily Journal*, February 8, 1853. This article is also reprinted in Allen, *American Prejudice*, 76–77.

60. Rev. Thomas Henson was the pastor of the Zion Baptist Church of New York from 1851 to 1855. See C. Peter Ripley et. al., eds., *The Black Abolitionist Papers*, vol. 5, *The United States, 1859–1865* (Chapel Hill: University of North Carolina Press, 1992), 348 n. 24.

61. Allen, *American Prejudice*, 86. Despite his former patron's disapproval of his marriage, Allen notified Gerrit Smith about his marriage and departure. William G. Allen to Gerrit Smith, April 9, 1853, in *Calendar of the Gerrit Smith Papers in the Syracuse University Library*, vol. 2 (Albany: Works Projects Administration, 1942), 149.

62. "Prof. Allen Is Married," *Liberator*, May 6, 1853; reprinted from the *Syracuse Weekly Star*.

63. *Liberator*, May 6, 1853; reprinted from the *Utica Gazette*.

64. Allen, *American Prejudice*, 91.

65. "A Brutal and Scandalous Outrage," *Frederick Douglass' Paper*, March 4, 1853.

66. "Prof. Allen's Case," *Frederick Douglass' Paper*, March 11, 1853.

67. Ibid.

68. Allen, *A Short Personal Narrative*, 23.

69. A[sa]. Caldwell, "New York Central College," *Frederick Douglass' Paper*, April 1, 1853.

70. "Letter from L. D. Tanner," *Frederick Douglass' Paper*, April 29, 1853.

71. Stafford Green to Asa Caldwell, September 24, 1852, Cortland County Historical Society.

72. Asa S. Wing to Gerrit Smith, May 5, 1853, in *Calendar of the Gerrit Smith Papers*, 149.

73. William G. Allen to Gerrit Smith, January 24, 1854, in *Calendar of the Gerrit Smith Papers*, 160.

74. "Letter from Prof. Wm. G. Allen," *Frederick Douglass' Paper*, August 5, 1853.

75. William Wells Brown, "Fugitive Slaves in England," *Frederick Douglass' Paper*, July 24, 1851.

76. Intro. to *Black Abolitionist Papers*, 1:10–11. See also Audrey Fisch, *American Slaves in Victorian England: Abolitionist Politics in Popular Literature and Culture* (New York: Cambridge University Press, 2000).

77. "Prejudice against Colour," *Anti-Slavery Reporter*, June 1, 1853, BAP, microfilm, 8: 0274. Lady Byron wanted to hire Allen as a lecturer for the Moral Reformatory School movement. Attempting to start this career, in January 1854 he wrote to Horace Mann asking for his endorsement. See R.J.M. Blackett, "William G. Allen: The Forgotten Professor," *Civil War History* 26, no. 1 (1980): 46–47; William G. Allen to Horace Mann, January 24, 1854, Horace Mann Papers, Massachusetts Historical Society, Boston. Publication is by permission of the Massachusetts Historical Society.

78. "Letter from William W. Brown," *Liberator*, June 3, 1853, BAP, microfilm, 8:0276; "Anniversary of West Indian Emancipation," *Patriot*, August 8, 1853, BAP, microfilm, 8: 0395.

79. R.J.M. Blackett, *Building an Antislavery Wall: Black Americans in the Atlantic Abolitionist Movement, 1830–1860* (Ithaca: Cornell University Press, 1983), 145; William G. Allen to Gerrit Smith, January 24, 1854, BAP, microfilm, 8:0608.

80. Speech by William G. Allen, document 58, in *Black Abolitionist Papers*, 1:372–78.

81. Blackett, "William G. Allen," 48. As the British abolitionist Richard D. Webb wrote to a friend, "He has had a hard turn of it—and her fate has been [worse?] for she is a lady in manner and feelings and she has had to endure great poverty." Richard D. Webb to "my dear Friend," March 6, 1859, Anti-Slavery Manuscripts, Ms. A.9.2.29 p. 65, Boston Public Library, Rare Books Department. Courtesy of the Trustees.

82. Allen to Gerrit Smith, May 14, 1859, BAP, microfilm, 11:0739.

83. *Anti-Slavery Reporter* (London), July 1, 1863; quoted in Benjamin Quarles, "Ministers without Portfolio," *Journal of Negro History* 39 (1954): 36.

84. Blackett, "William G. Allen," 51–52; Allen to Gerrit Smith, January 24, 1854, BAP, microfilm, 8:0608; Allen to Gerrit Smith, February 23, 1858, BAP, microfilm, 11:0152.

85. Dunn, "Early Academies of Cortland County," 75–76; Hanchett, "Dedicated to Equality and Brotherhood," 8.

86. Quarles, "Ministers without Portfolio," 35.

87. Intro. to *Black Abolitionist Papers*, 1:19–21; Marcus Wood, " 'All Right!' The Narrative of Henry Box Brown as a Test Case for the Racial Prescription of Rhetoric and Semiotics," *Proceedings of the American Antiquarian Society* 107 (1997): 65–104.

88. Blackett, *Building an Antislavery Wall*, 198.

89. One question that remains is whether Allen's books were available in the United States. In an article on the readership of *Our Nig*, Eric Gardner argues "not only that abolitionists knew about the book but that they may have consciously chosen *not* to publicize it" because its indictment of Northern racism was not what they wanted to hear. Eric Gardner, " 'This Attempt of Their Sister': Harriet Wilson's *Our Nig* from Printer to Readers," *New England Quarterly* 66 (1993): 227. This may also have been the case with Allen; given his ties to abolitionists in Boston and upstate New York, it is hard to believe that he would not have sought their patronage.

90. See chap. 1 in Robert B. Stepto, *From Behind the Veil: A Study of Afro-American Narrative*, 2d ed. (Urbana: University of Illinois Press, 1991).

91. Frances Smith Foster, *Witnessing Slavery: The Development of Antebellum Slave Narratives*, 2d ed. (Madison: University of Wisconsin Press, 1994), 4, 55.

92. Allen, preface to *A Short Personal Narrative*.

93. Hazel V. Carby, *Reconstructing Womanhood: The Emergence of the Afro-American Woman Novelist* (New York: Oxford University Press, 1987), 43.

94. Gardner, "This Attempt of Their Sister," 243.

95. William Wells Brown, "Memoir of the Author," in *The Black Man, His Antecedents, His Genius, and His Achievements* (New York: Thomas Hamilton, 1863), 11.

96. Frederick Douglass, *Narrative of the Life of Frederick Douglass, An American Slave, Written by Himself*, in *Frederick Douglass: The Narrative and Selected Writings*, ed. Michael Meyer (New York: Modern Library, 1984), 18.

97. Allen, *A Short Personal Narrative*, 5–7.

98. Foster, *Witnessing Slavery*, 76.

99. Allen, *A Short Personal Narrative*, 12.

100. Foster, *Witnessing Slavery*, 124–25.

101. Allen, *American Prejudice*, 1–2.

102. Intro. to *Black Abolitionist Papers*, 1:4–5.

103. Allen, *American Prejudice*, 98.

104. Allen, *Short Personal Narrative*, 25.

105. Ibid., 30.

106. Ibid., 28.

107. Allen, *American Prejudice*, 107.

108. Douglass, *Narrative*, 74.

109. Allen, *Short Personal Narrative*, 7.

110. Rev. J. W. Loguen, *The Rev. J. W. Loguen, as a Slave and as a Freeman. A Narrative of Real Life* (Syracuse: J. G. K. Truair, 1859), 402.

111. "New York Central College (from the Albany State Register)," *Liberator*, July 18, 1851.

Chapter Five

An earlier version of this chapter appeared in *Legal Studies Forum* 24 (2000): 133–55. Reprinted by permission of the publisher.

1. William G. Allen, *The American Prejudice Against Color. An Authentic Narrative, Showing How Easily the Nation Got into an Uproar. By William G. Allen, A Refugee from American Despotism* (London: W. and F. G. Cash, 1853), 1–2.

2. Joanne Pope Melish, *Disowning Slavery: Gradual Emancipation and "Race" in New England, 1780–1860* (Ithaca: Cornell University Press, 1998), 2.

3. Rachel F. Moran, *Interracial Intimacy: The Regulation of Race and Romance* (Chicago: University of Chicago Press, 2001), 19.

4. A. Leon Higginbotham Jr. and Barbara K. Kopytoff, "Racial Purity and Interracial Sex in the Law of Colonial and Antebellum Virginia," *Georgetown Law Journal* 77 (1989): 1967–2029. For an overview of miscegenation laws in the South, see chap. 2, "Antimiscegenation Laws and the Enforcement of Racial Boundaries" in Moran, *Interracial Intimacy*.

5. Kathleen M. Brown, *Good Wives, Nasty Wenches, and Anxious Patriarchs: Gender, Race, and Power in Colonial Virginia* (Chapel Hill: University of North Carolina Press, 1996), 116, 126.

6. William Walter Hening, comp., *The Statutes at Large: Being a Collection of All the Laws of Virginia* (1619–1792), 13 vols. (Richmond, 1809–23), 2:26; A. Leon Higginbotham Jr., *In the Matter of Color: Race and the American Legal Process: The Colonial Period* (New York: Oxford University Press, 1978), 33–34; Edmund S. Morgan, *American Slavery, American Freedom: The Ordeal of Colonial Virginia* (New York: W. W. Norton, 1975), 311.

7. Brown, *Good Wives*, 195.

8. Hening, *Statutes at Large*, 2:170; Higginbotham and Kopytoff, "Racial Purity," 1993–95.

9. Hening, *Statutes at Large*, 2:260, 270; A. Leon Higginbotham Jr., *Shades of Freedom: Racial Politics and Presumptions of the American Legal Process* (New York: Oxford University Press, 1996), 47, 51.

10. Higginbotham and Kopytoff, "Racial Purity," 1973.

11. Hening, *Statutes at Large*, 2:170, 260.

12. Higginbotham and Kopytoff, "Racial Purity," 1970.

13. Morgan, *American Slavery*, 328. See also Morgan's discussion of the emergence of American slavery and racism in chaps. 15 and 16.

14. James Hugo Johnston, *Race Relations in Virginia and Miscegenation in the South, 1776–1860* (Amherst: University of Massachusetts Press, 1970), 185.

15. Brown, *Good Wives*, 181.

16. Higginbotham, *In the Matter of Color*, 39.

17. Brown, *Good Wives*, 196.

18. Hening, *Statutes at Large*, 3:86–87.

19. Higginbotham, *In the Matter of Color*, 44–45.

20. Higginbotham and Kopytoff, "Racial Purity," 1996; Hening, *Statutes at Large*, 3: 86–87.

21. H. R. McIlwaine, ed., *Legislative Journals of the Council of Colonial Virginia*, 3 vols. (Richmond, 1918), 1:262; Brown, *Good Wives*, 202.

22. Hening, *Statutes at Large*, 3:447–61; Higginbotham, *In the Matter of Color*, 50–55.

23. Hening, *Statutes at Large*, 3:333.

24. Ibid., 3:252; Thomas D. Morris, *Southern Slavery and the Law, 1619–1860* (Chapel Hill: University of North Carolina Press, 1996), 22–23; Higginbotham and Kopytoff, "Racial Purity," 1976–77.

25. Hening, *Statutes at Large*, 4:126–33; Higginbotham, *Shades of Freedom*, 35.

26. Brown, *Good Wives*, 218–19.

27. In the last major development in the regulation of interracial relationships during the colonial period, in 1753 the prohibition of Indian-white marriages was omitted from the law. This prohibition only of black-white marriages was part of an omnibus act "for the better government of servants and slaves." Indians may have been overlooked because the colony had made the transition to African slave labor. See Hening, *Statutes at Large*, 6:361–62; David H. Fowler, "Northern Attitudes towards Interracial Marriage: A Study of Legislation and Public Opinion in the Middle Atlantic States and the States of the Old Northwest" (Ph.D. diss., Yale University, 1963), A97.

28. Hening, *Statutes at Large*, 12:184; Higginbotham, *Shades of Freedom*, 39.

29. Werner Sollors, *Neither Black Nor White Yet Both: Thematic Explorations of Interracial Literature* (New York: Oxford University Press, 1997), 398.

30. Peter W. Bardaglio, *Reconstructing the Household: Families, Sex, and the Law in the Nineteenth-Century South* (Chapel Hill: University of North Carolina Press, 1995), 62.

31. Byron Curti Martyn, "Racism in the United States: A History of the Anti-miscegenation Legislation and Litigation" (Ph.D. diss., University of Southern California, 1979), 228–29.

32. Higginbotham and Kopytoff, "Racial Purity," 1985–86.

33. Ariela J. Gross, "Litigating Whiteness: Trials of Racial Determination in the Nineteenth-Century South," *Yale Law Journal* 108 (1998): 129–30.

34. Higginbotham and Kopytoff, "Racial Purity," 1979, 2007.

35. Ibid., 2020–21.

36. 388 U.S. 1 (1967). For an excellent discussion of the *Loving* case (which is even cited in the Supreme Court decision), see Walter Wadlington, "The *Loving* Case: Virginia's Anti-miscegenation Statute in Historical Perspective," *Virginia Law Review* 52 (1966): 1189–1223.

37. Fowler, "Northern Attitudes," 41–49, A48–50; Winthrop D. Jordan, "American Chiaroscuro: The Status and Definition of Mulattoes in the British Colonies," *William and Mary Quarterly* 19 (1962): 184 n. 2.

38. Fowler, "Northern Attitudes," 56–60.

39. Higginbotham, *In the Matter of Color*, 151–59; Fowler, "Northern Attitudes," A82; Morris, *Southern Slavery*, 46.

40. Higginbotham, *In the Matter of Color*, 216–18, 248–51.

41. Fowler, "Northern Attitudes," 61–62, A23–24.

42. Fowler, "Northern Attitudes," A40; Ira Berlin, *Many Thousands Gone: The First Two Centuries of Slavery in North America* (Cambridge: Belknap Press of Harvard University Press, 1998), 78.

43. Berlin, *Many Thousands Gone*, 207–8.

44. Fowler, "Northern Attitudes," A40.

45. Johnston, *Race Relations in Virginia*, 231.

46. Higginbotham, *In the Matter of Color*, 71, 98.

47. James Oliver Horton and Lois E. Horton, *In Hope of Liberty: Culture, Community, and Protest among Northern Free Blacks, 1700–1860* (New York: Oxford University Press, 1997), 10. This was the fate of Sedgwick's characters Magawisca and Oneco (see chapter 3).

48. Higginbotham, *In the Matter of Color*, 61–62; *The Colonial Laws of Massachusetts* (1889; reprint, Littleton, Colo.: Fred B. Rothman, 1995), 53.

49. Horton and Horton, *In Hope of Liberty*, 10, 21.

50. Higginbotham, *In the Matter of Color*, 63, 80–81.

51. Fowler, "Northern Attitudes," 67–68. Judge Samuel Sewall's famous antislavery pamphlet *The Selling of Joseph* appeared in 1700.

52. *Acts and Resolves, Public and Private, of the Province of Massachusetts Bay, 1692–1780*, 21 vols. (Boston: Wright and Potter, 1869–1922), 1: 578–79.

53. Higginbotham, *In the Matter of Color*, 75–78.

54. Henry W. Farnam, *Chapters in the History of Social Legislation in the United States to 1860* (Washington, D.C.: Carnegie Institution of Washington, 1938), 438.

55. Higginbotham, *In the Matter of Color*, 72; Horton and Horton, *In Hope of Liberty*, 10–11; Melish, *Disowning Slavery*, 25–26, 212.

56. Higginbotham, *In the Matter of Color*, 96–97. On the question of how abolition was accomplished in Massachusetts (whether by judicial, economic, or individual means), see Elaine MacEacheren, "Emancipation of Slavery in Massachusetts: A Reexamination, 1770–1790," *Journal of Negro History* 55 (1970): 289–306; Arthur Zilversmit, "Quok Walker, Mumbet, and the Abolition of Slavery in Massachusetts," *William and Mary Quarterly* 25 (1968): 614–24; William O'Brien, "Did the Jennison Case Outlaw Slavery in Massachusetts?" *William and Mary Quarterly* 17 (1960): 219–41.

57. *Acts and Laws of the Commonwealth of Massachusetts* (1786; reprint, Boston: Wright and Potter, 1893), 10.

58. Fowler, "Northern Attitudes," 107.

59. See chapter 6 for a detailed discussion of the campaign for the repeal of the Massachusetts intermarriage law.

60. *The Public Laws of the States of Rhode Island and Providence Plantations, 1798* (Providence: Carter and Wilkinson, 1798), 483. The law was repealed in 1881.

61. *Maine Laws*, chap. 70, sec. 2 (1821); quoted in Martyn, "Racism in the United States," 322; Fowler, "Northern Attitudes," 109.

62. Higginbotham, *In the Matter of Color*, 269.

63. Horton and Horton, *In Hope of Liberty*, 5–6.

64. Fowler, "Northern Attitudes," 54–55; Higginbotham, *In the Matter of Color*, 284–86.

65. Higginbotham, *In the Matter of Color*, 301.

66. Fowler, "Northern Attitudes," 84–87; Horton and Horton, *In Hope of Liberty*, 73.

67. Higginbotham, *In the Matter of Color*, 103–6.

68. Fowler, "Northern Attitudes," A67; Higginbotham, *In the Matter of Color*, 108, 110, 114–15.

69. Fowler, "Northern Attitudes," 88–92; Berlin, *Many Thousands Gone*, 237; Horton and Horton, *In Hope of Liberty*, 73–74.

70. David G. Croly, *Miscegenation: The Theory of the Blending of the Races, Applied to the American White Man and the Negro* (New York: H. Dexter, Hamilton, 1864), 18; Sidney Kaplan, "The Miscegenation Issue in the Election of 1864," *Journal of Negro History* 34 (1949): 274–343; Martha Hodes, *White Women, Black Men: Illicit Sex in the Nineteenth-Century South* (New Haven: Yale University Press, 1997), 144.

71. Fowler, "Northern Attitudes," 220–21, 264–66.

72. Quoted in Alfred Avins, "Anti-miscegenation Laws and the Fourteenth Amendment: The Original Intent," *Virginia Law Review* 52 (1966): 1243–44.

73. Fowler, "Northern Attitudes," 264–65. For an analysis of Southern postbellum trends in miscegenation law, see Julie Novkov, "Racial Constructions: The Legal Regulation of Miscegenation in Alabama, 1890–1934," *Law and History Review* 20, no. 2 (Summer 2002): 225–78. Charles F. Robinson II, in "The Antimiscegenated Conversation: Love's Legislated Limits, 1868–1967" (Ph.D. diss., University of Houston, 1998), studies trends in Texas, Louisiana, Alabama, and Oklahoma.

74. Hodes, *White Women, Black Men*, 6, 147.

75. *Loving v. Virginia*, 388 U.S. 1 (1967).

76. Berlin, *Many Thousands Gone*, 1.

77. Higginbotham, *Shades of Freedom*, 46.

78. Ibid., 31–32.

79. Reginald Horsman, *Race and Manifest Destiny: The Origins of American Anglo-Saxonism* (Cambridge: Harvard University Press, 1981), 101; Audrey Smedley, *Race in North America: Origin and Evolution of a Worldview* (Boulder: Westview Press, 1993), 205; Berlin, *Many Thousands Gone*, 358–65.

80. Smedley, *Race in North America*, 234–37. For an excellent overview of the polygenesis debate, see chap. 2, "American Polygeny and Craniometry before Darwin: Blacks and Indians as Separate, Inferior Species," in Stephen Jay Gould, *The Mismeasure of Man*, rev. and expanded ed. (New York: W. W. Norton, 1996).

81. Melish, *Disowning Slavery*, 38, 86, 238.

82. Berlin, *Many Thousands Gone*, 245–46.

83. Martyn, "Racism in the United States," 194.

84. Benjamin C. Howard, *Report of the Decision of the Supreme Court of the United States, and the Opinions of the Judges Thereof, in the case of Dred Scott v. John F. A. Sanford* (December term 1856) (Washington, D.C.: Cornelius Wendell, 1857), 15. The standard citation is *Scott v. Sanford*, 60 U.S. 393 (1857).

85. Howard, *Dred Scott*, 19–22.

86. Don E. Fehrenbacher, *The Dred Scott Case: Its Significance in American Law and Politics* (New York: Oxford University Press, 1978), 429.

87. Higginbotham, *Shades of Freedom*, 67.

Chapter Six

1. Regardless of their differing viewpoints on intermarriage, it is important to remember that the authors in this chapter were all dedicated to the fight against slavery. Their writings reveal the dynamic interracial dialogue occurring within this struggle: between David Walker and William Lloyd Garrison; among Webb, Harriet Beecher Stowe, and the English abolitionists; and between Harper and Child.

2. "An Act for the Better Preventing of A Spurious and Mixt Issue, Etc.," in *Acts and Resolves, Public and Private, of the Province of Massachusetts Bay, 1692–1780*, 21 vols. (Boston: Wright and Potter, 1869–1922), 1:578; quoted in Byron Curti Martyn, "Racism in the United States: A History of the Anti-miscegenation Legislation and Litigation" (Ph.D. diss., University of Southern California, 1979), 121; David H. Fowler, "Northern Attitudes towards Interracial Marriage: A Study of Legislation and Public Opinion in the Middle Atlantic States and the States of the Old Northwest" (Ph.D. diss., Yale University, 1963), 50–52.

3. "Act for the orderly Solemnization of Marriages" providing that "no person authorized . . . to marry shall join in marriage any white person with any Negro, Indian, or Mulatto, under penalty of fifty pounds; and all such marriages shall be absolutely null and void." *Acts and Laws of the Commonwealth of Massachusetts* (1786); reprint, Boston: Wright and Potter, 1893), 10.

4. The intermarriage law became a factor in a dispute between towns over poor relief. In the 1810 Massachusetts case *Inhabitants of Medway v. Inhabitants of Natick*, the question of which town was responsible for the Vickons family rested on the racial identity of Roba Vickons. The court ruled that, as the child of a mulatto man and a white woman, Roba was not a mulatto, as the town of Natick claimed, and therefore her marriage to a white man was legal. The court dodged the issue of whether the miscegenation law of 1786 was constitutional, but it set the important precedent that a person with 50 percent or more "white blood" was white in the eyes of the law. In an 1819 case, *Inhabitants of Medway v. Inhabitants of Needham*, a suit involving the poor relief of Roba Vickons's mulatto and white parents, the court ruled that Massachusetts had to uphold their marriage. At the time of their marriage in the 1760s, such unions were legal in Rhode Island, and so Ishmael Coffee and his future wife had crossed the border in order to have a legal marriage before returning to Massachusetts to live. See Fowler, "Northern Attitudes," 107–8, A53; Martyn, "Racism in the United States," 274–76.

5. As editor of the *Genius of Universal Emancipation* in Baltimore, Garrison had previously addressed the question of intermarriage. In response to the marriage of a Haitian leader's daughter to a Prussian colonel, Garrison declared, "The time is to come when all the nations of the earth will intermarry, and all distinctions of color cease to divide mankind." *Genius of Universal Emancipation*, February 5, 1830; quoted in Henry Mayer, *All on Fire: William Lloyd Garrison and the Abolition of Slavery* (New York: St. Martin's Press, 1998), 82.

6. *Liberator*, January 15, 1831, 3.

7. Donald M. Jacobs, "David Walker and William Lloyd Garrison: Racial Cooperation and the Shaping of Boston Abolition," in *Courage and Conscience: Black and White Abolitionists in Boston*, ed. Donald M. Jacobs (Boston Athenæum; Bloomington: Indiana University Press, 1993), 1–2.

8. David Walker, *David Walker's Appeal, In Four Articles; Together with a Preamble, to the Colored Citizens of the World, but In Particular, and Very Expressly, to Those of the United States of America* (1830; Baltimore: Black Classic Press, 1993), 28–29.

9. "The Marriage Law," *Liberator*, May 7, 1831, 75.

10. "The Marriage Law," *Liberator*, May 21, 1831, 83.

11. William Lloyd Garrison, *Thoughts on African Colonization* (1832; reprint, New York: Arno Press, 1968), 120.

12. "The Intermarriage Law," *Liberator*, February 24, 1843, 31.

13. "Corinthian Editors, or a Specimen of Royal Blood, and Proof of the 'March of Mind,'" *Liberator*, April 2, 1831, 55.

14. Jacobs, "David Walker and William Lloyd Garrison," 13, 15.

15. Debra Gold Hansen, *Strained Sisterhood: Gender and Class in the Boston Female Anti-Slavery Society* (Amherst: University of Massachusetts Press, 1993), 18.

16. Louis Ruchames, "Race, Marriage, and Abolition in Massachusetts," *Journal of Negro History* 40 (1955): 250–63.

17. "Lynn Female Anti-Slavery Society," *Liberator*, April 12, 1839, 57.

18. Hansen, *Strained Sisterhood*, 20–21.

19. Reprinted in the *Liberator*, February 8, 1839, 23.

20. House of Representatives, "Report on the Petition of S. P. Sanford and Others Concerning Distinctions of Color," Legislative Documents, no. 74, April 3, 1839, 8–10. The U.S. Supreme Court made the same argument in *Pace v. Alabama* (1882), upholding the "'separate but equal' principle" in Alabama's miscegenation law. See Rachel F. Moran, *Interracial Intimacy: The Regulation of Race and Romance* (Chicago: University of Chicago Press, 2001), 80.

21. Lydia Maria Child, *An Appeal in Favor of That Class of Americans Called Africans*, ed.

Carolyn L. Karcher (1833; reprint, Amherst: University of Massachusetts Press, 1996), 125, 187–88.

22. Lydia Maria Child, "Anti-Slavery Catechism," *National Anti-Slavery Standard*, October 14, 1841, 74.

23. "The Spirit of Caste," *National Anti-Slavery Standard*, July 15, 1841, 22.

24. Lydia Maria Child, "To the Legislature of Massachusetts," *Liberator*, April 26, 1839.

25. "The Quadroons" first appeared in the *Liberty Bell* (Boston: Massachusetts Anti-Slavery Fair, 1842), 115–41. Quotations (cited in the text) are taken from a more readily available reprint, in *Rediscoveries: American Short Stories by Women, 1832–1916*, ed. Barbara H. Solomon (New York: Mentor, 1994), 88–98.

26. Child, *An Appeal*, 188.

27. Literary annuals and gift books were very popular in antebellum America: over a thousand were published between 1825 and 1865. There were at least seven antislavery annuals, but the *Liberty Bell* was the most successful. See Ralph Thompson, "The *Liberty Bell* and Other Anti-slavery Gift-Books," *New England Quarterly* 7 (March 1934): 154–68.

28. Hansen, *Strained Sisterhood*, 134; Thompson, "The *Liberty Bell*," 154–56, 160.

29. Eliza Lee Follen, "Women's Work," in *Liberty Bell* (Boston: Massachusetts Anti-Slavery Fair, 1842), 6–8.

30. *Colonial Records, of the state of Georgia, 1752–1782* (Atlanta, 1904–16), 1: 59–60; quoted in Fowler, "Northern Attitudes," A23.

31. Carolyn L. Karcher, *The First Woman in the Republic: A Cultural Biography of Lydia Maria Child* (Durham: Duke University Press, 1994), 337.

32. Ibid., 336–37.

33. See Joanne Pope Melish, *Disowning Slavery: Gradual Emancipation and "Race" in New England, 1780–1860* (Ithaca: Cornell University Press, 1998) for an account of the virtual amnesia about the local experience of slavery.

34. *Acts and Resolves Passed by the Legislature of Massachusetts, in the Year 1843* (Boston: Dutton and Wentworth, 1843), 4. David Fowler notes that the Whigs would not have repealed the law; it was the election of a Democratic House and a Democratic governor, Marcus Morton, in 1842 that made the repeal politically possible ("Northern Attitudes," 151).

35. Melish, *Disowning Slavery*, 277.

36. Frank J. Webb, *The Garies and Their Friends*, ed. Robert Reid-Pharr (Baltimore: Johns Hopkins University Press, 1997); hereafter cited in the text.

37. There is some controversy over the year of Webb's birth. Rosemary Faye Crockett says that he was born in 1828, while the back jacket of the Johns Hopkins edition of his novel says that he worked for *Freedom's Journal* in the late 1820s. Crockett's account is the more convincing, especially because, in her 1857 introduction to the novel, Harriet Beecher Stowe describes him as a "young man" (*Garies*, xix).

38. Elise Virginia Lemire, "Making Miscegenation: Discourses of Interracial Sex and Marriage in the United States, 1790–1865" (Ph.D. diss., Rutgers University, 1996), 111.

39. Rosemary Faye Crockett, "*The Garies and Their Friends*: A Study of Frank J. Webb and His Novel" (Ph.D. diss., Harvard University, 1998), 148–49; Lemire, "Making Miscegenation," 110–13.

40. Crockett, "*Garies and Their Friends*," 22–25.

41. Quoted in Joan D. Hedrick, *Harriet Beecher Stowe: A Life* (New York: Oxford University Press, 1994), 249–50.

42. Crockett, "*Garies and Their Friends*," 25.

43. Ibid., 203–4.

44. Robert Reid-Pharr, intro. to Webb, *Garies*, xi.

45. Fowler, "Northern Attitudes," A80.

46. Noel Ignatiev, *How the Irish Became White* (New York: Routledge, 1995), 155–56. Fears of abolitionism and amalgamation also sparked riots in other cites. For a discussion of the New York City and Utica riots, see chap. 2 of Lemire, "Making Miscegenation."

47. Ariela J. Gross, "Litigating Whiteness: Trials of Racial Determination in the Nineteenth-Century South," *Yale Law Journal* 108 (1998): 129.

48. Melish, *Disowning Slavery*, 274.

49. Lyde Cullen Sizer, *The Political Work of Northern Women Writers and the Civil War, 1850–1872* (Chapel Hill: University of North Carolina Press, 2000), 223.

50. See Kathleen Diffley, *Where My Heart Is Turning Ever: Civil War Stories and Constitutional Reform* (Athens: University of Georgia Press, 1992).

51. Sizer, *Political Work of Northern Women Writers*, 224.

52. Eric Foner, *A Short History of Reconstruction, 1863–1877* (New York: Harper & Row, 1990), 12.

53. David W. Blight, *Race and Reunion: The Civil War in American Memory* (Cambridge: Belknap Press of Harvard University Press, 2001), 57.

54. Foner, *Short History of Reconstruction*, 84.

55. W.E.B. DuBois, *Black Reconstruction in America* (New York: Russell & Russell, 1962), 282–83; Foner, *Short History of Reconstruction*, 113.

56. Blight, *Race and Reunion*, 101; Foner, *Short History of Reconstruction*, 145.

57. Foner, *Short History of Reconstruction*, 84–85, 93; see chaps. 5 and 6 for a discussion of presidential and radical Reconstruction.

58. Lydia Maria Child to Samuel J. May, January 11, 1866, in *The Collected Correspondence of Lydia Maria Child, 1817–1880*, ed. Patricia G. Holland, Milton Meltzer, and Francine Krasno (Millwood, N.Y.: Kraus Microform, 1980), microfiche 64/1700.

59. Karcher, *First Woman in the Republic*, 490–500. As Child wrote to her publisher James T. Fields: "The book is written expressly *for* the Freedmen; intended to stimulate and encourage them, by accounts of what colored people *have* done, and by the best speciments of colored authors. . . . I myself think the book would help to remove prejudice from the minds of white people" (August 23, 1865, ibid., microfiche 63/1678).

60. Frances Smith Foster, intro. to *A Brighter Coming Day: A Frances Ellen Watkins Harper Reader* (New York: Feminist Press at the City University of New York, 1990), 19–20. To make a fair comparison of Child's and Harper's activities, it is important to realize that Harper was forty years old at the end of the Civil War, while Child was sixty-three. Also, Child was never a public speaker; she always reached her audiences through her writing.

61. Melba Joyce Boyd, *Discarded Legacy: Poetics and Politics in the Life of Frances E. W. Harper, 1825–1911* (Detroit: Wayne State University Press, 1994), 119–120.

62. Foster, *Brighter Coming Day*, 33.

63. Lydia Maria Child to William P. Cutler, July 10, 1862, in *Collected Correspondence*, microfiche 52/1417.

64. Lydia Maria Child to Francis Shaw, July 28, 1867, ibid., microfiche 67/1789.

65. Lydia Maria Child, *A Romance of the Republic* (Lexington: University Press of Kentucky, 1997), 185; hereafter cited in the text.

66. Dana D. Nelson, intro., ibid., xxvi.

67. Ibid., xiii.

68. "Two Books by Mrs. Child," *The Nation*, August 15, 1867, 127–28.

69. Review of *A Romance of the Republic*, by Lydia Maria Child, *National Anti-Slavery Standard*, August 10, 1867, 3.

70. Karcher, *First Woman in the Republic*, 530.

71. Lydia Maria Child to Eliza Scudder, July 8, 1869, in *Collected Correspondence*, microfiche 71/1901.

72. Frances Smith Foster, intro. to *Minnie's Sacrifice, Sowing and Reaping, Trial and Triumph: Three Rediscovered Novels by Frances E. W. Harper* (Boston: Beacon Press, 1994), xii–xiii; quotations from *Minnie's Sacrifice* are cited in the text.

73. Boyd, *Discarded Legacy*, 40. See William Goodell, *The American Slave Code in Theory and Practice: Its Distinctive Features Shown by Its Statutes, Judicial Decisions, and Illustrative Facts* (New York: American and Foreign Anti-Slavery Society, 1853): "Should a colored citizen of Maryland cross its boundary, . . . on returning home, more than a month after, he is liable to be seized and SOLD" (360).

74. Frances Smith Foster, "Gender, Genre, and Vulgar Secularism: The Case of Frances Ellen Watkins Harper and the AME Press," in *Recovered Writers/Recovered Texts: Race, Class, and Gender in Black Women's Literature*, ed. Dolan Hubbard (Knoxville: University of Tennessee Press, 1997), 51; Foster, intro. to *Minnie's Sacrifice*, xxv, xxx.

75. Boyd, *Discarded Legacy*, 130–32.

76. Frances E. W. Harper, "Mrs. Harper—Affairs in South Carolina," *National Anti-Slavery Standard*, August 10, 1867.

77. Boyd, *Discarded Legacy*, 130.

78. For an excellent reading of *Iola Leroy*, see Elizabeth Young, *Disarming the Nation: Women's Writing and the American Civil War* (Chicago: University of Chicago Press, 1999).

79. Boyd, *Discarded Legacy*, 80.

80. Frances E. W. Harper, "Our Greatest Want," *Anglo-African Magazine*, May 1859, BAP, microfilm, 11:721.

81. See Boyd, *Discarded Legacy*, 145, for a good argument for this reading. For an explanation of the missing chapters, see Foster's introduction to *Minnie's Sacrifice*.

82. Hazel Carby, *Reconstructing Womanhood: The Emergence of the Afro-American Woman Novelist* (New York: Oxford University Press, 1987), 89.

83. Frances Harper to William Still, March 1871, quoted in Boyd, *Discarded Legacy*, 145.

84. *Waiting for the Verdict* (1867) by Rebecca Harding Davis and *What Answer?* (1868) by Anna Dickinson also pose the question about the fate of the former slaves in American society. The taboo against intermarriage plays a central role in both novels, and the writers do not share Child's optimism. For readings of these novels, see Karcher, *First Woman in the Republic*, and Sizer, *Political Work*.

Epilogue

1. "Vote Yes on Amendment Two," *Mobile Register Online*, October 22, 2000, *www.al .com/cgi-bin/printer/printer.cgi*; "Alabama to Vote on Ending Interracial Marriage Ban during November Elections," *Jet*, October 23, 2000, 4; Somini Sengupta, "Removing a Relic of the Old South," *New York Times*, November 5, 2000, sec. 4, 5; Somini Sengupta, "Marry at Will," *New York Times*, November 12, 2000, sec. 4, 2.

2. See Gary B. Nash, "The Hidden History of Mestizo America," in *Sex, Love, Race: Crossing Boundaries in North American History*, ed. Martha Hodes (New York: New York University Press, 1999), 10–32.

3. *Pace v. Alabama*, 106 U.S. 583 (1883). From the *Loving* decision: "In [*Pace v. Alabama*], the Court upheld a conviction under an Alabama statute forbidding adultery or fornication between a white person and a Negro which imposed a greater penalty than that of a statute proscribing similar conduct by members of the same race. The Court reasoned that the statute could not be said to discriminate against Negroes because the punishment for each participant in the offense was the same." *Loving v. Virginia*, 388 U.S. 10 (1967).

4. Eva Saks, "Representing Miscegenation Law," in *Interracialism: Black-White Intermarriage in American History, Literature, and Law*, ed. Werner Sollors (New York: Oxford University Press, 2000), 65.

5. *Perez v. Lippold*, 198 P. 2d 17 (1948). The case is also known as *Perez v. Sharp* and *Perez v. Moroney*. In the *Loving* case, the Supreme Court noted that in *Perez*, California's was the first state court to recognize that miscegenation statutes violate the equal protection clause. Peggy Pascoe complicates this simplistic account, countering that while the outcome of the case was clear, "the rationale for this outcome was a matter of considerable dispute"; See her "Miscegenation Law, Court Cases, and Ideologies of 'Race' in Twentieth-Century America," *Journal of American History* 83, no. 1 (June 1996): 63. Pascoe notes that the original case was argued on the basis of freedom of religion: "Because both Perez and Davis were Catholics and the Catholic Church did not prohibit interracial marriage, California miscegenation law was an arbitrary and unreasonable restraint on their freedom of religion" (61).

6. *Brown v. Board of Education of Topeka*, 347 U.S. 483 (1954); Richard Kluger, *Simple Justice: The History of* Brown v. Board of Education *and Black America's Struggle for Equality* (New York: Alfred A. Knopf, 1976), 491, 494.

7. Kluger, *Simple Justice*, 750–51.

8. Walter Wadlington, "The *Loving* Case: Virginia's Anti-miscegenation Statute in Historical Perspective," *Virginia Law Review* 52 (1966): 1211.

9. Patricia Penn Hilden, *When Nickels Were Indians: An Urban, Mixed-Blood Story* (Washington, D.C.: Smithsonian Institution Press, 1995), 155.

10. Chadwick Allen, "Blood (and) Memory," *American Literature* 71, no. 1 (March 1999): 96–97.

11. Fergus M. Bordewich, *Killing the White Man's Indian: Reinventing Native Americans at the End of the Twentieth Century* (New York: Doubleday, 1996), 78, 329.

12. Allen, "Blood (and) Memory," 93–94, 97, 111.

13. Jacky Rowland, "Georgia Kids Dance Away Race Taboos," *BBC News Online*, May 6, *http://news.bbc.co.uk/1/hi/world/americas/1970266.stm*; Patrik Jonsson, "Integration Finally Gets a Dance Card at Georgia Prom," *Christian Science Monitor*, May 3, 2002, *www.csmonitor.com/2002/0503/p01s02-ussc.htm*; Elliott Minor, "Rural County High School Holds First Integrated Prom," *Savannah Now*, May 5, 2002, *www.savannahnow.com/stories/050502/LOCintegratedprom.shtml*; "Georgia High School Students Plan White-Only Prom," *CNN Student News*, May 2, 2003, *http://www.cnn.com/2003/EDUCATION/05/02/separate.proms.ap*.

INDEX

58, 168–69; fornication, 45–46, 50, 126, 134, 136, 138; freedom of religion, 205n. 5; and gender, 42, 45–46, 55, 60–61, 127–28, 140, 146, 149, 163; inheritance, 131, 134–35, 151, 158; marriage, 45–46, 50, 52, 128–29, 131–38; null and void, 51–52, 92–93, 131, 134–35, 137–38; overruled by courts, 171–72; and poor relief, 201n. 4; penalty for celebrants, 51, 129, 131, 133, 137–38; purpose of, 34, 38–45, 125–27, 130, 132–36, 138; racial definitions, 35–38, 45–47, 51, 57–59, 129–33, 137, 147; repeal of, 51–52, 132, 137, 139–40, 171, 173; and slave law, 55–58, 125–40, 198n. 27; twentieth century, 131–32. *See also Dred Scott;* interracial marriage: and Indian land; *Johnson v. McIntosh; entries for individual states*

Leather-stocking novels (Cooper), 81–84, 87, 90

Liberator, 147–48

Liberty Bell, 152–53, 202n. 27

Liberty Party, 101, 114

Limpieza de Sangre, 36

Loguen, Rev. J.W., 123

Loring, Ellis Gray, 108

Louisiana, 134–35, 163

Louisiana Purchase, 59, 82–83, 135

Loving v. Virginia, 132, 140, 144, 171–72, 204n. 3

Mahican Indians, 68

Maine, 50–52, 138, 140

Malachi, 41

Mann, Horace, 195n. 77

Marshall, John, 87–88

Maryland, 132–33, 140, 143, 165, 204n. 73

"Mary Rescue," 102, 112–17, 123. *See also* "Jerry Rescue"

Massachusetts: abolition of slavery, 137, 199n. 56; Declaration of Rights, 137, 148; miscegenation law, 46, 50–51, 135–37, 143, 147; repeal campaign, 137, 146–54, 202n. 34

Massachusetts Journal, 97

May, Rev. Samuel J., 102

"Memoirs of Henry Obookiah" (Dwight), 188n. 42

Michigan, 140

Minnie's Sacrifice (Harper), 135, 160, 165–68

"miscegenation," 7, 139–40, 160. *See also* law, miscegenation

Mississippi, 140

Missouri, 140

Mohawk Indians, 69

Momaday, N. Scott, 173

Monroe, James, 13

Moriscos, 35

Morse, Rev. Jedidiah, 18

Morton, Thomas, 41

Moses, 41, 166–67

Mott, Lucretia, 102

Mtohksin, Jehoiakim, 71, 188n. 30

mulatto, 107, 128–31, 133; "tragic mulatta," 134, 152–53, 157, 162, 167. *See also* law, miscegenation: racial definitions

Muslims, 35

narrative of control. *See* interracial marriage: narrative of control

narrative of disruption. *See* interracial marriage: narrative of disruption

Narrative of the Life of Frederick Douglass (Douglass), 121, 123

The Nation, 165

National Anti-Slavery Standard, 150, 165

National Watchman, 108

Nehemiah, 41

A New-England Tale (Sedgwick), 76

New Hampshire, 50

New Jersey, 50

New York, 124, 139

New York Central College: closure of, 119; founding of, 103–107, 193n. 16, 193n. 18, 193n. 19; and integrated education, 106, 108, 193n. 22; and race, 107; reaction to intermarriage scandal, 102, 116–17, 124

New York Evening Post, 66

Nicholas V, Pope, 43

Niles' Weekly Registrar, 18, 49

North American Review, 66, 82